An Archaeology of Disbelief

The Origin of Secular Philosophy

Edward Jayne

EDITED BY ELAINE ANDERSON JAYNE

Hamilton Books

Lanham • Boulder • New York • Toronto • Plymouth, UK

Copyright © 2018 by Hamilton Books
4501 Forbes Boulevard, Suite 200, Lanham, Maryland 20706
Hamilton Books Acquisitions Department (301) 459-3366

Unit A, Whitacre Mews, 26-34 Stannary Street,
London SE11 4AB, United Kingdom

Library of Congress Control Number: 2017955105
ISBN: 978-0-7618-6966-5 (cloth : alk. paper)—ISBN: 978-0-7618-6967-2 (electronic)

∞™ The paper used in this publication meets the minimum requirements of American National Standard for Information Sciences Permanence of Paper for Printed Library Materials, ANSI/NISO Z39.48-1992.

To Elaine

Without her help this book would not have been possible

Contents

Preface

Socrates was executed for atheism in Athens, and other ancient philosophers such as Theophrastus and even Aristotle were confronted by the same possibility. Several centuries later many libraries seem to have been destroyed by fire in order to eradicate all texts suggestive of secular philosophy, and still later medieval Christian scribes and scholars resorted to textual censorship with comparable results. Such extremes have of course been abandoned since the Renaissance, but modern classical scholarship has effectively sustained this dubious effort by ignoring or deemphasizing the materialist perspective of ancient secularists such as Democritus, Strato, Carneades and even Aristotle despite ample textual evidence to the contrary.

At the turn of the twentieth century, the eminent classicist John Burnet went so far as to explain that the primary achievement of early Greek philosophers consisted of "the faith that reality is divine" in the shared "effort to satisfy what we call the religious instinct."[1] In effect he proposed that ancient Greek philosophy served as an early version of religion dedicated to the concept of existence as a product of one or more gods. The no less eminent scholar, W.K.C. Guthrie, apparently shared this assumption as suggested by his reluctance to acknowledge secular analysis. His five-volume set, *A History of Greek Philosophy*, provides an outstanding historical analysis of ancient classical philosophy, but his convictions as a lay minister at his college chapel may have biased his analysis more than he realized. This tendency seems likely, for example, when he suggested the possibility of shared ambivalence toward religious belief by both of the pre-Socratic philosophers, Parmenides and Melissus:

> Against those who speak of mysticism and proofs of the existence of God, it is
> necessary to point out that, even if Parmenides and Melissus retained, almost

vii

automatically, this legacy from earlier thought, their remains show that it was of little importance to them.[2]

In simpler terms, religion was presumably retained by both philosophers at least as common assumptions otherwise of little importance later in their lives. Guthrie could obscure the religious disbelief of Melissus, as indicated in a passage quoted by Diogenes Laertius in *Lives of Eminent Philosophers*:

> Moreover, he [Melissus] said that we ought not to make any statements about the gods, for it was impossible to have knowledge of them."[3]

This was a succinct admission of agnosticism--if not atheism--and in fact it anticipated the viewpoint of modern logical positivists including Bertrand Russell, Guthrie's colleague at Cambridge.

In contrast, Theodor Gomperz, the eminent Austrian classicist who lived at the same time as Burnet seems to have suggested the likelihood of Melissus' impiety when he accused him of an inexcusable transgression, but without going so far as to identify it:

> Grave fallacies must be laid to his charge, but there is not the least ground to impute to him any deliberate imposture or any deception save the deception of himself.[4]

Grave fallacies indeed! One can only suppose that Melissus' refusal to concede the necessary existence of gods was considered so extreme that it had to be ignored except as an unspeakable transgression. Unfortunately, however, this avoidance that Gomperz shared with Burnet and Guthrie served to obscure the pivotal significance of Melissus' primary assumption—the recognition that the combination of spatial and temporal infinitude, the latter as already suggested by Parmenides, seems to eliminate the likelihood of transcendental godhead. Of necessity a functional god along with the promise of an afterlife could only be possible as co-extensive portions of material existence in its entirety. Melissus accordingly declared an assumption implicit in ancient Greek philosophy from its very beginning, and in doing so he bridged the gap from Parmenides' holistic perspective asserted by classical goddesses at least for literary effect to the outspoken atheism of Democritus, Protagoras, and an assortment of Athenian Sophists, followed by Aristotle and still later by Strato, Carneades and even Cicero. Unfortunately, modern ignorance of this predominant secular assumption throughout ancient Greek philosophy obscures an important historic linkage between what might seem two separate periods in the history of ancient Greek philosophy—pre-Socratic secular philosophy and Aristotelian cosmology that turns out to have been equally secular once submitted to close examination.

In fact careful analysis of early Greek philosophical texts discloses that pre-Socratic philosophers were almost unanimous in their disdain for both Homeric polytheism and the cult worship of later years. Today their arguments continue to be ignored or willfully misinterpreted precisely because they explain the physical universe on a materialist basis at odds with Platonism and modern Christianity. Even prominent modern secular philosophers have more or less shared this perspective as illustrated by Bertrand Russell's qualified praise of Aristotle's theoretical contribution in his standard history of western philosophy. More recently, Tim Whitmarsh maintains in *Battling the Gods: Atheism in the Ancient World*, a text for the most part supportive of ancient freethought, that ancient material philosophers lacked a genuine tradition of their own despite their interesting lives and opinions. But not true. Except for the Platonists and Neoplatonists, ancient Greek philosophers more or less shared Melissus' rejection of the orthodox god concept, and in fact their version of materialism was surprisingly in accord with the most advanced findings of modern science. This is why it seems useful to reconstruct their shared perspective by integrating on a holistic basis their few texts and fragments that still exist despite the library fires, medieval censorship, and modern scholarship devoted to its misinterpretation.

I.

My reconstruction of ancient disbelief begins as a summary of the roughly fifteen major pre-Socratic natural philosophers who sought to explain a physical universe devoid of supernatural intervention. The second chapter thereupon features the Age of Pericles, when Platonism took root as a reaction against Athenian Sophists who promoted uncompromising doubt regarding all matters, including religion. The text also takes into account Protagoras' secular achievement as a skeptic, and then summarizes Plato's effort to renew the god concept based on a theory of ideal forms earlier suggested by Anaxagoras. The next two chapters document how Aristotle's effort to formulate a cosmology in the probable sequence of his texts from *Physics* and *Metaphysics* to *De Caelo, Generation and Corruption,* and finally *De Anima* effectively unified and consolidated pre-Socratic secular assumptions based on the likelihood that the universe consists of mass in infinite cyclical motion. Pious references to monotheistic godhood are conceded now and again throughout Aristotle's argument, but most are identified as obvious interpolations by medieval scribes.[5]

The fifth chapter discusses Theophrastus and Strato as Aristotle's two principal successors at the Lyceum. Theophrastus' primer on metaphysics-- all that remains of his ample scholarship on cosmology--is discussed as a summary of Aristotle's assumptions that set the stage for Strato's more strident atheistic approach. Also taken into account are Strato's invention of experimental science and his unsuccessful use of a primitive vacuum jar to reconcile Democritus' atomism with Aristotle's concept of spatial continuity. Apparently this is the first scientific experiment on record, and despite its unavoidable failure it seems to have inspired Bacon's later dependence on experimentation that is now generally considered to have initiated modern science. As suggested in greater detail (and for the first time), Bacon himself very likely suggested his debt to Strato in his Preface to *Novum Organum* without specifically identifying him by name.

In the sixth chapter, the shared version of natural philosophy proposed by Epicurus and Lucretius is shown to provide what amounts to an alternative version of materialism that featured Democritus' assumptions rather than those of Aristotle. In my seventh chapter, Academic Skepticism is explored pertaining to both Arcesilaus' emphasis on common sense and Carneades' more rigorous emphasis on probability as well as his strident misuse of Aristotelian logic to reduce orthodox religious assumptions to absurdity. All evidence of these atheistic arguments was later destroyed except for several passages quoted by Sextus Empiricus, who undoubtedly refrained from admitting their authorship by Carneades in order to guarantee publication and/ or to avoid prosecution.

The eighth chapter examines Cicero's sophisticated comparison among these various approaches and their comparative validity. In his final remarks that have been either overlooked or misinterpreted, he expresses his willingness to modify Carneades' version of skepticism in light of Aristotelian assumptions as formulated by his former tutor Posidonius. In effect his perspective was both skeptical and Aristotelian, a combination that anticipated modern secular philosophy. Finally, the Epilogue provides an abbreviated history of western civilization's loss and recovery of secularism since the Roman Empire.

Altogether as many as two dozen ancient philosophers are interpreted in light of their shared commitment to a secular explanation of the universe. The skeptics are shown to include Protagoras, Aenisidemus, Arcesilaus, and Cicero, while outspoken atheists include Anaximander, Democritus, Strato, Carneades, and Lucretius. A mixed viewpoint can be attributed to Xenophanes, Heraclitus, and Anaxagoras, and natural philosophers with obvious atheistic tendencies include Theophrastus, Epicurus, and especially Aristotle during his thirteen years at the Lyceum in Athens. Aristotle's cosmology is conceded to be obscure in at least a few contexts, but, as I try to demonstrate, its cumulative analysis compels a strictly secular explanation once understood based on his theoretical advance from *Physics* and *Metaphysics* to his later texts in their obvious combination, *De Caelo, On Generation and Corruption,* and *De Anima.*

II.

I myself am not a professional classicist versed in Greek and Latin, but instead a retired English professor who spent several years teaching lecture courses about the literary history of western civilization. My syllabus included *Gilgamesh* followed by a quick unit upon Greek genius that featured Homer, Greek tragedy, and Plato's "Allegory of the Cave" before my analysis advanced to the Bible, Shakespeare, and various modern authors. Totally omitted from my lectures was Greece's remarkable assortment of secular thinkers. This was partly because their textual record is necessarily scattered, but also because I did not recognize its central importance relevant to the history of western civilization.

On the other hand, my graduate seminars in literary criticism featured literary deception as "substitutive enhancement" much as explained in my book, *Negative Poetics* dealing with the pursuit of pleasant alternatives—the testament of love as opposed to indifference, the vision of evil as opposed to severe misbehavior, etc. Later I applied this veridical methodology to both literary and non-literary texts, whether by Kant, Shakespeare, or the original authorship of American constitutional law. The archaeology I am proposing here brings this analysis into play once again, this time as an antidote to the reluctance of modern classical scholarship to accept pre-Socratic secular assumptions that culminated with Aristotle's impressive version of materialism. In effect my task has been to disclose Greek philosophy's remarkable theoretical achievement as the primary source of modern secularism.

As for the title of this book, it speaks for itself. Just as the field of archaeology features the recovery of prehistoric artifacts that bear religious implications, my effort is to perform essentially the same service relevant to ancient disbelief. Just as shards of pottery and occasional temple ruins exemplify the findings of archaeology, the task of this book features the analysis of scattered philosophical fragments additional to the only available complete texts by three ancient secularists--Aristotle, Lucretius, and Cicero. In combination, these provide sufficient evidence toward a systematic understanding of a thriving secular tradition a couple thousand years ago.

Introduction

The practice of religion may be traced back as many as 300,000 years, and identifiable religious groups existed during the Neolithic Age perhaps 30,000 years ago. On the other hand, there is no evidence of outspoken religious disbelief until the sixth century BC, roughly twenty-five hundred years ago. This repudiation first occurred in ancient Greece when so-called natural philosophers began to engage in speculative inquiry more or less a century before the Age of Pericles.[1] By most accounts the original individual to engage in philosophical speculation, Thales—supposedly the most eminent of the seven wise men—would seem to have conceded the existence of gods, but he also suggested the possibility that the entire universe consists of water. His disciple Anaximander took the next step by instead proposing the likelihood of an unknown substance that eliminated the necessity of gods, and later philosophers mostly concerned themselves with a variety of materialist cosmologies until the inception of Platonism followed by Aristotle's more inclusive synthesis. Much later, Greek secularism declined during the Roman Empire and finally terminated during the so-called Dark and Middle Ages. At least a thousand years passed before the Renaissance attained what has been described as a rebirth of Greco-Roman civilization, and not surprisingly a major aspect of this achievement was the rediscovery of secular philosophy in light of ancient Greek findings.

Comparable periods of doubt can also be detected at about the same time in the ancient civilizations of China, India, and Iran, when such figures as Confucius and Lao'tze likewise questioned orthodox religion. However, their disbelief does not seem to have inspired any significant speculation by their followers. Why was Greek civilization unique as the source of this remarkable secular revolution? In the final analysis an economic explanation seems the most plausible. Earlier civilizations enjoyed high levels of agricultural prosperity on the fertile river plains of Egypt, Mesopotamia, China, and India, and their economies seem to have depended on collective obedience ensured by shared religious convictions. The supernatural authority of gods played an essential role in helping to guarantee obedience and sustain received expectations. To this extent the promotion of belief was more important than the pursuit of knowledge that might possibly be in conflict with belief.

I. AN ECONOMIC EXPLANATION

Eventually, however, mercantile trade throughout the eastern Mediterranean region became more profitable relative to agrarian productivity, and cognitive skills became more important than cooperative submission. Phoenician trade thrived by the twelfth century BC, and its obvious success inspired Greek competition that led to the founding of Greek city-states similarly dependent on trade. On the coast of Turkey the port city of Miletus played a dominant role until Persian armies sacked it in 494 BC, whereupon regional leadership shifted to Greece, and Athens came to the fore. Here Greek traders expanded the use of coinage invented in Lydia in the early seventh century. The nearby silver mines of Laurion provided ample precious metal for this purpose, and primitive banks were founded to help subsidize transactions linked with trade. Coastal agricultural regions from Italy to the Black Sea also benefitted from this commercial network. In exchange for food--primarily consisting of grain—Grecian port cities engaged in primitive manufacture that included the sale of tools, weapons, pottery, clothing, jewelry, and leather, as well as slaves obtained from lands conquered by others. Almost all urban dwellers in these cities—even a few of the slaves--somehow shared in this affluence.

A rapidly growing leisure class soon emerged that adopted a wide variety of cultural innovations, particularly in Athens during the fifth century BC. [2] As explained by Carroll Quigley in *The Evolution of Civilizations*, "We might say that the Age of Expansion in the eastern Mediterranean was from about 850 B.C. to about 450, while in the western basin it was about 700 to 250 BC[3] As perhaps the most consequential outcome of this prosperity, a highly articulate minority became interested in philosophy as a theory of existence more credible than Homeric mythology. Of course priests and traveling bards continued to promote religious belief among the populace, but an expanding number of philosophers and their disciples joined in the pursuit of a credible explanation of the physical universe in and of itself. As later explained by Aristotle, "It was when almost all the necessities of life and the things that make for comfort and recreation were present, that such a knowledge began to be sought."[4] Eventually this speculative inquiry led to both science and the field of philosophy. As Hegel explained many centuries later, "idea stepped into existence" for the first time, and "universal mind" became rooted in the capacity for sustained analysis rather than unexamined credulousness. Just as religion had played a useful role in the accumulation of agrarian wealth, secular philosophy was the most remarkable product of mercantile wealth. Hegel also declared that this pivotal achievement served to demarcate the transition when "unhistorical history" came to an end in Europe--in other words when meaningful antithesis emerged between "the divine . . . and the human subject as an individual." Though Hegel himself would have vigorously rejected such a possibility, this transformation en-acted an advance from collective religious orthodoxy to genuine intellectual freedom rooted in the substantiation of individual judgment.[5]

According to the Marxist philosopher Karl Kautsky in *Foundations of Christianity*, this conceptual breakthrough was strictly the result of the accu-mulation of sufficient wealth to produce an independent leisure class, and according to Karl Marx himself early in his career, this financial achievement very likely had a "civilizing influence" as best confirmed at the time by the rapid increase in the pursuit of secular inquiry. The classical Greek econo-mist H. Michell also suggested in more general terms that the most important byproduct of this influence was an "era of intellectual alertness" in the pur-suit of truth at the expense of conformity rooted in unexamined credulous-ness. In effect inquiry supplanted belief, and there was less resistance to the pursuit of a better and more credible explanation of cosmic design than the erratic—at times preposterous--reign of Homeric gods.[6]

II. LOSS OF TEXTUAL EVIDENCE

Unfortunately, most of the textual evidence of this intellectual freedom has disappeared in a process of attrition beginning with the Roman Empire. This was when the enforcement of shared belief once again played a major role in social control, and it intensified with the advent of Christianity in the fourth century AD. Secular analysis at odds with religious orthodoxy was preserved on a limited number of scrolls that were too often consigned to wholesale destruction in later centuries. There were several ways this happened, but the most effective choice--whether intended or not--seems to have been through the destruction, usually by fire, of ancient libraries that housed these scrolls. The first perpetrators seem to have been pagan sects and Roman conquerors, but within a few centuries a succession of righteous Christian emperors took on the task on a more systematic basis. Of course many library fires may have been accidental, but too many occurred not to have been intentional, and it is all but impossible today to know, since there is no record of scrolls that might have been salvaged and transported to other libraries. The very information that a library was destroyed seems to suggest the likelihood that its entire contents were thereby eliminated. That at least a few scrolls might have been saved was of course a possibility, but this is never mentioned.

While the Villa of the Papyri at Herculaneum, containing about 1,800 papyrus scrolls, was buried by the eruption of Vesuvius in 79 AD, the eradication of too many other ancient libraries resulted from obvious human involvement. The Phoenician libraries at Tyre and Carthage as well as their temples and palace archives were destroyed by Roman and Macedonian armies, and the library at Pergamon (with an estimated 200,000 rolls) was destroyed by Mark Antony. Similarly, the Library of Domitian was destroyed during the reign of Commodus, and both the Forum of Trajan (with from 10 to 20 thousand rolls) and Library of Hadrian in Athens were severely damaged during the Herulian invasion in 267 AD. In addition, Rome's citywide conflagration during Nero's reign included the perhaps accidental destruction of many smaller libraries as well as having damaged the Library of Palatine Apollo and the library for the palace of Tiberius.

The destruction of scrolls at odds with religious orthodoxy even seems to have been encouraged during the earliest stage in the history of Christianity. As the Apostle Paul recounted with obvious approval in Acts 19:18-20, a large heap of scrolls was submitted to a bonfire at Ephesus in order to celebrate a particular group's conversion to Christian faith. These scrolls supposedly encouraged "curious arts" [*perierga*] somehow linked with magic, possibly suggesting that the specific impiety worthy of destruction was not to be identified in the very act of destroying texts that might have advocated it. The English translation of the Bible's estimate that the texts were worth five thousand pieces of silver—accidentally multiplied by ten in both the German and English translations of the passage--suggests the likelihood that at least a few of the scrolls that were destroyed might have been relevant to natural philosophy.[7]

Once in power, the Christian Emperor Constantius initiated the wide-scale burning of pagan libraries and books in general across the Roman Empire. A decade later, in 364 AD, the Christian Emperor Jovian ordered the burning of the library at Antioch as well as the systematic destruction of books across the eastern region. In 370 the Christian Emperor Valens did the same, as did Theodosius II in 448 and Justinian in 556. The destruction of Rome's largest library at Trajan's Forum (10,000 rolls) seems to have been ordered by Pope Gregory I in the sixth century and/or by Pope Gregory VII in the eleventh century. According to John of Salisbury, Pope Gregory I explained his effort was to encourage piety, "for fear the secular literature might distract the faithful from the contemplation of Heaven." However, both Popes may have taken this course to destroy whatever of the collection remained after earlier damage during the reign of Commodus, as possibly the result of lightning. On the other hand, all twenty-nine of the public libraries that existed in Rome as late as 350 AD seem to have disappeared by the seventh century, but they might simply have been dismantled as was likely with the smaller libraries at many of the city's public baths. [8]

The biggest and most impressive library of all, at Alexandria, was severely damaged three times. In 48 BC a substantial portion of its contents was accidentally destroyed by Julius Caesar when he burned his fleet to prevent its flight from conflict. In 273 AD, the library once again caught fire during the Emperor Aurelian's invasion to capture the city, and its later and more severe destruction was ordered by the Christian Emperor Theodosius in 391, undoubtedly on religious grounds. The library was finally entirely destroyed in 642 as ordered by the Caliph Omar, this time in the cause of Muslim purity. Altogether, perhaps a half-million rolls were lost at this one site over a period of seven hundred years. A large portion of ancient Greek philosophy was undoubtedly eradicated in these many fires.

The much later destruction of the Library of Constantinople in 1453 by Muslim fanatics completed the task, whether intended or not, of demolishing whatever remained of the textual record of secular philosophy in ancient Greece. Of course the ruins of many of the buildings that housed these ancient libraries survive today, but their destruction was secondary to the loss of the scrolls themselves and their written contents. As a result, many dozens of ancient authors can be identified only by name or because of the remaining existence of small portions of their texts described as fragments.

As to be expected, scrolls of secular philosophy by particular individuals were particularly vulnerable to wholesale eradication throughout this period. For example, the entire output of Democritus and Strato relevant to natural philosophy was lost, as was that of Theophrastus except for a small assortment of scientific writings and one short essay on metaphysics. Also destroyed was the complete output of Clitomachus, who was Carneades' scribe and supposedly the most prolific author in ancient times. Only three essays remain by Epicurus, who was generally ranked next unto Clitomachus in ancient times for his level of productivity. In contrast, Plato's dialogues as well as Homer's two monumental epics steeped in mythology have endured twenty-five centuries almost in their entirety.

III. FIVE SECULARISTS WHO SURVIVED

Ancient texts relevant to secular philosophy that continue to exist today are strikingly few as compared to the output of ancient authors in other areas of inquiry, most notably dealing with such fields history, mythology, political considerations, etc. Nevertheless, incidental references to secular theory by Plato, Cicero, Plutarch, and others are useful in the attempt to resurrect ancient philosophy, as was the effort of so-called ancient doxographers who collected earlier philosophical passages they considered worth preserving—fragments that are seldom more than a couple sentences long. From the first through the third centuries AD, one or more individuals identified as "Aetius" (if such a person existed) exercised this laudable pursuit, as did such figures as Philodemus, Pseudo-Plutarch, Clement of Alexandria, Antisthenes, Aristoxenus, Porphyry, Stabaeus, and perhaps a dozen others as well as Aristotle himself. It was not until the late nineteenth century, however, that the German classicist Hermann Diels finally gathered all the existing fragments to compile a single standard text later translated into English by Kathleen Freeman as *Ancilla to the Pre-Socratic Philosophers.*[9] Diels referred to as many as 103 ancient Greek philosophers, but he could only quote fragments by thirty-eight of them, and most fragments were not more than a couple of sentences long. Significantly, the entire collection fills just 162 pages in Freeman's translation.

Also useful are incidental commentaries by scholastic philosophers in later centuries such as Alexander of Aphrodisias, Ammonius, Philoponus, Themistius, and especially Simplicius. In fact, it was Simplicius' effort to resurrect Aristotelian theory that was said to have provoked the Roman emperor Justinian into outlawing the pursuit of Athenian philosophy in 529 AD. From this historic juncture onward, godless inquiry was actually against the law, and many thousands of heretics were later tortured and burned at the stake for transgressing this prohibition. St. Thomas Aquinas sought to revive Aristotle during the thirteenth century, but his successful effort was to harness Aristotle's analytic freedom in support of religious orthodoxy. In contrast, a formidable task that confronts modern scholarship dealing with ancient secular philosophy is to piece together as well as possible the essential theoretical sequence that took place in the collective advance from Thales to Plato, Aristotle, and their Hellenistic successors. In retrospect many of their insights are remarkably sophisticated, and their theoretical synthesis in its entirety suggests a remarkable level of secular enlightenment at the inception of western civilization.

Not more than five ancient textual sources that escaped destruction either promoted secular assumptions or took them into account on a sympathetic basis. Most conspicuous was Cicero's sequence of two dialogues, *Academica* and *De Natura Deorum*, probably written during the last two years of his life. Probably because of his popular but unsuccessful historic effort to preserve the Roman Republic, most of Cicero's writings were preserved, even including these two scrolls except for deletions pertaining to Carneades. On the other hand, the other four ancient textual sources that escaped destruction by accident could easily have been expunged from history. Their recovery was entirely accidental, and without their wealth of supportive information the secular achievement of ancient philosophy could easily have been lost to modern research.

Most remarkable, of course, was Aristotle's mature output of writings, which was described as oral doctrine—*acroamata*—that was specifically intended for his disciples alone. These texts were intentionally excluded from publication during his lifetime, but they comprise almost his entire output that exists today. This unique trove of restricted theoretical analysis was discovered as a bundle of lecture notes in the basement of the descendants of one of his disciples roughly two centuries after his death. According to Plutarch, the Roman general Sylla brought the entire lot to Rome in 86 BC, and Andronicus the Rhodian was able to put Aristotle's various texts in print. At about the same time copies were supposedly brought to Alexandria, Egypt, to provide the nucleus for the famous Alexandrian library. Until then Aristotle's reputation had been as a gifted advocate of Plato's ideas, but most of his earlier output as a member of Plato's Academy seems to have been all but forgotten without much of a sense of loss. His future reputation accordingly rested upon his confidential output at his own institute--the Lyceum--that was much later salvaged and published. As I try to demonstrate, deletions and interpolations were brought to play over many centuries afterwards to obscure the secular implications of Aristotle's philosophy. Once these alterations are taken into account, his secular viewpoint becomes obvious as a unique and remarkable synthesis of pre-Socratic concepts.

The second of the stray "finds" was *Lives of the Eminent Philosophers* by the historian of philosophy Diogenes Laertius (often simply described as Diogenes), who lived between the first and fourth centuries. A single copy of *Lives* was recovered in the ninth century AD, and all later editions were based on this single copy. Diogenes Laertius summarized the lives and ideas of as many as 82 early Greek philosophers. Altogether, he included 1,186 references to 365 books authored by roughly 250 philosophers. Especially important was his inclusion of an appendix including three complete essays by Epicurus, the only record that has survived of his authorship. Moreover, he mentioned five earlier historians of philosophy who are now altogether forgotten--Sotion, Dinon, Manetho, Hecataeus, and Hippobotus—all of whom probably referred to other philosophers equally forgotten. Much of this information is unavailable elsewhere and must be considered unsubstantiated, most notably pertaining to biographical matters such as the supposedly colorful deaths of Heraclitus, Zeno, and Empedocles.

The third stray "find" was the single volume of Lucretius' epic *De Natura Deorum,* which was discovered by the papal secretary, Poggio Bracciolini, in a remote German monastery in 1417. As many as fifty additional copies of this epic history of the physical universe were later discovered during the fifteenth and sixteenth centuries, but only after Poggio's achievement afforded theological respectability by an officer of the Vatican. Today the most authoritative manuscripts, the O and Q codices in Leiden, are dated from the ninth century. Several decades ago earlier papyrus manuscripts of the first century were found in Herculaneum that had been buried as early as the 79 A.D. volcanic eruption of Mount Vesuvius. However, their condition is so fragile that they still defy reconstruction at this time. In any case, the recovery of a complete text in the early fifteenth century pertaining to natural philosophy was of unique value preliminary to Bruno's speculation toward the end of the sixteenth century. Soon afterwards, Gassendi also seems to have been inspired by Lucretius when he modernized the theory of atomism on a more scientific basis.

The fourth and last inclusion in this category, more a fortunate acquisition than a stray "find," was a history of skeptical ancient philosophy by the second century skeptical philosopher Sextus Empiricus. This thorough assessment was only brought to light among European scholars when it was included among an assortment of books transported from Constantinople's libraries to Venice to prevent their destruction by Muslim fanatics during the successful invasion of 1453. Perhaps a generation older than Diogenes Laertius, Sextus Empiricus emphasized the ancient history of skepticism, and here alone several of Strato's atheistic arguments may be examined, if without any reference to his identity as their author.

Without full access to all of these five early sources whose survival seems in retrospect to have been entirely accidental, the piecemeal record of ancient secularism could more likely have been ignored, and its unique secular perspective might not have been renewed by the Italian Renaissance—at least not to the same extent.

Chapter One

The Pre-Socratic Philosophers

At least fifteen ancient Greek thinkers played significant roles in the abandonment of polytheistic religion featured by such classical authors as Homer and Hesiod. During the early sixth century BC, these so-called pre-Socratic materialists—more simply described as natural philosophers—became active in a variety of separate Grecian coastal cities scattered across the eastern Mediterranean region. Beginning in Miletus on the coast of Turkey, their shared inquiry spread to Croton and Elea near the foot of Italy, then Abdera on the northern Aegean coast, and finally to Athens. The early attempt to isolate a single underlying substance in the universe led to an emphasis on cosmic infinitude as well as the pursuit of relevant mathematical analysis. Holistic and cyclical theories were also proposed as well as the concept of atomism. Radical skepticism later emerged in Athens, setting the stage for the grand cosmologies of Plato and Aristotle that would later be expanded upon by various disciples and followers over the next few centuries. Except for the works of Plato and Aristotle, little textual evidence exists today to document the first stages of this remarkable intellectual breakthrough beyond a few hundred random passages. Nevertheless, the movement as a whole arrived at a loose synthesis of cosmologies that ultimately provided the basis for modern secular assumptions. Only by piecing together the assortment of fragments that remain linked with their probable authorship can this collective achievement be fully recognized as the origin of western civilization's unprecedented materialist perspective that continues to flourish in modern times.

I. THALES (CA. 624 - 546 BC)

Greek philosophy seems to have begun during the sixth century BC at Miletus, a Greek city-state on the coast of Turkey. Generally considered the first
philosopher, Thales was by all accounts the founder of the so-called Milesian
school. He was possibly of Phoenician descent but spent most of his adult
years as a wealthy citizen in Miletus. He was also honored as the most
eminent of the ancient world's seven wise men, and among his accomplish-
ments cited by Diogenes Laertius, he supposedly introduced to the Greek
world the conceptual advances in geometry and astronomy that he had acquired while in Egypt. He wrote treatises on the solstice and equinox, established the length of both the year and a 30-day month, and accurately predicted an eclipse of the sun in 585 BC. He also calculated the sizes of the sun
and moon, and succeeded in measuring the height of Egyptian pyramids by
their shadows. Moreover, he demonstrated how a right-angled triangle could
be inscribed in a circle. Relevant to governance, he served as an advisor to
his friend Thrasybulus, the benevolent tyrant of Miletus, and he was said to
have anticipated the consequences of a drought soon enough to capitalize on
the increased price of olives the next year by buying up all the available oil
mills. On the other hand, it is said he once fell into a ditch as he watched the
stars, whereupon an old woman asked him how he could expect to know
about the heavens if he couldn't even see beneath his feet!

Six centuries preceding Christ, Thales supposedly formulated his own
version of the Golden Rule--to refrain from doing what we blame in others.
When asked what is most difficult in life, he replied, "To know oneself."
Asked what is easiest, he replied, "To give advice to another." Moreover, he
warned, "Avoid ill-gotten gains," an edict worthy of consideration even today. He was also said to have asserted that in the final analysis there is no
difference between life and death, possibly suggesting the immortality of the
soul, and when asked what is the divine, he replied with a pantheist assertion
that anticipated the cosmologies of both Parmenides and Aristotle, "that
which neither begins nor ends, suggestive of eternity without divine authority." In a slightly different light he explained the world is animate and full of
divinities. It is anybody's guess, of course, how many of these ideas were
proposed by Thales or were later attributed to him because of his status as the
"wisest man of his age."[1]

According to Aristotle, Thales also held that that the soul and thought are
identical, suggesting Aristotle's later equation between the human mind and
mental behavior. Relevant to the physical universe, Thales actually suggested
that a magnet has motive force comparable to the soul in the sense that it
draws iron to it, thereby producing physical motion.[2] He also suggested
Anaxagoras and Plato's concept of a spiritual universe, for example by having advanced the pantheistic assumption that "all things are full of gods." As

explained by Plutarch in *Moralia*, "Thales had set forth the excellent hypothesis that soul exists in all the most dominant and most important parts of the universe." In light of his earlier remark that divinity consists of eternity, Thales also anticipated the notion of soul central to Anaxagoras' philosophy that later inspired Platonism.[3]

Thales was mostly famous for his theory that the first principle of the universe (*arche*) consists of water, the thinnest of all liquids according to Aristotle.[4] Today the concept seems somewhat credible in light of recent astronomical findings that water is a product of ice molecules from vast cosmic clouds that existed before the creation of the sun. According to Aristotle, Thales argued both that the earth floats on water and that water suffuses the existence of all matter, not merely the liquid realm supposedly occupied by aquatic gods such as Poseidon and Amphitrite. Just as ice and steam possess fluidity, so does life itself and indeed everything that plays a role in the world about us as later explained by Aristotle:

> Thales, the founder of this school of philosophy [materialism], says the [basic] principle is water (for which reason he declared that the earth rests on water), perhaps getting the notion from noticing that the nutriment of all things is moist, and that heat itself is generated from the moist and kept alive by it (and that which they come to be is a principle of all things). He got this notion from this fact, and from the fact that the seeds of all things have a moist nature, and that water is the origin of the nature of moist things.[5]

Thales exaggerated the role of water as the single basic element that happened to be capable of motion that can be observed, but more important was his explanation of the universe in monistic terms free of anthropomorphic mythology typical of the Homeric gods as well as Orphic belief. This was a significant advance. Whatever the primary element (or substrate) might consist of, Thales' proposal suggested for the first time the possibility of a strictly physical universe governed by a single basic principle. Of course water is essential to human survival and biology in general, but more important yet, he suggested, it provides the substance of everything else. It effectively bridges the animate and inanimate realms of the universe. Of course Thales' theory can be criticized as having been a gross simplification, but it initiated the pursuit of a holistic theory more credible than Homer's extravagant fabrications about the gods. This was effectively the first step toward a consistent theory of materialism as an explanation of the universe independent of religion.

II. ANAXIMANDER (ca. 610 – 546 BC)

Anaximander, Thales' disciple and successor in Miletus, took a more inclusive approach by proposing the possibility of an unknown universal substrate
(*apeiron*) that comprises the primary "stuff" of existence but with specific
characteristics as yet undetermined. He did not deny that this basic element
might consist of water, but there were other possibilities as well. He suggested, for example, that the human soul seems air-like, a concept that anticipated the cosmology of Anaximenes. As later explained by Cicero, Anaximander simply proposed *arche* to consist of "an infinity of substance." By
implication, it has no spatial or temporal edge and its existence is necessarily
identical throughout.[6] Anaximander did not try to identify this basic universal "stuff" as a visible element, for example by accepting Thales' suggestion
of water or some kind of a fluid, air as later proposed by Anaximenes, or
earth as still later proposed by Xenophanes. Instead, he suggested that this
substance very likely consists of something entirely different and yet to be
determined, for example the concept of an atomic field of atoms proposed by
Leucippus and Democritus more than a century later.

Anaximander also explained how everything that occurs in the universe
emerges from infinitude through a process of opposition beginning with the
simple but all-purpose binary distinction between heat and cold. This concept
of sustained dualism anticipated the dialectics later featured by Plato and
Aristotle. As briefly explained by Aristotle in a single sentence, Anaximander had maintained, " . . . that [all] contrarieties are contained in the one and
emerge from it by segregation."[7] Hence any particular thing or event necessarily partakes of the universe as a whole through its divergence from another equally pronounced aspect that serves as its opposite. On this basis all
things and events throughout the universe participate in a complex interaction with alternatives equally derived from the whole. Differences in temperature sustain this process as a whole, thereby setting the stage for all other
phenomena to occur in any number of ways through binary opposition.

Little textual evidence of Anaximander's assumptions has survived, and
his explanation is limited to a single passage that can easily be misinterpreted. Here he featured the universal existence of material substance that
undergoes incessant creation and destruction in a cyclical manner:

> The Non-Limited is the original material of existing things; further, the
> source from which existing things derive their existence is also that to which
> they return at their destruction, according to necessity; for they give justice and
> make reparation to one another for their injustice, according to the arrange-
> ment of Time.[8]

Thus, "things make reparation, and therein do justice to one another according to the order of time."[9] By implication ceaseless motion takes place in a steady advance from one extreme to its opposite—from growth to decay, from life to death--without the intervention of a creator identified with a god or gods.

As later suggested by Aristotle in *Physics*, Anaximander might conversely have been willing to identify God with the complete universe in the sense that its physical existence is no less infinite:

> Further, they [all pre-Socratic philosophers] identify it [the universe] with the Divine, for it is deathless and imperishable as Anaximander says, with the majority of the physicists.[10]

Thales had perhaps already implied this, but here Aristotle attributed the acceptance of pantheism to Anaximander, as well as asserting that this possibility was shared by most of the pre-Socratic materialists as well as himself.

On the other hand, Anaximander also seems to have anticipated the theory of evolution by suggesting that all life began in the sea as a product of moisture that evaporates because of heat from the sun. Thereafter, he suggested, it continued to advance and culminated with the creation of mankind. He made no effort to provide a specific explanation of this evolutionary transition, but his proposal obviously anticipated the findings of Darwin many centuries later. More specifically, he proposed a cyclical model of the universe that may have inspired the later cyclical theories proposed by Empedocles and Aristotle. According to Anaximander, the initial opposition between hot and cold throughout the universe lapsed into a complex cycle between wet earth, hot fire, cold air, wet water, dry earth, and finally somehow a broken ring of water and a ring of fire that divides into three subsequent rings. Both Anaximander's evolutionary model and the cyclical cosmology it suggested were described at length in a lost Milesian philosophical text that Theophrastus summarized two centuries later and in turn, his text was summarized by Simplicius six centuries later. [11]

Anaximander also invented the gnomon used for a sundial, and he supposedly constructed a clock to tell the time. Moreover, he devised the first map as a depiction of geographical space, and he was said to have constructed the first artificial globe, thereby suggesting the possibility of the earth's spherical shape later described by Pythagoras. Both Parmenides and Empedocles described a monotheistic god in the shape of a globe, and later Plato and Aristotle adopted Anaximander's concept of the globe as a model equivalent to the earth's shape.

III. ANAXIMENES (ca. 585 - 528 BC)

As an associate of Anaximander and very likely his disciple, Anaximenes specified air as the most likely substrate for the universe because its density is far lower than that of Thales' water. Whereas water's flotation is almost limited to the surface of the earth, air provides a universal medium for the sky as well. Moreover, air almost always involves a high level of motion as compared to water and earth on a graduated scale. Anaximenes also qualified Anaximander's concept of indeterminate space by insisting that it is undetectable except as the result of motion, moisture, or extreme temperature. He apparently explained that air provides the underlying nature of the universe, converting to fire when it becomes finer, then wind, cloud, water, earth, and even stones. The third century theologian, Hippolytus, suggested that Anaximander treated air as the source of all existence including the gods and that its medium supports perpetual motion, perhaps even to the universe as a whole. [12]

Anaximenes' theory is defensible to a certain extent even today. Modern biology confirms that water provides an essential component of the human body, and recent research suggests the likelihood that water existed in a cosmic cloud preceding the creation of the sun. On the other hand, according to a third-century Christian theologian, Hippolytus, Anaximenes went on to suggest that perpetual motion can occur in such a medium, arguably lending support to Anaximander's theory of infinitude and anticipating Aristotle's later theory of mass in incessant motion. [13]

Anaximenes' choice to give air a central role instead of water seemed to make perfect sense at the time. If the universe primarily consists of sky, air can be interpreted as a medium for the universe more relevant to space in general. Three levels of density can be taken into account—air, water, and finally earth and things in general later described as matter. As a possible fourth element, fire—a visible manifestation of heat—could then be added to the hierarchy as first suggested by Anaximander and later emphasized by Heraclitus, on the assumption that heat rises through air as air does through water. Moreover, Thales' concept of water could be described as a tangible manifestation of air, for the seeming interaction between the two could be explained by what we term condensation and rarefaction. Later both Heraclitus and Empedocles went on to combine air with earth, fire and water on a cyclical basis, and still later, its role was enlarged by Diogenes of Laertius in a new level of interpretation that enlarged air's essential role as being relevant to life itself. [14]

IV. XENOPHANES (CA. 570 – 475 BC)

Thought to be a contemporary of Anaximenes, Xenophanes was respected primarily as a religious poet who wrote in epic meter and was said to have lived into his nineties. He was born in the Ionian city of Colophon, roughly fifty miles southeast of Miletus, and the influence of Milesian philosophers, especially Anaximander, influenced his intellectual development. He seems to have fled the region to escape invaders in 546 BC and spent most of his life in exile, having traveled as far as the Sicilian towns of Zancle and Catana. He lived for a while in Elea, where he tutored Parmenides, thereby linking the so-called Eleatic school on the coast of Italy with Thales' Milesian school on the coast of Turkey.

As inspired by Xenophanes and led by Parmenides, the Eleatic school featured a strictly holistic perspective rather than an emphasis on the identity and interactive function of the universe's primary elements. However, Xenophanes was far more concerned about religion than his Milesian precursors. He referred to polytheism at least thirteen times in the fragments available today, as well as having made at least as many as six monotheistic references to a single God. On one hand, Xenophanes' orthodox description of a dominant God surrounded by others of his kind who are less powerful seems obviously polytheistic:

> There is one god, among gods and men the greatest, not at all like mortals in body or in mind.

Then again, a monotheistic version of God seems obvious in other fragments.

> He sees as a whole, thinks as a whole, and hears as a whole.

> But without toil he sets everything in motion, by the thought of his mind.

> And he always remains in the same place, not moving at all, nor is it fitting for him to change his position at different times. [15]

Here a monotheistic God is described with specificity, but Xenophanes also proposed the concept of the universe as a "whole" in "motion." The emphasis on motion suggests the influence of both Anaximander and Anaximenes of the Milesian school, and the emphasis on a "whole in motion" suggests a concept later featured by Parmenides of the Eleatic school as well as Aristotle's mature cosmology.

Xenophanes also emphasized the singular identity of the physical universe much as would later typify Biblical sagacity as well as deist assumptions popular in the eighteenth and nineteenth centuries:

For everything comes from earth and everything goes back to earth at last.

This is the upper limit of the earth that we see at our feet, in contact with the air; but the part beneath goes down to infinity.

All things that come into being and grow are earth and water. [16]

The first of these, "from earth to earth, etc." is obviously identical with Genesis 3.19, suggesting the possibility of a shared source as early as the sixth century BC. On the other hand, the first and third of these fragments anticipate Empedocles' later cyclical model of the universe, while the second and third apparently accept Anaximander's emphasis on earth itself as a basic stuff—in effect an entirely new element comparable to Thales' concept of water and in a supplementary combination different from the earth-air binarism suggested by Anaximenes.

Xenophanes also drew upon Anaximander's concept of a sphere to describe supernatural omniscience with human organs of perception:

God's shape is spherical, altogether different from man. He can see and hear, but does not breathe; he entirely consists of mind and thought, and is eternal. [17]

This concept of God seems to have been intended to provide a spatial analogy that depicts God's comprehensive authority. Just as the center of a sphere is equidistant from all points on its surface, he suggested, God's authority is equally relevant to all things and events in the universe. The infinitude of God's authority can be understood on the assumption that everything that exists is equally determined by the central authority of godhead.

What Xenophanes despised was the Homeric conception of gods as a mixed assortment of anthropomorphic deities that displayed the most reprehensible level of human behavior:

Homer and Hesiod have ascribed deeds to the gods that are a reproach and disgraceful: theft, adultery, and deception.

No less absurd in his opinion was the anthropomorphic depiction of gods based on human appearance and behavior:

Mortals believe the gods are born and have human clothing, voice and form.

Ethiopians say that their gods are flat nosed and dark, Thracians that theirs are blue eyed and red haired.

If oxen and lions had hands and could draw with their hands . . . horses would draw the shapes of gods to look like horses, and oxen to look like oxen, and each would make the gods' bodies have the same shape as they themselves had.[18]

On the whole, Xenophanes seems to have believed in an abstract God or gods somehow identified with the earth and less personified than popular deities at the time.

He also proposed his own version of a secular binarism—effectively a substratum that enlarged Thales supposition to include a binary opposition between earth and water as the two basic elements: "We all have our origin from earth to water," and "All things that come into being and grow are earth and water." By treating water as the "source of wind" he also suggested as many as three primary elements--water, earth, and air.[19] The addition of fire as the fourth basic element would later be adopted by both Heraclitus and Empedocles. The inclusion of earth as one of the primary elements took on even more significance once Melissus effectively substituted the generic concept of mass, anticipating Aristotle's still later concept of binary interaction between mass and motion essential to his final cosmology.

Finally, Xenophanes seems to have anticipated the skeptical assumptions of Sophists several decades later by having declared the inevitability of ignorance, including the knowledge of gods. As possibly the final fragment of his philosophical book, he argued, "Let things be believed for at least seeming to be true."[20] In effect, Xenophanes maintained that individuals deserve the freedom to entertain their own suppositions because there is no absolute verification of the truth relevant to any of them. For even those who may stumble on the truth have no assurance of its veracity. Xenophanes was even willing to extend this caveat to religious belief:

> Yet with respect to the gods and what I declare about all things, no man has seen and no man will know the truth in its clearness. Nay, for e'en should he chance to affirm what is really existent, he himself knoweth it not; but opinion holds sway over all things.[21]

In sum, all presumably valid knowledge necessarily remains opinion, a skeptical stance as later insisted by Athenian Sophists as well as Cicero's generation and beyond.

V. PHERECYDES OF SYROS (CA. 580-520 BC)

An often overlooked early Greek thinker, Pherecydes of Syros seems to have been younger than Thales, but he can be credited with having sought in his own fashion to bridge the gap between Homeric mythology and secular materialism. Like Thales, he was identified as one of the seven wise men, and he bore the distinction of having been the teacher of Pythagoras. He was

also credited with having expressed himself in prose instead of poetry perhaps for the first time among ancient Greek authors. His principal astronomical achievement was his successful determination of the annual turning point
of the sun between winter and summer, and in his lost book *Pentemychos* he
proposed an ambitious metaphysical system that blended science, allegory,
and mythology. Moreover, he was said to have been the first to suggest the
immortality of the soul and the central importance of earth, and a cyclical
cosmology—perhaps the first of its kind--that involved various gods based
on five elements--aether, fire, air, water, and earth. Somehow all of these
were linked with the permanent role of three divine principles--Zeus, earth,
and time. He was said to have initiated the exploration of immortality
through metempsychosis from one mind to the next, as well as a concept of
endless time that seems to have anticipated the later theories of Parmenides,
Melissus and Aristotle. Much of Pherecydes' thinking was compatible with
pre-Socratic assumptions, but his sustained effort to take mythology into
account apparently diminished his contribution as compared to the more
stringent ideas of Thales and his successors. Unfortunately, as with too many
others, nothing he wrote has survived.

VI. PYTHAGORAS AND THE PYTHAGOREANS (ca. 570 - 495 BC)

According to Diogenes Laertius, Pythagoras was born on the island of Samos, and traveled to such regions as Lesbos, Cronos, and Egypt before
returning to Samos, then went into exile as the result of disagreement with its
tyrant, Polycrates. He might have met Thales during his teens and later
visited both Egypt and Babylonia before settling in Croton, a Greek city on
the coast of southern Italy, where he spent the rest of his life. He became a
cult leader with a large following dedicated to a special admixture of mathematical philosophy and his own version of religion derived from Egyptian
mysticism. He promoted the notion of an afterlife and reincarnation before
final union with a universal soul equivalent to a monotheistic God. His core
doctrine was kept a guarded secret by his followers and has for the most part
been lost. Like later philosophers such as Socrates, Arcesilaus, and Carneades, he was said to have taken pride in having written nothing himself, so
the record of his arguments was entirely the product of later disciples. According to Diogenes Laertius, Pythagoras did in fact author at least three
texts—*On Education, On Nature,* and *On Statesmanship*—but was sufficiently embarrassed by his stylistic deficiencies to have prevented their circu-
lation. Modern scholars, however, have rejected this likelihood. [22] Texts identified with his authorship might well have been modified or augmented by
later followers who were probably linked with one of the competitive schools
based on his teachings--the "Acousmatics" (or "Pythagorists"), who featured

his mystical teachings as opposed to the so-called "Mathematicians," who featured his scientific assumptions.

Pythagoras is generally credited with having invented the world *philosopher*. When asked by Leon, the tyrant of Phlius, exactly who he was, Pythagoras supposedly answered with a word that was as a combination of the words *philo* (love) and *sophos* (wisdom), by implication not pertaining to "useful" or "comfortable" truths, but instead the "hard" truths that cannot be denied.[23] He was also said to have invented the word *cosmos* to describe the universe as a whole, and the word *harmony* as a description of music that could be applied to every aspect of life. Moreover, he invented the word *monads* that was later supplanted by Leucippus and Democritus' word *atoms*.

Pythagoras' particular historic achievement was his effort to explain the physical universe on a strictly mathematical basis that was best illustrated by geometry as the analysis of spatial relationships. Most famous was his theorem that the square of any right triangle's hypotenuse is always equal to the combined squares of its two rectangular sides divided in half. Instead of adhering to the Milesian effort to isolate a single physical element comparable to water, air, or earth, he argued that the basic root of physical existence—in effect Anaximander's principle of *arche*—primarily derives from complex mathematical quantification.

As explained by his disciple, Alexander, in *Successions of Philosophers*, Pythagoras proposed the monad as a basic unit of existence, from which derives the dyad as a binarism that links monads, followed by all the rest of the numbers and valid equations that put them into play. He argued that from simple numbers, he argued, derive in succession the point, the line, the solid figure, sensible bodies, and the four elements, fire, water, earth and air, all of which combine to produce the universe as a whole with the earth at its center.[24]

Pythagoreans went so far as to argue that a void equivalent to the number of zero exists which separates all things and even numbers from each other as later explained by Aristotle:

> The Pythagoreans held that void exists and it enters the world from the infinite air, the world inhaling also the void which distinguishes the natures of things, as if it were what separates and distinguishes the terms of a series. This holds primarily in the numbers; for the void distinguishes their nature..[25]

This preliminary aspect of Pythagoras' cosmic model might well have inspired the later concept of particles suspended in a void that was debated by the atomists and Anaxagoras followed by Aristotle and Strato's effort to obtain a defensible synthesis.

Like Anaximander and Xenophanes, Pythagoras was fascinated by the sphere and even considered it the most beautiful solid figure and comparable to the circle as the most beautiful plane figure. He was the first to describe the earth as being spherical well before the astronomical findings of the Alexandrian astronomer Hicetas, who inspired Copernicus' heliocentric theory many centuries later.

The basic and most accessible evidence Pythagoras used to support his elaborate cosmology was the harmonious relationship among intervals on a musical scale as illustrated by the length and tightness of strings. He proposed the concept of *harmonia* to designate an integrated relationship on such a scale relevant to all phenomena and then drew upon this principle to define odd and even numbers, prime and composite numbers, and square numbers in the realm of arithmetic. He also identified this harmony on a celestial scale as a cosmic music of the spheres. In medicine he proposed his own version of homeopathy, using opposites to stabilize physical disorders. One's physical health, he suggested, depends on the effective sustenance of an appropriate balance that can be quantified on an arithmetic basis: "Health means the retention of the form, disease its destruction."[26]

As later mentioned by Aristotle, Pythagoras' disciples--described as Pythagoreans--used Anaximenes' concept of air in their explanation of music as a universal principle that might also explain human behavior as it relates to other and more inclusive aspects of cosmology:

> The theory handed down from the Pythagoreans . . . [they] declared that the soul is identical with the particles in the air, and others with what makes these particles move. These particles have found their place in the theory because they can be seen perpetually in motion even when the air is completely calm . . . for they all seem to assume that movement is the distinctive characteristic of the soul, and that everything else owes its movement to the soul . . ."[27]

The Pythagoreans seem to have anticipated Anaxagoras and Plato's cosmology of a universal soul, Leucippus and Democritus' cosmology of incessant atomic interaction, and even Aristotle's cosmology of mass in perpetual motion as explained in *De Caelo*.

Pythagoras rejected the Homeric gods, but he continued to accept the concepts of prophecy, divination, and the transmigration of souls, and he argued that the sun, moon, and stars might be considered gods because they generate heat as suggested by Anaximander's cosmology. He correctly proposed that the sun illuminates the moon and that "gods and man are akin inasmuch as man partakes of heat." Fate is the cause of things, he maintained, and all things that live partake of heat. Moreover, he suggested, biological reproduction results from germination, and the entire soul comprises three parts—intelligence, reason, and passion. He also argued that consciousness draws nourishment from the blood supply to the brain; and since reason alone is immortal, he proposed, only the human soul is immortal. This particular assumption confirmed the link between reason and mathematics as well as having anticipated both Platonic metaphysics and Aristotle's assumption of graduated human consciousness. Also implicit in Epicurus' cosmology was a theory of order and logic seemingly at odds with Anaximenes' theory of air that implied limitless boundaries. In contrast, Pythagoras' alternative emphasis on number and mathematical exactitude featured forms accessible to cognitive recognition.

There were several accounts of Pythagoras' death, but most likely he and as many as forty of his disciples seem to have been murdered by the inhabitants of the neighboring town of Croton. It seems these angry townsmen resented what seemed the arrogance of Pythagoras and his followers that culminated in the school's effort to impose its own government on the entire community. In a public confrontation, an angry throng of hostile Crotons supposedly cut Pythagoras' throat, then slaughtered all but two of his followers.

Later disciples who adhered to Pythagorean doctrine continued to conceal its wide assortment of assumptions from the scrutiny of others. Those who broke this rule were subject to punishment and even expulsion as illustrated by the harsh treatment of Hippasus when he disclosed some of its mathematical secrets. Even Empedocles seems have been expelled several decades later when he sought to incorporate some aspects of Pythagorean doctrine into his writings. The accurate perpetuation of Pythagorean assumptions seems to have been the intention of this enforced secrecy, but their secrecy also seems to have permitted continuous revisions in response to the theoretical stance of later pre-Socratic philosophers.

By some accounts, the eminent philosopher-scientist Alcmaeon lived in Croton in the second half of the sixth century BC and was a student of Pythagoras and was considered a Pythagorean by Diogenes Laertius and others. This possibility seems to have been ignored by sources preceding Diogenes Laertius and to be disputed by a variety of modern classicists. However, the possibility of his personal relationship, his residence in Croton, and the dedication of his single book *On Nature* to Pythagoreans suggest the likelihood of his connection with the movement. He wrote mostly on medical issues, for example an analysis of the brain as the seat of consciousness, the essential role of sensation, and the necessity of balance between excess and deficiency in the sustenance of the body. He was also credited, however, with first suggesting the immortality of the soul, very likely having inspired Plato's later explanation of the soul in *Phaedrus*. He extended this principle to the "justice" of the whole universe as a conflict between opposites, most notably between earth and fire as complementary basic elements. That Xenophanes featured earth just as Heraclitus featured fire suggests the possibility of a chronological sequence among the three theories, but at this time there is no evidence to determine their order.

There was no confirmed textual record of Pythagorean doctrine until the publication of the treatise *On the Universe* by Philolaus, a contemporary of Socrates whose mentor Lysis was one of the two disciples to have survived the massacre at Croton. Philolaus apparently retained Pythagoras' mathematical perspective, for example, featuring the unique status of the number ten and the concept of a harmonic mean as illustrated by musical figures. However, he also seems to have addressed Heraclitus' concept of fire, Parmenides' holistic concept of the universe, and Empedocles' cyclical model. Moreover, he argued, the cube represents geometric harmony that suggests Pythagoras' concept of a harmonic mean.

According to Diogenes Laertius, Philolaus also proposed the creation of an expanding circular universe with symmetrical thickness: "The universe is one, and it began to come into being from the centre, and from the centre upwards at the same intervals as those below." On the other hand, he described the sun as a celestial lens that transmits both the light and heat of the rest of the universe on the earth, a concept not entirely without merit if the sun sustains the heat and light first produced by the Big Bang.[28] Perhaps inspired by Philolaus, Plato later offered the concept of a single god at the center of such an eruption, as opposed to Aristotle's concept of perpetual orbits devoid of central godhead.[29]

In a possibly spurious fragment, Philolaus' cosmology also seems to have provided a broad synthesis of an inclusive cyclical realm as earlier suggested by Parmenides, one that anticipated both Plato's transcendent aspect of soul and universal mind and Aristotle's more secular concept of modification in a strictly physical universe:

> But since the moving part circles from everlasting to everlasting, and the part that is moved is disposed in whatever way the moving part carries it, it follows necessarily that one is ever in motion and the other ever passive. And the one is wholly the dwelling of Mind and Soul, and the other of Becoming and Change; and the one is first in power and superior, and the other is second and inferior. But that which is made of both these, namely the ever-running (*circling*) Divine and the ever-changing Mortal, is the universe.[30]

The passage seems to have anticipated both the theories of Plato and Aristotle. However, any effort to distinguish its accuracy relevant to this choice is necessarily speculative as a summary of Pythagoras' original doctrine.

There is no clear evidence of Philolaus' influence on Plato despite the likelihood that he acquired a copy of *On the Universe* and wrote *Timaeus* in response to its ideas. He mentioned Philolaus by name only once in his writings—an incidental reference in *Phaedo*, an entirely different text. According to Diogenes Laertius, Philolaus nevertheless advocated an abstract deterministic cosmology that possibly inspired Platonism to a certain extent, "that all things are brought about by necessity and harmonious inter-relation." However, this intention also seems to have anticipated Aristotle's assumptions as suggested by Philolaus' first sentence of his book quoted by Diogenes Laertius, "Nature in the ordered universe was composed of unlimited and limiting elements, and so was the whole universe and all that is therein."[31] In effect, Philolaus seems to have enlarged and updated Pythagoras' theory to justify the concept of a self-sufficient universe relevant to later and more advanced theoretical contributions. By doing so he helped to set the stage for the more inclusive formulations of both Plato and Aristotle.

VII. HERACLITUS (CA. 540 - 480 BC)

Heraclitus was born about sixty miles north of Miletus in the port city of Ephesus to an aristocratic family from whom he inherited considerable wealth. He lived to about the age of sixty, supposedly transferred his endowment to his younger brother, abandoned all social connections, and became increasingly misanthropic toward the end of his life. His single reference to Ephesus suggests implacable hostility, "May wealth not fail you, men of Ephesus, so that you may be convicted of your wickedness!"[32] There is no indication he was directly connected with the Milesian school or with any major philosopher at the time, but he seems to have been aware of the earlier arguments of Xenophanes and Pythagoras. While he never mentioned Parmenides' arguments, Parmenides seems to have been aware of his.

Heraclitus seems to have authored a single text with three sections loosely devoted to the topics of religion, statecraft, and cosmology, and one hundred-forty passages have been preserved as aphorisms rather than portions of longer texts. Perhaps ironically, he warns in fragment 47, "Let us not conjecture at random about the greatest things," though he himself confronts exactly this risk. His topics exhibit little continuity, justifying Aristotle's complaint that he failed to prolong any argument, but his ability to encapsulate a theoretical paradox within the fewest possible words was exceptional.

At first many of these aphorisms might seem self-evident, but upon further consideration take on deeper significance. For example, the obvious insight of fragment 12, "Those who step into the same river have different waters flowing ever upon them," enlarges Anaximenes' concept of incessant motion by suggesting sustained interaction between change and stasis. Plato later suggested a slight modification, "All things are in motion and nothing is at rest," and in turn Aristotle proposed the universal principle of all things caught up in eternal motion.[33] Aristotle extended this to a cyclical explanation of the seasons, astronomical phenomena, and the cycle of life and death, all of which seems anticipated by fragment 103 of Heraclitus, "Beginning and end are general in the circumference of the circle."[34]

In *Metaphysics* Aristotle attributed to Heraclitus two obviously linked paradoxical aphorisms: (1) "all things are and are not," and (2) "all things are true and all are false." These seemingly empty maxims suggest the frequent contradiction that what seems valid relevant to one perspective can be rejected in light of another.[35] Also insightful is Heraclitus' notion that the transition from one state of affairs to another is a stable aspect of existence:

> The sun is new each day.

> The way up and down is one and the same. [36]

Relevant to change as a discernible process, Heraclitus proposes fire to be the fourth and most basic substance additional to water, air, and earth:

> Fire lives the death of earth and air lives the death of fire; water lives the death of air, earth that of water. [37]

However, fire seems to have taken on a double and therefore even more important role. Both Anaximander and Pythagoras had already featured the vital necessity of warmth, but Heraclitus enlarges the principle by identifying fire itself—presumably the agent of warmth--as the primary source of transition among the other elements. In its double role as both one of these four stages in perpetual sequence but also as effectively the agent that imposes this transition, he apparently suggests that fire is the dominant aspect of the universe, as indicated by three additional fragments:

> There is an exchange: all things for Fire and Fire for all things, like goods for gold and gold for goods.

> Fire, having come upon them, will judge and seize upon (condemn) all things.

> Need and satiation. [38]

More specifically, Heraclitus identified lightning as a particularly dramatic version of fire launched from the sky with great power:

> The thunder-bolt (*i.e. Fire*) steers the universe. [39]

Elsewhere Heraclitus substituted "soul" for "fire," suggesting the possibility that the two are different versions of the same principle in sequence with earth, air, and water, and with each phase destroyed with the inception of the next:

To souls it is death to become water; to water, it is death to become earth. From earth comes water, and from water, soul.[40]

Heraclitus even substituted soul for air, featured by both Anaximenes and Empedocles, setting the stage for Anaxagoras' later concept of *Nous* as a principle of universal mind later essential to Platonic metaphysics.

Just as earth, air, and water in combination antedates Aristotle's later concept of matter, Heraclitus' theory of fire can also be understood to have anticipated the concept of energy as a basic process equivalent to the other three as substances collectively identified as mass. Also suggestive of at least the inevitable effect of fire, Heraclitus proposed elsewhere that the world is in such total flux that the truth can never be fully disclosed:

The hidden harmony is stronger (or 'better') than the visible.

Nature likes to hide.[41]

For the sake of argument, modern naturalists might be willing to accept a slightly different sequence that identifies fire with the Big Bang, followed by earth identified with planetary matter, and water and air as basic elements that support life. In as many as three fragments—31, 36, and finally 76—Heraclitus took into account Anaximander's theory of cycles to suggest a relatively complicated life-and-death sequence that also anticipated the four-stage cycle that Empedocles adopted in his later circular cosmology. Then death itself becomes the principal agent of transition, and the reference to soul (or consciousness) identified with air in this fourfold cycle of transitions renews the original concept of Anaximenes without reference to fire.

Heraclitus also reexamined the destructive aspect of conflict on both a negative and positive basis:

War is both king of all and father of all, and it has revealed some as gods, others as men; some it has made slaves, others free.

One should know that war is general (*universal*) and jurisdiction is strife, and everything comes about by way of strife and necessity.[42]

Struggle and its result in destruction are inevitable aspects of the universe according to Heraclitus' cosmology. Yet he also suggested harmony plays a universal role, and by implication the universe somehow manifests the inter-action between conflict and harmony at the most basic level. Heraclitus proposed a countervailing holistic theory of the universe that depends on more inclusive harmony linked with soul, identified as *Logos* ("the word" or any logical argument that can be verbalized on a more inclusive basis) as explained in several of his fragments:

The Law (*of the universe*) is as here explained; but men are always incapable of understanding it, both before they hear it, and when they have heard it for the first time. For though all things come into being in accordance with this Law, men seem as if they had never met with it, when they meet with words (theories) and actions (processes) . . .

That which is in opposition is in concert, and from things that differ comes the most beautiful harmony.

Joints: whole and not whole, connected-separate, consonant-dissonant.

You could not in your going find the ends of the soul, though you travelled the whole way: so deep is its Law (*Logos).*

When you have listened, not to me but to the Law (*Logos)*, it is wise to agree that all things are one.

For all human laws are nourished by one, which is divine. For it governs as far as it will, and is sufficient for all, and more than enough. [43]

Heraclitus anticipated the later concept of a unified universe of Parmenides and Aristotle by explaining the universe based on the principle of *Logos*--the "purpose which steers all things through all things."[44] Though fire both sustains and participates in cyclical interaction with earth, air, and water as components of the physical universe, an even more basic factor plays the most dominant role, a holistic organization akin to human intelligence imbedded in the universe. As opposed to a process identified with fire, Heraclitus thus seems to have proposed *Logos* as a more inclusive principle of stasis that both dominates and stabilizes the universe. The dialectic opposition between the two—fire and *Logos*—presented at an entirely new level Anaximander's initial theory of binarisms that predominate in the universe as a whole.

By having advanced the notion of *Logos*, Heraclitus may be said to have invented his own version of metaphysics as a dialectic explanation of the complete universe. Plato seems to have been inspired by his theory of *Logos,* and Aristotle, followed by Sextus Empiricus and others, seem to have been influenced by Heraclitus' dialectic if without fully supporting it.[45] Even the New Testament's Gospel of John starts with wording possibly inspired by Heraclitus, "In the beginning was the Word [i.e. *Logos*], and the Word was with God, and the Word was God." John's specific use of the Greek word *Logos* in this passage seems entirely in accord with Heraclitus' use of the word five centuries earlier.

In a couple of passages, Heraclitus seems to have explained *Logos* on a strictly religious basis, for example by accepting the notion of a "divine law" as a single principle relevant to the universe:

> If we speak with intelligence, we must base our strength on that which is common to all, as the city of the Law (*Nomos*), and even more strongly. For all human laws are nourished by one, which is divine. For it governs as far as it will, and is sufficient for all, and more than enough. [46]

Divine law can be identified with an orthodox concept of God's authority, and by implication such a God becomes a benevolent figure who exudes charity necessarily misunderstood by mankind:

> God is day-night, winter-summer, war-peace . . . but he changes like (fire) which when it mingles with the smoke of incense is named according to each man's pleasure.
>
> To God all things are beautiful, good and just; but men have assumed some things to be unjust, others just. [47]

It seems possible that these fragments were later interpolations, but Heraclitus can be said to have rejected orthodox religious observances at least to the extent that they consist of "rites accepted by mankind in the Mysteries are an unholy performance"[48] Neither Orphic practices nor Homeric mythology seem to have had any particular appeal to him. Like his predecessors Xenophanes and Epicurus, he did not entirely abandon religion but sought to explain the physical universe based on ultimate authority, perhaps but not necessarily, identified with a deity. His ambivalence is shown in two fragments in which he linked "that which is wise is one" first with Zeus identified by name and later with the more abstract reference to a "purpose which steers all things through all things." He declared in the first fragment that singular wisdom is both willing and unwilling to be called by the name of Zeus," and in the second he took a more abstract stance by declaring "That which is wise is one: to understand the purpose which steers all things through all things."[49] In the second passage, final authority consisted of the capacity for imparting both motion and direction to everything in the universe. This primal source can be considered a God or gods, or Plato's spiritual authority, or even Aristotle's altogether secular concept of mass in perpetual motion. To this extent at least, Heraclitus' arguments anticipated both science and metaphysics supportive of religion.

Few if any scholars accept the bizarre account of Heraclitus' death as told by Diogenes Laertius, especially since its singular violence might seem to have been fabricated in the effort to ridicule his theories. Supposedly Heraclitus sought to cure a skin affliction by pasting a mixture of animal feces over his entire body. He then lay in the sun to let the mixture dry out, but it hardened to such an extent that he was unable to protect himself when a pack of hungry dogs devoured him alive! It should be acknowledged that Diogenes Laertius was alone in having recounted this as well as a few other such bizarre death stories--respectively of Strato and Empedocles. However, in all three instances no one else has left an alternative version.

VIII. PARMENIDES (ca. 515 - 450 BC)

Parmenides effectively marks the midpoint of pre-Socratic philosophy, having been born as many as five decades after Xenophanes and five decades before Democritus. Like Heraclitus he was the product of a wealthy family and was raised in Croton near the Sicilian communal site of Pythagoras and his disciples. He also seems to have been familiar with the ideas of Heraclitus, who was perhaps a generation older, and in his youth he had a Pythagorean teacher, Ameinias, as well as Xenophanes, who was still alive when Parmenides eventually became the founder and principal philosopher of the so-called Eleatic school located near Rome at Elea. He played a central role in the advance of Greek philosophy and perhaps lived long enough to meet the youthful Socrates, as Plato indicates in his dialogue *Parmenides.*

Whereas earlier Milesian philosophers had emphasized matter or the "stuff" of the universe, under his influence the Eleatic school emphasized the temporal and spatial limitlessness of the universe—effectively an absence of any kind of an edge or boundary relevant to timeless infinitude as maintained by Parmenides himself or on both a temporal and spatial basis as maintained by Melissus. In a single large fragment preserved by Sextus Empiricus recorded by Simplicius, Parmenides accepted a holistic concept of the universe as earlier suggested by Anaximander and Xenophanes, but he also sought to revise and enlarge Heraclitus' concept of *Logos* by depicting the universe as a limitless but indivisible and self-sufficient whole that was devoid of motion. Stasis dominated rather than alteration on the assumption that all changes cancel each other out. Otherwise, he both accepted and superseded the physical reductionism in the Milesian tradition and the mathematical emphasis of Pythagoras.

In the approximately two dozen fragments available today, Parmenides began his analysis with a mythical vision of a Homeric goddess who delivered him by chariot into a supernatural realm where his many questions could be answered by rejecting all "things that seem" and rejecting those without proof. Needless to say, his use of a fictive goddess to declare the necessity of truth could well have been an intentional contradiction:

> Thou shall inquire into everything: both the motionless heart of well-rounded Truth, and also the opinions of mortals, in which there is no true reliability.

But nevertheless thou shalt learn these things (*opinions*) also—how one should go through all the things-that-seem, without exception, and test them. [50]

His supernatural guide then gives guidance to Parmenides on how to tell truth from falsehood:

> You must accept my word when you have heard it—the ways of inquiry which alone are to be thought: the one that IT IS, and it is not possible for IT NOT TO BE, is the way of credibility, for it follows Truth; the other, that IT IS NOT, and that IT is bound NOT TO BE: this . . . is a path that cannot be explored; for you could neither recognize that which is NOT, nor express it. [51]

Parmenides also highlighted the importance of temporal continuity with his insistence that "Being has no coming-into-being and no destruction, for it is whole of limb," and effectively endless. At the risk of contradicting himself, he argued, that nothing can come "into being, beside Being itself, out of Not-Being." [52] The implication seems obvious that existence never began nor will it ever end. Also that the universe was never created nor is there any prospect of its termination. Therefore, existence can only be explained in and of itself, and truth ultimately accords with existence. The countless assortment of untruths that deviate from this principle of existence—for example the vivid possibility of an enormous turtle with earth perched on its shell—simply do not exist except in their lively depiction.

Parmenides capped his description of the universe in a passage with the anthropomorphic concept of a ruling goddess might well have been intended as a parody of Heraclitus' earlier depiction. Just as a relatively minor goddess supposedly first confronted with the truth, a higher goddess—presumably the highest—actually informs him of this truth in light of Heraclitus' depiction of fire:

> For the narrower rings were filled with unmixed Fire, and those next to them with Night, but between (*these*) rushes the portion of Flame. 'And in the centre of these is the goddess who guides everything; for throughout she rules over cruel Birth and Mating, sending the female to mate with the male, and conversely again the male with the female. [53]

Parmenides quickly simplified the most basic task of this goddess as the principle of love: "First of all the gods she devised Love." [54] Here love once again plays a pivotal role, perhaps as inspired by the early Greek poet Hesiod.

Perhaps inspired by Xenophanes, Parmenides declared that the earth is spherical and located in the center of the universe, and first emphasized that sensation can only be inexact, confirming the necessity of reason, for example in determining the most basic truths of nature such as, " . . . how earth and sun and moon, and the aether common to all, and the Milky Way in the heavens, and outermost Olympus, and the hot power of the stars, hastened to come into being."[55] But like Heraclitus, Parmenides also proposed that the soul and mind are effectively identical, and he advocated the necessity of reason "instead of imagination's deceit" in deciding whether "the generation of man" ultimately derives from the sun as an effect of heat that "surpasses the sun itself." As later explained by Diogenes Laertius, he suggested the paradox as justified by his own example that only human reason can equal or exceed the physical manifestation of the universe.[56]

As Aristotle noted, Parmenides' ultimate contribution was his simple implication--apparently inspired by Xenophanes--that the One is God, a monist concept that anticipated both Plato's theory of spiritual infinitude and even Aristotle's theory of an endless physical universe.[57] However, Parmenides also seems to have divided the universe into the "flaming fire in the heavens" (or light) as depicted by Heraclitus and what might be construed as its polar opposite, either earth or "dark Night, a dense and heavy body" as depicted by Xenophanes. Both are equal, Protagoras proposed, "because to neither of them belongs any share of the other." He also explained in materialist terms that suggest Anaximander's dichotomy, "Everything is full equally of Light and invisible Night, as both are equal, because to neither of them belongs any share (of the other)."[58]

Despite its apparent contradictions, Parmenides work seems to have inspired later scientific and philosophical inquiry at an abstract level of analysis. On the other hand, his cosmology also anticipated the concept of a spiritual universe later emphasized by Anaxagoras and Plato, and it is not surprising that it was later featured in Plato's dialogue, "Parmenides," in which he submitted to elaborate explanation the axiom, "If there is no one, there is nothing at all." As explained by Parmenides, Heraclitus' concept of *Logos* with an identity as "one"—had become the ultimate issue.

IX. ZENO OF ELEA (ca. 490 – 430 BC)

Zeno seems to have been born in Elea in 489 BC, roughly twenty-five years after Parmenides. He was possibly an adopted son of Parmenides as well as his disciple and, according to Plato in his dialogue *Parmenides*, they journeyed together to Athens to meet Socrates. By 446 BC Zeno's first book, *Disputations,* was apparently published against his will with the subtitle *Against the Philosophers* and/or *Treatise on Nature*. It was a highly argumentative book, and his principal target seems to have been the Pythagoreans, the first of the pre-Socratic cosmologists to have called themselves philosophers. Though Zeno, like Parmenides, might have been exposed to Pythagorean doctrine at an early age, later Pythagoreans seem to have rejected the holistic emphasis of Parmenides, and Zeno came to his defense by challenging the inescapable limitations of their mathematical Pythagorean assumptions.

According to Aristotle, Zeno was the first to employ dialectic analysis just as Empedocles was said to be the first to discover rhetoric. Zeno's specific approach can be described as having been dialectic in the sense that he used logic on a negative basis in order to deny one thesis in order to demonstrate its opposite. By disproving X, he proved the opposite of X. In effect he sought to reduce supposedly credible theories to absurdity (e.g. the Pythagorean assumption that discrete numbers are imbedded in the universe) in order to demonstrate their inadequacy. He was credited with the first use of logical analysis one that Aristotle went on to substantially enlarge and formalize for a more comprehensive theory of deductive logic. Zeno's most famous use of this strategy was his rejection of the Epicurean notion that all "things are a many" in a numerical sense, since they may be described as an infinitude of discrete entities identified as limits. To demonstrate his thesis, Zeno suggested that anybody who advances to a distant goal must first advance half the distance, but earlier by a fourth, earlier yet by an eighth, and so on. Therefore, an infinite number of intermediate stages--each of them effectively a point on a line--must first be completed in the effort to attain the final goal, and as a result nothing in motion can reach its destination. Other such paradoxes described by Aristotle included determining the exact location of a place and even the sound of millet seeds when they hit the floor. As explained by Aristotle, Zeno suggested infinite divisibility might seem to preclude actualization, but of course it does not, demonstrating that mathematical calculation alone cannot fully describe a continuous and essentially holistic universe. Zeno did not believe any of the paradoxes he proposed, but used them as hypothetical examples to discredit what he thought was facile mathematical analysis.

For his successors, Zeno's primary theoretical contribution was to have featured this paradox and others like it, which were probably proposed in the single book he wrote early in his career as mentioned in Plato's dialogue "Parmenides." Later Aristotle took into account this particular example of Zeno's argumentation several times, but without otherwise mentioning his theoretical assumptions. Even today Zeno's paradox is generally understood as an absurdity, but this was intended by Zeno himself who used it to demonstrate the inadequacy of mathematical exactitude to explain physical process on a holistic basis.

Ironically, the deviation of reality from its numerical calculation was perhaps best illustrated by Zeno's experience with death as his own personal transition—how and in what sequence nobody can be sure. As told by Diogenes Laertius, whose story can neither be confirmed nor rejected by consulting alternative sources, one of three possibilities transpired when he lost his life. As a prisoner standing before the throne of Demylus, Elea's tyrant at the time, Zeno was said to have offered to whisper the names of his fellow collaborators in the ear of Demylus, who supposedly accepted his offer. But then Zeno bit his ear and would not release his grip until he himself was stabbed to death by loyal soldiers. Another possibility suggested by Diogenes Laertius, however, was that Zeno bit Demylus' nose, not his ear, and was killed for having done so, or, as a third possibility, he might have instead bitten off his own tongue and spit it in Demylus' face, whereupon an angry crowd murdered Demylus.[59] There is no historic evidence which, if any of these accounts was true, but in all three instances a transition occurred whereby life was followed by death for one or both of the two individuals, Zeno and Demylus. Needless to say, as with Diogenes Laertius' account of the deaths of both Heraclitus and Empedocles, there seems ample room for skepticism among modern scholars.

X. MELISSUS OF SAMOS (WON SEA BATTLE IN 441 BC)

Like Pythagoras, Melissus was born in Samos and in his maturity he supposedly became a respected statesman. As the admiral of Samos' fleet during the Peloponnesian War, he was celebrated for having broken an Athenian blockade against the island in 441-40 BC. His status as a philosopher, on the other hand, seems to have been almost incidental, despite the importance of his assumptions. There is no clear evidence that he had any direct link with Parmenides or with any of the other philosophers at the time, and little is known about his theoretical achievement beyond his prose treatise *On Being*, even though it enlarged the Eleatic concept of existence as a unified whole. His brief reference to earth, air, fire, and water as elements suggests he was aware of Empedocles' assumptions.[60] However, he ignored the theories of both Empedocles and Anaxagoras.

His primary contribution seems to have been in extending Parmenides' concept of infinitude to apply to space as well as time. No boundaries exist, he asserted, that limit temporal or spatial infinitude. By implication, no exterior realm such as heaven, paradise, or Hades is possible as a separate realm from the physical universe. Whereas Parmenides conceded the possibility of spatial limitations of the universe by describing the universe as a sphere with all points equidistant from its center, as earlier suggested by Anaximander and Xenophanes, Melissus rejected the concepts of both spatial and temporal boundaries in a disconcertingly short sentence, "But as it [existence] is always, so also its size must always be infinite."[61] Both time and space are alike in that they are necessarily endless without a center or any kind of edge or perimeter.

Melissus also expanded Parmenides' holistic notion, "what exists is one" by emphasizing the importance of extension devoid of borders:

> If it were infinite, it would be One; for if it were two, (*these*) could not be (*spatially*) infinite, but each would have boundaries in relation to each other. [62]

This doubled concept of the infinitude of both time and space clarifies Melissus' agnostic supposition quoted by Diogenes Laertius that it is impossible to have knowledge of the gods. [63] Any thing or event—even one or more gods--might seem isolated by some kind of an edge or boundary, for example birth, death, or bodily mass, but its very occurrence situates it in the universe that as a whole possesses both temporal and spatial infinitude.

Melissus also offered a number of paradoxes that linked the concept of boundaries with the distinction between existence and non-existence. Several of these paradoxes can be quoted as examples that support Parmenides' primary assumptions:

> . . . before it came into being, Nothing existed. If however Nothing existed, in no way could anything come into being out of nothing. Nor is there any Emptiness; for the Empty is Nothing; and so that which is Nothing cannot be. And there can be no Dense and Rare.

> If Things were Many, they would have to be of the same kind as I say the One is.

> If Being Is, it must be One; and if it is One, it is bound not to have body. But if it had Bulk, it would have parts, and would no longer be.

> If Being is divided, it moves; and if it moved, it could not be. [64]

Melissus accepted the possibility of mixture among elements, though he seems to have rejected Democritus' notion of atoms as impenetrable matter surrounded by void as a state of absence that "cannot be." [65] Melissus argued in a different context, "If Things were Many, they would have to be of the same kind as I say the One is." [66] Thus the principle of unbounded limits that applies to the universe as a whole also applies to all atoms within the universe. In effect a void cannot exist in interior space any more than in the universe as a whole. [67] With this wording Melissus seems to have suggested difficulties with Leucippus' notion of atomism that anticipated Strato's later effort to obtain a synthesis between the two.

Aristotle was highly critical of Melissus' arguments in several contexts, suggesting at the very beginning of *Physics*, " . . . the argument of Melissus is gross and offers no difficulty at all: accept one ridiculous proposition and the rest follows--a simple enough proceeding." Later in the text Aristotle took

Melissus' thesis more seriously by offering the dubious refutation, "But there is no necessity for there being a void if there is movement. It is not in the least needed as a condition of movement in general, for a reason which escaped Melissus: viz. that the full can suffer qualitative change." Significantly, Aristotle revisited these considerations in *De Caelo* and seems to have considerably modified his stance by conceding that Melissus' arguments, like those of Parmenides, were defensible on a metaphysical basis though he could not be "held to speak as a student of nature."[68] Arguably this obvious threefold stair-step sequence of responses by Aristotle supports the likelihood that *Physics* was a relatively early work as compared to *De Caelo*, in which he seems to have consolidated his cosmology by more effectively obtaining a synthesis between metaphysics and the science of physics as justified by Melissus' pivotal insight regarding infinitude.

XI. EMPEDOCLES (CA. 492 – 432 BC)

Empedocles was born in Sicily, and was about a generation younger than Parmenides and a generation older than Anaxagoras. He was a mystic, physician, poet, dramatist, political activist, and what might be described as an eclectic philosophical genius. He was supposedly expelled from the Pythagorean society during his youth for having incorporated passages from their secret discourses into his early poetry, and, according to Diogenes Laertius, he later studied as a fellow student of Zeno under Parmenides. He admired Parmenides and supposedly imitated his poetry in declaring his own philosophical ideas. During his life his fame rested as much on his poetic eloquence as his contribution to philosophy, and much of his philosophy was appreciated at the time as a prose version of poetry. He was said to have written as many as forty-three tragedies as well as a 600-line book pertaining to medicine. Also, he may have been the first philosopher to take an interest in botany, and Aristotle later described him as the inventor of rhetoric.

In opposition to autocratic power Empedocles seems to have played a populist role in local politics and at one point was offered the kingship of the city, which he refused. Also, he supposedly wore extravagant clothing, became wealthy in his old age, and took pride in his status as a prophet. He seems to have been describing himself when he wrote:

> There was living among them a man of surpassing knowledge, who had acquired the extremest wealth of the intellect, one expert in every kind of skilled activity. For whenever he reached out with his whole intellect, he easily discerned each one of existing things, in ten and even twenty lifetimes of mankind.[69]

Empedocles supposedly even went so far as to encourage many compatriots to believe that he was a god.

Almost a fifth of Empedocles' philosophical writings are estimated to have survived, including a variety of fragments quoted by as many as fifteen later authors—eleven fragments by Aristotle, eight by Simplicius, six by Plutarch, etc. This is more than for any of the other pre-Socratic philosophers, despite the likelihood that he wrote not more than one or two books on cosmology, *On Nature* and *Purifications*. These are usually mentioned as unrelated texts, but it has been suggested that they might have been separate titles for the same text. There is a striking contrast among his fragments between a religious and secular perspective, and it cannot be discounted that he might have sought to mingle the two viewpoints in a single book.

Empedocles' religious convictions are on frequent display in his fragments, for example, in his passage, "Happy is he who enjoys the wealth of divine thoughts, but wretched the man whose mind emphasizes obscure opinion about the gods!" In the same context he also suggested a surrealistic depiction of a particular God, possibly Apollo, who combined Parmenides and Anaxagoras' principle of universal mind with Xenophanes concept of spherical manifestation:

> It is not possible to bring God near within reach of our eyes, nor to grasp him with our hands, by which route the broadest road of Persuasion runs into the human mind. [70]

> But he (God) is equal in all directions to himself and altogether eternal, a rounded Sphere enjoying a circular solitude. [71]

Empedocles' identification of God with mind anticipated the more elaborate suppositions of both Anaxagoras and Plato, but there is no clear evidence whether his incidental suggestion preceded or followed Anaxagoras' more elaborate explanation.

Like Parmenides, on the other hand, Empedocles insisted on the eternal existence of the universe without any necessary reference to one or more gods:

> But that which is lawful for all extends continuously through the broad-ruling Air and through the boundless Light. [72]

A universal law was also an issue of utmost importance to both Plato's later concept of godhead as eternal mind and, still later, Aristotle's concept of an eternal physical universe which is modified solely by motion. Also possibly influenced by Parmenides, Empedocles suggested the temporal infinitude of the universe:

. . . it is impossible for anything to come into being; and for Being to perish completely is incapable of fulfillment and unthinkable; for it will always be there, wherever anyone may place it on any occasion. [73]

By implication, such endlessness necessarily precludes the role of a God or gods in having created it. Empedocles insisted on this likelihood at least twice again as applied to human destiny:

There is no creation of substance in any one of mortal existences, nor any end in inexecrable death, but only mixing and exchange of what has been mixed; and the name 'substance' is applied to them by mankind. [74]

Empedocles rejected the concept that non-existence both precedes birth and follows death for the individual human being: ". . . before mortals were combined (*out of the Elements*) and after they were dissolved, they are nothing at all." [75] The obvious compromise among these variant assumptions, as later suggested by Aristotle, would be that individuals do in fact die but not the species as a whole.

At times Empedocles seems entirely confident of a received monotheistic viewpoint. Elsewhere, however, his attitude seems pantheistic, for example when he declares his acceptance of Anaxagoras's assumption, "For all things . . . have intelligence and a portion of Thought." [76] Often his rhetorical skills obscure the contradictions implicit in his arguments, and well enough for him to have avoided the prosecution that seemed more likely for outspoken atheists such as Democritus and Protagoras.

Empedocles addressed his book(s) to his disciple Pausanias with a conventional invocation to his own Muse with knowledge as "divine law [that] allows us creatures of a day to hear." He asked Pausanias to grasp his true assumptions in his "inner heart," but also to protect them "within [his] silent bosom," apparently to prevent their disclosure. It remains to be seen whether these feelings supported popular religion or his materialist assumptions, such as appeared in one of his published texts that attracted more readers than those of most of his contemporary philosophers. Elsewhere Empedocles called upon Pausanias to "hear" Zeus, Hera, Aidoneus, and Nestis," but he also took the risk articulating current secular assumptions. Not that Empedocles totally rejected religion. Rather, he seems to have sought to bridge the gap between received belief and secular possibilities. Like Anaximander and Pythagoras, he took satisfaction in a unified physical universe that could be analyzed on a consistent basis, but like Anaxagoras and later, Plato he sought a strictly spiritual explanation for this transcendent outcome.

Like Parmenides, Empedocles sought to link endlessness with cyclical behavior whereby various stages "perish into one another." While Heraclitus had already suggested such a cyclical explanation, Empedocles enlarged the concept based on an elaborate four-stage transition among earth, air, fire, and water.[77] Unlike Heraclitus, he explained the cause of this sequence as the outcome of love rather than fire. Empedocles instead proposed a functional dichotomy between love and hate that seems to suggest a more basic interaction between attraction and repulsion and is reminiscent of Anaximander's earlier concept of cyclical interplay between hot and cold as the primary cause of sustained motion in the physical universe. Further, by featuring Heraclitus' concept of incessant conflict between love and hate, Empedocles proposed what must have seemed an all-inclusive grand synthesis of pre-Socratic materialism--a cyclical interaction among the four supposedly basic elements--water as suggested by Thales, air as suggested by Anaximenes, earth as suggested by Xenophanes, and fire as featured by Heraclitus. Moreover, Empedocles agreed with both Anaximander and Parmenides that this grand cosmic cycle has persisted throughout eternity kept in motion by a binary interplay between love and hate attraction and repulsion) in a grand cyclical transition more inclusive than Anaximander's dualism between hot and cold and Heraclitus' dualism between fire (or war) and *Logos*. Empedocles depicted this cosmic momentum as a timeless cyclical struggle among the most basic elements: "In turn they get the upper hand in the revolving cycle, and perish into one another and increase in the turn appointed by Fate."[78] His cyclical hypothesis seems to have been popular among contemporaries, and others suggested several relatively simple alternatives, for example Hippo of Rhegium's binary cycle between fire and water; Oenopides of Chios' cycle between fire and air; and Onomacritus' cycle among fire, water, and earth without air.[79]

Perhaps of philosophical significance was Empedocles' suicide. As with the deaths of Heraclitus and Zeno recounted by Diogenes Laertius, Empedocles was said to have killed himself in a singular fashion, in his case by having jumped into Mount Etna's volcano in order to confirm his status as a god. However, this final choice is entirely conjectural, and he might instead have later died at Peloponnese or Thurioi. The primary evidence of suicide was supposed to have been the discovery of his sandals carefully arranged at the volcano's rim.[80]

XII. ANAXAGORAS (ca. 500 – 428 BC)

Born in Ionia, Anaxagoras traveled to Athens and was the first major philosopher to reside there. He was said to have arrived at the age of twenty and to have spent three decades in the city during the early reign of Pericles. He was supposedly Pericles' teacher as well as the city's unofficial "resident" philosopher until his trial for impiety for having maintained that the sun and moon are celestial bodies rather than gods. After his acquittal, the result of an eloquent defense by Pericles, he retired to the city of Lampsacus on the

Hellespont, where he later died. By some accounts his death occurred at about the time of Plato's birth. At one time he was supposedly on friendly terms with the dominant Sophist, Protagoras, as well as the tragedian Euripedes, both of whom were suspected of religious disbelief by fellow citizens. There is no evidence, however, that he had any direct relationship with Socrates aside from his influence regarding the concept of higher consciousness as suggested by Socrates at his trial. Anaxagoras and Democritus never met, and they both admitted that they avoided each other. Democritus was much younger and undoubtedly less well-known at the time, but their aversion might well have resulted from theoretical differences.

As suggested by the title of his single published text, *Physica* (translated as *On Natural Science)*, Anaxagoras pursued both science and philosophy, and he seems to have played a singular role in having exposed Athenians to both of these fields of inquiry for the first time. His philosophical debt was eclectic, but his version of materialism seems to have been primarily inspired by the theoretical assumptions of Anaximenes, who had died a few decades earlier. As documented by Diogenes Laertius, Anaxagoras' cosmology was supported to a large extent by empirical observation, for example his suppositions that the sun is an enormous mound of red-hot metal more massive than the Peloponnesus mountain range and that its radiation is powerful enough to illuminate the moon as well. He also proposed that the Milky Way exists as the light of stars not illuminated by the sun, that wind occurs when air is rarified by the sun's heat, that the collision among clouds causes thunder and lightning, that earthquakes result from air descending into the earth, and that mammalian procreation is caused by the combination of heat, moisture, and an unknown "earthy substance."

At the very beginning of *Physica*, Anaxagoras advanced a defensible cosmology inspired by Anaximenes, which later influenced both Plato and Aristotle. He asserted that the universe consists of air and aether, which partake of infinitude in both the number and minute size of countless particles similar to each other:

> All things were together, infinite in number and in smallness. For the Small also was infinite. And since all were together, nothing was distinguishable because of its smallness. For Air and Aether dominated all things, both of them being infinite. For these are the most important (*Elements*) in the total mixture, both in number and in size. [81]

Just as Parmenides and Melissus had ascribed infinitude to both time and space, Anaxagoras extended the principle to the microscopic in size. Anaxagoras' concept of a minute substance might seem to have been suggested by the atomism advocated by Leucippus followed by Democritus, but he also argued, contrary to their assumptions, that mixtures might occur among these elements, and that particles are not separated by any kind of a void at the smallest level. Instead, he proposed that the universe consists of an infinite medium of aether as earlier suggested by Anaximenes. He also argued the possibility that growth and nutrition occur at the atomic level and the likelihood that all things differ to the extent that that they involve different mixtures of identical ingredients as suggested by the modern theory of atomic structure with its electrons, neutrons, etc.

He identified all basic elements as seeds: "the seeds of all Things, which contain all kinds of shapes and colours and pleasant savours."[82] He went on to describe the visible universe as a realm occupied by a large assortment of "composite products" comprising an infinitude of perceptible shapes and colors, since "all things contain a portion of everything," a principle that still remains defensible. He enlarged Heraclitus' thesis that the unity of opposites is universal based on the assumption that all of the most basic elements "circulate and are separated off by force and speed." On the other hand, he seems to have accepted Heraclitus' two concepts regarding a concentric deity and the central role of *Logos* as cosmic law dominant in the universe. He even anticipated Aristotle's assumption that motion alone produces force, but he seems to have linked this with a presumably subatomic velocity many times faster than the visible universe, thereby anticipating the modern acceptance of the speed of light as many times faster than the speed of stars and planets.[83]

Anaxagoras also adopted Anaximander and Empedocles's emphasis on rotary motion by suggesting that the universe as a whole is incessantly rotating with enough rapidity for it to cohere. His assumptions here become debatable based on modern analysis. However, he also proposed a spatial continuity whereby air and aether are separated from the surrounding multiplicity, as perhaps suggested by Anaximenes, and he went on to argue, "all things are together" and "forever equal" as already suggested by his principle that "all things contain a portion of everything."[84] He further proposed that each physical substance is distinct from others because one component predominates in its mixture with other elements, and he explained that the interaction among these particles can ultimately be traced to attraction and repulsion. He even declared his acceptance of Parmenides principle that nothing can be added to the totality of all things and likewise that nothing can pass away, and, as later summarized by Aristotle, he asserted, "Almost all things that are homogeneous are generated and destroyed only through aggregation and segregation, and are not in any other sense generated or destroyed but remain eternally."[85] In modern terms, the atoms and molecules of any particular body can be transferred one way or another among various compounds in a potentially endless sequence.

Many of Anaxagoras' assumptions are useful as a complex synthesis of earlier theories, but he took a further step by linking them based on his own

theory of *Nous*, the transcendent manifestation of mind more unified than the
binary opposition of love and hate. If earth, air, fire, and water occur in
sustained motion by an interaction between the strictly mental principles of
love and hate as proposed by Empedocles, this interaction can be subsumed
to *Nous* as human consciousness on a more holistic basis. Thought itself
became the most basic element, rather than any of the various alternatives
suggested by his predecessors. As explained by Anaxagoras, *Nous* is effectively "the finest of all things," a manifestation of thought that necessarily
exists both in and beyond the physical nature. In effect, *Nous* is the only
element that both participates in nature and exceeds it: "And nothing is
absolutely separated off or divided the one from the other except Mind
[*Nous*]."[86]

Heraclitus had already proposed the notion of *Logos* as a mental function
imbedded in the universe, and Empedocles had featured the dichotomy between the mental dispositions of love and hate. In turn, Anaxagoras proposed
the more inclusive existence of *Nous* as transcendent mind—possibly a universal agent of law suggesting supernatural authority. As possibly suggested
by Melissus' concept of a unified physical existence with no boundaries,
Anaxagoras suggested the manifestation of transcendent existence identified
as Mind, which is paradoxically "mixed with no Thing, but is alone by
itself," yet with ultimate authority over the universe as a whole.[87] As much
later explained by Cicero, Anaxagoras was "the first pre-Socratic philosopher to hold that the orderly disposition of the universe is designed and
perfected by the rational power caused by mind, called *Nous*."[88] *Nous* was
identified as a shared principle that comprises both the entire universe and a
mental capacity independent of the universe that it has effectively created.

As proposed by Aristotle, this cosmic authority also bore a substantial
ethical aspect, for Anaxagoras argued that a single deity exists comparable to
the "good" identified with appropriate mental behavior.[89] Now an entirely
new concept of religion became possible in strictly monotheistic terms that
was obviously more credible than the Homeric mythology of Zeus and his
fellow gods and goddesses. This spiritual version of pre-Socratic cosmology
effectively provided the foundation for a more advanced version of religion
as a monotheistic alternative to the Homeric gods. No longer did deity consist of anthropomorphic mythical figures, but instead it entailed an embodied
universal consciousness both in and of itself and as an intrinsic manifestation
of the universe. This was the principle that Socrates had in mind when he
asserted the religious implications of Anaxagoras' notion, "that it is mind
that produces order and is the cause of everything."[90] This also helps to
explain why Socrates felt he did "know" on a spiritual plane aside from his
frequent insistence in public debate that he knew he didn't know. Many
centuries later at the Council of Nicaea, the concept of *Nous* seems to have
inspired the Christian notion of a Holy Ghost as a particular aspect of God

imbedded in the universe as a whole. Obviously, however, *Nous* as transcendent consciousness differs from the modern Darwinian explanation of human intelligence as the outcome of biological evolution in which the human mind is a product of the universe, not its essence, as Aristotle also seems to have asserted in his pivotal text *De Anima*.[91]

In several pages preserved by Simplicius, Anaxagoras had no difficulty in accepting the paradox that transcendent mind is both perfect and the ultimate source of conscious mistakes and the world's countless imperfections. Unlike the sustained trial-and-error mistakes typical of normal mental behavior, the perfection of higher consciousness is supposedly singular and unassailable. Anaxagoras even went on to suggest that a transcendent version of mind achieves total purity as opposed to everything else that is otherwise independent of full control:

> Other things all contain a part of everything, but Mind is infinite and self-ruling, and is mixed with no Thing, but is alone by itself. . . . For it is the finest of all Things, and the purest, and has complete understanding of everything, and has the greatest power.[92]

An entirely new version of supernatural authority identified with godhead then seemed possible based on this definition of universal mind (*Nous*). Anaxagoras also suggested that transcendent creationism was a product of Mind by having made things "revolve from the outset," apparently the agent of both creation and circular revolution as already suggested by Empedocles and Parmenides and later featured by Aristotle:

> For it [Mind, or *Nous*] is the finest of all Things, and the purest, and has complete understanding of everything, and has the greatest power. All things which have life, both the greater and the less, are ruled by Mind. Mind took command of the universal revolution, so as to make (*things*) revolve at the outset. And at first things began to revolve from some small point, but now the revolution extends over a greater area, and will spread even further. And the things which were mixed together, and separated off, and divided, were all understood by Mind. . . . And nothing is absolutely separated off or divided the one from the other except Mind. Mind is all alike, both the greater and the less.[93]

He then suggests that the entire universe came into existence much as explained by earlier pre-Socratic philosophers:

> It was this revolution which caused the separation off. The dense and moist and cold and dark (*Elements*) collected here, where now is Earth, and the rare and hot and dry went outwards to the furthest part of the Aether. . . . Earth solidifies . . . water is separated off. From water comes earth, and from earth stones are solidified . . . [94]

This genetic explanation by Anaxagoras simplified and smoothed over Empedocles paradigm on what seems a more credible basis.

Despite all seeming disparities, Anaxagoras explained, transcendent mind is the primary agent that harmonizes contradictory aspects of the universe as well as all motion among celestial bodies in the sky. He concurred with Leucippus and Democritus' thesis that nature consists of an infinitude of seemingly mindless and therefore chaotic microscopic interactions. However, he also insisted that this perceived disorder produces overall harmony, the product of higher mental behavior. Just as Empedocles subsumed the cyclical momentum of natural elements depicted by earlier philosophers to the binary opposition between love and hate, Anaxagoras subordinated this entire hierarchy to an even higher singular authority--*Nous* itself--an inclusive principle of transcendent consciousness that could later be identified as monotheistic godhead. His concept of mind's universal authority through the rapid expansion of the universe seems to have inspired Platonism's most basic assumptions as well as Christian theology's much later concept of God's transcendent authority. Thus, both Plato's idealism and Aristotle's naturalism can be traced to the influence of Anaxagoras. Plato's metaphysical assumptions seem to have been primarily inspired by Anaxagoras' concept of *Nous*, while Aristotle's later cosmology served as a synthesis of Anaxagoras' scientific perspective with that of both Leucippus and Democritus.

XIII. DIOGENES OF APOLLONIA (CA. 425 BC)

Raised in Apollonia on the island of Crete, Diogenes of Apollonia was younger than both Anaxagoras and Leucippus and perhaps slightly older than Democritus. Plato ignored him in his Dialogues along with Leucippus and Democritus, and among the ancient natural philosophers Diogenes shared with Socrates the distinction of having been ridiculed in public performances of comedies during his lifetime. Yet his philosophy played an important, if limited, role in bridging the gap between the early Milesian school—particularly Anaximenes—and Aristotle's mature cosmology in *De Caelo* and *De Anima*. All of the earlier pre-Socratic philosophies anticipated Aristotle's theoretical synthesis, some more than others, but it was Diogenes who effectively summarized pre-Socratic assumptions, setting the stage for Aristotle's later and more sophisticated version of metaphysics.

Diogenes accepted the position of Thales and Anaximander that nature as a whole derives from a single basic substrate, thereby justifying a monistic theory of the physical universe. With this in mind, according to Aristotle, Diogenes sought to resurrect Anaximander's original concept of heat as a continuous activity of the universe:

Diogenes is right when he argues that unless all things were derived from one, reciprocal action and passion could not occur. The hot thing, e.g. would not be cooled and the cold thing in turn be warmed, for heat and cold do not change reciprocally into one thing, but what changes (it is clear) is the *substratum*. Hence, whenever there is action and passion between things, that which underlies them must be a single something. No doubt, it is not true to say that *all* things are of this character; but it is true of all things between which there is a reciprocal action and passion. [95]

In response to the interplay between heat and its absence Diogenes, who was familiar with human anatomy, pointed out the essential role of that lungs play in delivering air to the rest of the body. He revived the assumption of Anaximenes that air plays a basic role linked with heat as the source of incessant motion necessary for the sustenance of life.

As later explained by the Christian church father, Clement of Alexandria, Diogenes was willing to enlarge Anaximenes' choice of air in perpetual motion as a particular benefit of the sun and even the principle of motion in and of itself:

Diogenes postulates air as the element. Everything is in motion and there are innumerable worlds. He constructs the cosmos thus: the whole is in motion and becomes thin in one place and dense in another, and where the dense comes together it has formed a close mass, and so on with the rest of the same way: the lightest parts took the uppermost station and produced the sun. [96]

In effect mass is a product of density, and the least dense version of mass is to be found in the sun, the source of heat and the agent of energy distributed by air. Diogenes accepted Anaximenes' choice of air as the essential source of life and therefore the primary and most basic element of the universe derivative of heat. [97] He insisted, "Men and all other animals live by means of air, which they breathe in, and this for them is both Soul (Life) and Intelligence." Today, of course, oxygen's crucial role is in biological existence is recognized, but Diogenes extended the principle to explain the governance of the whole universe, by implication linking breath with the strictly physical manifestations of fire, conflagration, and even the power of the sun:

And it seems to me that that which has Intelligence is that which is called Air by mankind; and further, that by this, all creatures are guided, and that it rules everything; for this in itself seems to me to be God [sic] and to reach everywhere and to arrange everything and to be in everything. . . . Also in all animals, the Soul is the same thing, (*namely*) Air, warmer than outside in which we are but much colder than that nearer the sun. [98]

Perhaps something exists equivalent to a monotheistic God, but it entirely consists of air. In effect, Diogenes considered breath to be a more basic universal principle than Anaxagoras' concept of universal soul, suggesting that the metabolic function of neural performance is more basic than its cognitive manifestation. Anaxagoras had already proposed the existence of a single God, as had both Empedocles and even Xenophanes. However, Diogenes' explanation of godhood seems pantheistic and is in accord with Anaximenes' concept of air as the most basic medium of the universe, effectively linking mind and matter.

Diogenes conceded the basic necessity of a monistic universe—all things "the alteration of the same thing"—as first suggested by the Milesians preceding the binary and quaternary divisions of Heraclitus and Empedocles:

> It seems to me, to sum up the whole matter, that all existing things are created by the alteration of the same thing, and are the same thing. This is very obvious. For if the things now existing in this universe—earth and water and air and fire and all the other things which are seen to exist in this world: if any one of these were different in its own (*essential*) nature, and were not the same thing which was transformed in many ways and changed, in no way could things mix with one another . . .

Like Anaxagoras he identified the organization of the universe equivalent to human intelligence. Moreover, he even seems to have agreed with Anaxagoras that the universe is ultimately a product of consciousness with human behavior one instance of this inclusive capability:

> "All . . . things come into being in different forms at different times by changes of the same (*substance*) and they return to the same. Such a distribution would not have been possible without Intelligence."[99]

Diogenes' thesis linked Anaximenes' emphasis on the central role of air with mental capacity equivalent to Anaxagoras' concept of *Nous* and Plato's later insistence on a spiritual universe. Nevertheless, Diogenes subsumed mind to matter, not the other way around as Plato argued. In none of his existing fragments did he explicitly assert matter's dominant role, but its likelihood was everywhere implied. Significantly, Plato ignored Diogenes' theoretical contribution, whereas Aristotle took him into account at least five times.

XIV. LEUCIPPUS (ca. EARLY 5TH CENTURY BC)

Leucippus could have been born and raised in Miletus or Abdera, Elea or Melos, and it seems he spent his entire life as a teacher either in Miletus or Abdera on the northern coast of the Aegean Sea between Thrace and Macedonia. But possibly not. According to Diogenes Laertius, Epicurus later claimed that Leucippus never existed. Others however disagreed, and it seems likely that Leucippus did exist, that he was a pupil of Zeno or even Parmenides in Elea, which would account for his monist assumptions regarding a strictly physical universe. As an advocate of such a synthesis he was said to have written two scrolls, *The Great World Order* and *On Mind*, the first of which is now entirely lost. However, one sentence has survived from the second scroll, the compelling statement, "Nothing happens at random; everything happens because of reason and by necessity."[100] A determinist cause and effect relationship was therefore of paramount importance and suggests both the Milesian and Eleatic perspectives.

Yet, such an explanation would have been at odds with the basic argument for which Leucippus is primarily known, that of a seemingly random interaction among microscopic atoms, by definition the smallest particles in existence. In fact the paradox between a dominant cosmic logic (featured by Heraclitus' concept of *Logos*) and endless random motion among infinitesimal atoms was an essential consideration, for if such chaos predominates at the most basic level of existence, how can the whole universe function on a predictable basis? The effort to resolve this seeming contradiction that has persisted even in modern times became the essential goal of the atomists Leucippus and Democritus. Pythagoreans or perhaps the Phoenician, Mochus (or Moschus), might first have suggested the existence and behavior of such minute particles, but whatever Leucippus's source, if any, he himself primarily featured the possibility of countless atoms too small and chaotic to be observed by the naked eye, but in fact the universal stuff of the universe. Just as Parmenides and Melissus had assigned infinitude to time and space, Leucippus suggested its application strictly to microscopic events. Today, photons, electrons, or the so-called Higgs particles have been identified as even smaller bodies than atoms, but whatever microscopic stuff exists as the basic constituent of material existence, Leucippus identified it as atoms that compose larger entities, ultimately the whole universe.

Leucippus described the physical universe as a vast realm of mostly empty space filled with the incessant interplay of countless atoms in temporary combinations. As later explained by Diogenes Laertius, "The all includes the empty as well as the full," and the existence of matter is the combination of atoms through their network with each other suspended in space: "The worlds are formed when atoms fall into the void and are entangled with one another."[101] Aristotle more or less substantiated this explanation in his lost text, "On Democritus," later quoted by Simplicius. While he featured Democritus his summary applied to Leucippus' original theory as well:

> Democritus [i.e. Leucippus] thinks the nature of the divine entities consists of small substances infinite in number; he supposes a place for them, different

from them and infinite in extent, and to this he applies the names of 'void', 'nothing', and 'the infinite', while to each of the substances he applies the names 'thing', 'solid', and 'existent'. He thinks the substances are so small as to escape our senses have all sorts of shapes and figures, and differences of size. From these, then, . . . are generated and compounded perceptible masses. The substances are at variance and move in the void because of their dissimilarity . . . and as they move they collide with each other and interlock in such a way that . . . a single substance is never in reality produced from them; for it would be very simple-minded to suppose that two or more things could ever become one. . . . He thinks that they cling to one another and remain together until some stronger necessity . . . scatters them apart and separates them. He ascribes the genesis and the separation opposed to it not only to animals but also to plants, and to worlds, and generally to all perceptible bodies.[102]

Aristotle's principal disciple, Theophrastus, offered a slightly different but equally useful version of Leucippus' theory in the First Book of his *Opinions:*

Leucippus of Elea or Miletos (for both accounts are given of him) had associated with Parmenides in philosophy. He did not, however, follow the same path in his explanation of things as Parmenides and Xenophanes did, but, to all appearance, the very opposite. They made the All one, immovable, uncreated, and finite, and did not even permit us to search for *what is not*; he [Leucippus] assumed innumerable and ever–moving elements, namely, the atoms. And he made their forms infinite in number, since there was no reason why they should be of one kind rather than another, and because he saw that there was unceasing becoming and change in things. He held, further, that *what is* is no more real than *what is not*, and that both are alike causes of things that come into being: for he laid down that the substance of the atoms was compact and full, and he called them *what is*, while they moved in the void which he called *what is not*, but affirmed to be just as real as *what is.*[103]

Theophrastus primarily attributed variation to the structural differences between atoms themselves rather than their multiple combinations as later explained by Aristotle. Neither Aristotle nor Theophrastus sought to explain the cosmic explanation attributed to Leucippus whereby compound arrangements result from collisions and entanglements in an enormous whirl gathered around the earth, but still Theophrastus' passage provides a lucid explanation of the interaction between atoms and the void surrounding them.

In retrospect, the basic assumption of Leucippus'—the concept of particles suspended in a void—differed from Melissus' assumption that material continuity pervades the universe as an essentially continuous expanse of matter without any possibility for empty space. This emphasis upon continuity was later adopted by Aristotle as well, but what seemed a basic contradiction between continuity and the possibility of atomistic disjunction continued to defy synthesis, setting the stage for Strato's later unsuccessful effort to obtain a compromise based on experimental evidence. Both models seem defensible in light of modern physics in the sense that the entire universe can in fact be understood as an infinite force field much as Melissus proposed, but the microscopic space occupied by atomic particles is nevertheless vast compared to the size of their respective nuclei.

Leucippus suggested what might seem obvious—that motion as featured by Anaximenes would be impossible without empty space for things to move into. Dense atomic mass displaces (or pushes through) a comparatively rarified atomic mass of lesser density and, in the case of air and water, the rarified mass can be divided by anything of greater density, then almost immediately converges again. Air, for example, is full of atoms and molecules but contains far more empty space among these atoms and molecules than does a rock, so a rock can be thrown into the air without any difficulty. In effect, its tightly bound atoms and molecules displace the relatively sparse assortment of atmospheric atoms. Similarly, fish can swim in water, an axe can chop wood, and a diamond can cut glass. As a result, relative atomic density—i.e. greater mass relative to the space it occupies—is crucial to the possibility of motion.

Whatever the paradox between space and motion, Leucippus seems to have suggested that mass primarily exists as a multitude of tiny entangled atoms that occupy relatively little space. Leucippus was therefore able to treat atomic particles as the most basic element, and to explain the origin of celestial bodies—in fact the entire universe—relevant to the necessarily complex formation of these particles in what might seem an endless variety of substances:

> These [atoms] collect together and form a single vortex, in which they jostle against each other and, circling round in every possible way, separate off, by like atoms joining them. And the atoms being so numerous that they can no longer revolve in equilibrium, the light ones pass into empty space outside, as if they were being winnowed; the remainder keep together and, becoming entangled, go on their circuit together, and form a primary spherical system.[104]

With obvious reference to cyclical motion as already suggested by Heraclitus and Empedocles, Leucippus as summarized by Diogenes Laertius explained the entire universe as a more inclusive "entanglement of atoms" comprising a vast single vortex. At every level, bigger and more massive substances gather toward the center of spherical systems while lighter ones are thrust into outlying orbits.[105] Whether he recognized the fullest implications of his analysis, Leucippus also succeeded in helping to extend the earth's predictability to apply to the whole universe. Obviously the Milky Way fits this description, as do most other galaxies in the sky—as many as two trillion of them according to the most recent count.[106]

Leucippus was also correct in suggesting that the earth travels in orbit, but his notion that the sun itself orbits around the moon was of course mistaken. He also suggested the principle of gravity, maintaining that the earth was "formed by portions brought to the center coalescing," and he ventured to predict the eventual destruction of all celestial bodies, by implication including both the earth and universe: "As the world is born, so, too, it grows, decays and perishes, in virtue of some necessity," the nature of which he did not specify.[107] Here again Leucippus seems to have anticipated the assumption of modern astrophysicists that all stars and planets are just as susceptible to eventual destruction as people and animals.

Like the Milesian philosophers and Democritus, Leucippus excluded religion from consideration as compared to the other major pre-Socratic philosophers. He narrowed his theory to the universe as an objective realm that exists on a strictly physical basis from the bottom up. There was no opportunity for the presence and authority of one or more transcendent gods to be taken seriously according to his concept of infinitesimal existence. Leucippus' single presumably harmless fragment that has already been quoted, to the effect that "everything happens out of reason and by necessity," takes on new profundity in light of this cosmology. No matter how chaotic atomic entanglements might seem, existence is best understood as cosmic manifestation that endlessly replicates itself. In effect reason is imbedded in the universe, not the product of anthropomorphic intervention.

XV. DEMOCRITUS (CA. 460 – 370 BC)

Most historians link the final stage of pre-Socratic philosophy with Democritus, the so-called "laughing philosopher," who was a contemporary of Socrates as well as Leucippus' young co-author of the theory of atomism. Leucippus had first proposed such a possibility, but it was Democritus who effectively advanced its assumptions and took into account numerous concepts relevant to its implications. Later, Aristotle actually described him as a "man who had thought about everything," and, as suggested by Diogenes Laertius' bibliography, he seems to have authored as many as seventy-two scrolls upon a variety of fields including ethics, physics, astronomy, mathematics, logic, agriculture, medicine, epistemology, and even military tactics. Unfortunately, none of his complete works has survived, and the three hundred fragments included in Freeman's *Ancilla* are almost entirely limited to ethics and have no relevance to his theory of cosmology or atomism in particular, his most important philosophical contributions. The wide range of his theoretical inquiry was comparable to that of Aristotle, but unlike the fortunate recovery of Aristotle's writings, almost his entire output was lost except for numerous fragments almost all of which pertain to relatively inoffensive assumptions.

Democritus was born and raised in Abdera on the northern coast of the Aegean Sea, where Leucippus seems to have practiced philosophy and not far from where Aristotle was born perhaps seventy years later. He lived well into the fifth century and was said to have died at roughly the age of one hundred, by far the oldest of the major Greek philosophers. His family was quite wealthy and the Persian king Xerxes was said to have dined at their house while in transit from Greece to Persia. Perhaps impressed by the knowledge of Xerxes' staff regarding religion and astronomy, he himself supposedly traveled in his youth to Persia, Ethiopia, India, and Babylon, where he became acquainted with the Chaldean Magi. He was also said to have spent seven years with Egyptian geometers before returning penniless to Greece where he lived for a while in Athens, but there is no information on where he lived afterwards. He and Anaxagoras never met, and the chronology of his relationship with others in Athens is unclear. He later remembered having encountered Socrates, whereas Socrates in turn had no recollection of his presence or identity, suggesting he was older and more of a celebrity at the time. On the other hand, Democritus was said to have hired Protagoras as his secretary, then accepted him as a pupil despite the likelihood that Protagoras was a full generation older than Socrates.

The bulk of Democritus' theoretical arguments that we have today were preserved by Aristotle in fifty-seven passages relevant to cosmology, including eight in *Physics*, nine in *Metaphysics*, seven in *De Caelo*, three in *On Generation and Corruption*, and eight in *De Anima*. Other ancient authors who took his arguments into account included Sextus Empiricus (37 passages), and Cicero (17 passages listed). Plutarch's discussion of Democritus in "Against Colotes" also helps to confirm his reputation as a major philosopher several centuries after his death. Moreover, both Epicurus and the epic poet Lucretius seem to have based their shared secular perspective almost entirely on Democritus' assumptions. Unfortunately, most of Epicurus' cosmological analysis has been lost, and Lucretius' epic version seems to have been based on Epicurus' assumptions as much as those of Democritus.

The primary evidence of Democritus's theory of cosmology consists of a scroll called *The Great World-Order* (*Diakosmos*), which began with Leucippus's explanation of atomism in a preliminary section of the text, followed by his own smaller section identified as *Lesser World-Order*, which in a shortened version, enlarged the scope of Leucippus' theory. As neither portion of *Lesser World Order* has survived, Democritus' theory can only be reconstructed as a tentative likelihood based on the summaries of others. Fortunately, Aristotle wrote a précis summary of his theory that survived into the sixth century AD, long enough for Simplicius to have read and summarized its analysis in a long paragraph most of which can be quoted here in multiple translation:

As earlier indicated, Democritus proposed that all matter throughout the universe consists of atoms as an infinite number of minute particles that commingle with relative freedom in an otherwise infinite vacuum. The entirety of the visible universe accordingly consists of numerous combinations of these atoms that interact in relatively stable combinations. Moreover, a steady mixture of atoms is basic to all perceptible shapes and figures, and movement takes place among shapes and sizes resulting from this disparity. In effect heavy objects with relatively high atomic concentration can displace lighter substances (e.g. air or water) whose reduced density is necessarily less resistant. On the other hand, substances can interlock in relatively stable formations until an even "stronger necessity" is sufficient to scatter them. Democritus suggested this incessant modification derives from atomic interaction at the most basic level of manifestation relevant to vegetation, animal behavior, and in fact all perceptible and imperceptible existence. [108]

Obviously missing from the text is any reference to transcendent authority that might be identified with one or more gods. Unlike Anaxagoras, Democritus seems to have limited his analysis to a strictly physical explanation of a field of atoms as opposed to a more holistic analysis that linked physics with the possibility of universal consciousness.

According to Sextus Empiricus, Democritus was in full accord with Leucippus that the universe consists entirely of atoms suspended in empty space and that all else is nothing more than the necessarily limited perception of nature. To this extent their shared assumption enlarged Parmenides' description of existence as an endless unified realm. However, his version also featured physical determinism, since "all things happen by virtue of necessity." [109] An infinitude of atoms might seem to interact in random fashion, he conceded, but their cumulative manifestation occurs in a predictable manner just as seemingly irregular activity may be measured today by means of statistics. On a comparable basis, Democritus suggested, what might seem to consist of microscopic chaos must also be perceived as a more inclusive ordered system. He also proposed that countless other worlds exist across the universe, and that some of them "not merely resemble but completely and absolutely match each other in every detail . . . including human beings." [110]

To a limited extent Democritus accepted Anaxagoras' equation between soul and thought as particular aspects of a single universal substance relevant to mental behavior. In doing so he more specifically suggested, ". . . its power of originating movement must be due to its fineness of grain and the shape of its atoms." [111] By implication this caveat featured neural ingredients—today's concept of brain cells—that connect the transcendent aspect of consciousness with the physical behavior of the brain. In Book I of *De Anima*, Aristotle indicated that Democritus also identified soul as "a sort of fire or hot substance" [in modern terms metabolism as controlled oxidization] that is "linked with respiration as the characteristic mark of life." In effect his relatively simple proposal merged the earlier theories of such figures as Alcmaeon, Anaximenes, Anaxagoras, Diogenes Apollonius, and even Heraclitus. He also linked soul with mental behavior in general: "Soul and thought are, he says, one and the same thing." In effect, he suggested, soul is identical with human consciousness as a particular manifestation of the physical universe rather than supernatural intelligence as transcendent manifestation. This suggestion by Democritus as recounted by Aristotle might well have anticipated the later philosophical standoff between Platonism and Aristotle's natural philosophy—also between metaphysics and empiricism, ultimately between religion and science. [112]

According to Aristotle, Democritus also identified the soul with thought as human consciousness produced by "indivisible bodies" because of its atomic structure, effectively a concept of neural anatomy quite different from Anaxagoras' broad identification of soul with a single substance as "the principle of all things."[113] Democritus also seems to have anticipated Locke's epistemology by suggesting that soul is "identical with reason." Therefore, according to Aristotle, Democritus felt able to treat ideation as a product of sensation in response to the perceived environment:

> Democritus says that either there is no truth or to us at least it is not evident. And in general it is because these thinkers [inclusive of Democritus] suppose knowledge to be sensation, and this to be a physical alteration that they say what appears to our senses must be true. [114]

In other words, any change or movement observed in the environment necessarily produces a conscious response adequate to respond with appropriate behavior as later suggested by Lockean epistemology. Aristotle acknowledged that Empedocles and other pre-Socratic philosophers had also suggested this possibility, but maintained that it was Democritus who featured its central importance. According to Aristotle, Democritus even went on to suggest that all sensation—hence perception—is an advanced biological manifestation of touch as the simplest reflex at the most basic level of response. Aristotle mentioned this thesis in order to reject it, but modern research indicates its likelihood. For example, worms primarily depend upon tactile contact and perhaps odor as compared to more advanced response combinations of insects and animals. When an obstruction blocks the path of a worm, it possesses sufficient neural capability to recognize the impediment and move around it. The more refined senses of smell, sound, and sight may be identified as later additions acquired by more advanced species. [115]

As an arch-materialist obsessed with behavior of the physical universe, Democritus apparently had the reputation among most of his contemporaries as an outspoken atheist, as indicated by Cicero's brief remark at the beginning of *The Nature of the Gods*:

. . . his [Democritus'] denial of immutability, and therefore of eternity, to
everything whatsoever surely involves a repudiation of deity so absolute as to
leave no conception of a divine being remaining![116]

Few passages by Democritus that exist today confirm this radical stance
except for his expressed sympathy with Sophists who played a dominant role
in Athens at the time by promoting the assumption either that there is no
clear-cut truth or that it cannot be discerned. Democritus himself took this
argument to its limit by maintaining in at least one particular fragment ex-
cerpted from his lost text, *Canons*: "Truth is sunk in an abyss, opinion and
custom are all-prevailing, no place is left for truth, all things are successively
wrapped in darkness." As later explained by Cicero in *Academica,* "He [De-
mocritus] flatly denies that truth exists at all . . . and says that the senses are
'full of darkness.'"[117] Obviously this radical assertion of disbelief seems to
have been incompatible with Democritus' later reputation for encyclopedic
knowledge, so these particular remarks may be assumed to have typified an
early stance he later abandoned. In effect, his version of skepticism, very
likely inspired by Protagoras, might have justified an empirical thoroughness
later enlarged by Aristotle as opposed to Platonism's relatively simplistic
transcendental "truths" derivative of Anaxagoras' philosophy.

Democritus' only two comments that survive about contemporary religion are limited to his ridicule of its supposed social and psychological benefits quite aside from the likelihood of its validity as a credible explanation of
the universe. In the first of these remarks he identified religion as a primitive
effort to explain potential dangers in the physical universe that might have
been caused by gods:

> For when the men of old times beheld the disasters in the heavens, such as
> thunderings and lightnings, and thunderbolts and collisions between stars, and
> eclipses of sun and moon, they were affrighted, imagining the Gods to be the
> causes of these things.[118]

In the second passage Democritus proposed that the promotion of religion
had been an opportunistic ruse primarily beneficial to those who invented
and promoted it:

> When the life of mankind was without order, those who so far excelled the rest
> in strength and intelligence, that all men lived subservient to their commands,
> being intent to gain for themselves more admiration and veneration, invented
> for themselves a kind of superhuman and divine authority, and in consequence
> were by the populace accounted Gods.[119]

One suspects that Democritus mentioned this possibility with regards to early prophets who lived elsewhere in order to avoid the threat of public prosecution.

Democritus' religious disbelief seems a pivotal factor in helping to clarify his sustained hostility with Anaxagoras, then Plato during his residence in Athens. As Democritus explained at one time, Anaxagoras "did not take to him" upon his arrival in Athens, but he also offered a more benign explanation, "I came to Athens and no one knew me." Another possibility was the coincidence that both Anaxagoras and Democritus' tutor Leucippus sought at the same time to enlarge Eleatic cosmology by proposing competitive versions of microscopic infinitude with opposite attitudes toward the possible role of religion. Also Anaxagoras might have rejected Democritus simply because of his close relationship with Leucippus. In any case Plato seems to have sided with Anaxagoras by totally omitting any reference to both Leucippus and Democritus throughout his dialogues. In the single instance in which he was said by others to have mentioned Democritus by name, he declared his wish that all of Democritus' writings be burned. One of his disciples supposedly replied that Democritus' writings were already in such wide currency that the task would be difficult at best, which suggests the likelihood of a highly competitive relationship at the time. As mentioned by Diogenes Laertius, Plato also refused to enter into any kind of public debate with Democritus, very possibly because of his reputation as a formidable adversary:

> . . . obviously because he [Plato] knew that he would have to match himself against the prince of philosophers, described by Timon, 'Such is the wise Democritus, the guardian of discourse, keen-witted disputant, among the best I have ever read.'[120]

Ultimately Plato appears to have prevailed. His version of transcendent metaphysics obviously took precedence in later histories of philosophy at the expense of Democritus' radical empiricism, as much as anything because most of Democritus' writings upon cosmology were destroyed exactly as Plato had advocated, many of them probably by fire. To the extent that Democritus' general perspective has survived, it has been the result of his substantial influence upon three later authors—Epicurus, Lucretius, and especially Aristotle. Otherwise, record of his historic contribution would have been entirely limited to his relatively harmless ethical teachings featured by cautious ancient doxographers.

In retrospect, Democritus and Plato played complementary roles in their pursuit of basic philosophical truths. Plato advocated transcendent authority with obvious monotheistic possibilities as already inspired by Anaxagoras, whereas Democritus limited his perspective to empirical findings based on physical evidence that supported the rejection of godhood by such precursors as Anaximander and Melissus. In particular his concept of atomism encouraged a renewed pursuit of scientific investigation at odds with Plato's concept of ideal forms. Whereas Democritus explained human intelligence as complex mental behavior responsive to the objective world, Plato took up Anaxagoras' cause by featuring the importance of spiritual transcendence that presumably supersedes this level of knowledge relevant to the objective world. It was left to Aristotle, once Plato's favorite disciple, to bring Democritus' emphasis on materialism to a more advanced level through a close examination of early pre-Socratic assumptions.

In fact these two complementary strategies seem to have occurred in tandem. Just as Plato enlarged Anaxagoras' concept of *Nous* at the expense of Democritus, Aristotle enlarged the materialism of Democritus and many of his predecessors at the expense of Plato's concept of ideal forms. He submitted to analysis the formulations of both authors but increasingly sided with Democritus, especially in what would seem to have been his final three texts upon cosmology.[121] He continued to pursue the theory of physical continuity suggested by Anaxagoras, but also took into account the alternative hypothesis of Democritus and Leucippus regarding the analysis of spatial infinitude. This potential source of contradiction was much later explored by Aristotle's disciples, Theocritus and Strato, if without any success in obtaining a fully acceptable synthesis.[122] In any case, Democritus' achievement inspired the Epicureans and encouraged Aristotle's dependence on empirical investigation as well as his recognition that the god concept had little if any relevance to his effort to explain the universe as a whole.

XVI. FINAL CONSIDERATIONS

All of the pre-Socratic philosophers sought a holistic theory of the universe either by featuring a single element or as many as four in a functional combination. Godhead was not entirely omitted from consideration, but it was of secondary importance and often ignored, as were the various myths linked with the notion of supernatural deities. Monotheism and the transcendent authority of gods were suggested now and again--especially by Xenophanes, Parmenides, Empedocles, and Anaxagoras--but the strictly physical implication of their theories could easily be differentiated from their concessions to religion. On the other hand, many of the theories anticipated modern scientific concepts, for example when earth was explained as mass, fire as energy, and Pythagorean mathematics as a complex matrix of numerical relationships imbedded in nature as exemplified by the modern equations of gravity and the speed of light. For example, the concept of gravity was anticipated in a sense by Leucippus' notion that heavy objects fall because of their compact atomic arrangement as opposed to light elements that float or rise because they are effectively squeezed upward through the displacement of nearby heavier elements. In effect they retain their space by letting themselves be pushed upwards. Similarly, the concept of atomism advocated by Leucippus and Democritus anticipated modern particle physics, as did Anaxagoras' theory of sub-atomic continuity. In light of modern physics both theories turned out to be defensible. Moreover, Parmenides' concept of the universe as timeless spiritual existence bore useful implications for modern religion, as did Anaximander's concept of an unidentified substance within a potentially endless physical substratum.

It can be added that Heraclitus' notion of fire as sheer energy anticipated Farraday's theory of fire as rapid oxidization, the dependence of metabolism on oxidization proposed by Lavoisier, and even the splitting of atoms proposed by Einstein. Einstein's famous equation, e (energy) equals m (mass) times c squared (the speed of light times itself) can be loosely translated to the effect that fire (i.e. energy) equals earth (i.e. mass) times the square of a Pythagorean mathematical constant that somehow manifests the velocity of light. Ancient Greece's pre-Socratic materialists may be admired for having anticipated these factors as confirmed, for example, by the atomic bomb's instantaneous transition from mass (as suggested by Melissus), to energy (as suggested by Heraclitus). Even the recent discovery of the so-called Higgs particle can be explained by establishing a universal principle (Anaximander's concept of *arche)* that the entire universe (Parmenides' concept of its existence as a whole) consists of an enormous force field (again, Heraclitus' concept of fire) that produces matter (again Melissus' concept), whose existence consists of tiny particles (Democritus' concept of atomism) that result from the breakdown of "elegant symmetries" yet to be fully explained (Anaximander's principle of *arche* relevant to Pythagoras' theory of imbedded mathematics). On the other hand, Plato's version of Anaxagoras' concept of mind imbedded in the universe seems to have inspired the orthodox Christian binarism between transcendent spirit and the material universe as described by St. Augustine and still promulgated today by modern Christianity. Both ideological alternatives of science and religion can be traced to complementary aspects of pre-Socratic philosophy. What other ancient creed or system of belief bore any comparison to this collective achievement?

Chapter Two

Plato and the Age of Pericles

Radical doubt was fashionable among a generation of Sophists during the so-called Age of Pericles, which lasted roughly from 495-429 BC. The obvious absurdity of Greek mythology had finally provoked both outspoken skepticism and unrestrained secular speculation by many of the pre-Socratic philosophers. Disbelief came into vogue, and relevant to almost every issue the question boiled down to, "How can this assumption to be valid?" Or more to the point: "To what extent does it withstand sustained criticism?" Credible answers were formulated on a sustained basis to determine why or how any particular concept was worthy of consideration. Vigorous debate became commonplace as well as an enlarged emphasis on analytic skill that allowed more articulate and/or better-informed advocates to prevail at the expense of others. This pursuit of rhetorical advantage was perhaps best illustrated by an episode reported in Plato's dialogue *Protagoras*, when as a young dialectician Socrates fell into argument with Protagoras, the first and most successful proponent of Sophism. Supposedly their purpose was to explain the basic difference between virtue and knowledge. Much was said, and no decisive explanation finally prevailed. More important, however, the standoff confirmed that Socrates was a genuine contender quite aside from the seasoned capabilities of Protagoras.

I. SOPHISTS

It was almost inevitable that Sophism arose as a systematic commitment to disbelief. Sophists, however, took skepticism to excess, and it soon became almost a parody of itself. For example Gorgias, by many accounts the most eminent Sophist after Protagoras and Socrates, went so far as to insist that nothing exists, that if it did it would be unknowable, and if it were knowable it could not be communicated.[1] Even more radical was the argument by Xeniades of Corinth as late as 400 BC, later summarized by Sextus Empiricus:

> . . . that all things are false, and that every impression and opinion is false, and that all that becomes, becomes out of the non-existent, and all that perishes into the non-existent.[2]

Cratylus of the mid to late fifth century B.C. extended the principle to all acts of communication on the assumption that such behavior necessarily depends on telling lies. Later, Metrodorus of Chios, a friend and disciple of Epicurus, took skepticism to its ultimate limit:

I deny that we know whether we know something or know nothing, and even that we know the mere fact that we do not know (or do know), or know at all whether something exists or nothing exists.

This radical stance seems to have applied to religion, materialist philosophy, and just about everything else. Then again, Metrodorus could support the contrary proposition, "Everything exists which anyone perceives."[3] In combination, these complementary assertions confirmed that nothing is true, but also that everything submitted to discussion could be taken into account as a necessarily debatable version of truth.

Not surprisingly, the choice between religion and the pursuit of a secular alternative became a primary concern. Diagoras was obliged to flee from Athens in order to avoid prosecution as an atheist, but the poet Simonides appears to have been forgiven for the implicit agnosticism in his remark about the existence of the gods, "The longer I think about it, the fainter becomes my hope of an answer."[4] The philosopher Anaxagoras was prosecuted for atheism in a public trial, apparently because he proposed that the sun and moon were devoid of godhead, but fortunately he was acquitted as a result of Pericles' impassioned public defense. Pericles' mistress Aspasia was also tried, and she too was acquitted as the result of Pericles' eloquence in her defense. The eminent sculptor Phidias was less fortunate and died in prison, charged with obvious impiety for having portrayed Pericles and himself on Athena's shield in one of his statues.

Public trials with the possibility of execution obviously discouraged individuals from flaunting their disbelief, but less militant stances of deism, agnosticism, pantheism, and even theoretical complexity seem to have diminished the threat of prosecution, as illustrated by the later examples of Aristotle and Epicurus. Democritus and Euripides were suspected of atheism, and the more outspoken atheists who survived included such social outcasts as Prodicus of Ceos, Diagoras of Melos, Euhemerus of Tegea, and Theodorus of Cyrene.

Plato's cousin, the playwright Critias [*circa* 410 B.C.], also seems to have been notorious for his atheism. A relatively large fragment of his satiric play, "Sisyphus," displays impiety in its explanation of religion's origin. As summarized by Critias, a "wise and clever man" once invented both fear and religion by insisting that gods exist who know everything that people think or do and that it is impossible to escape the gods because of their surpassing intelligence. Mankind was so frightened by such a possibility that lawlessness ceased, and thus mortals came to believe in deities.[5] Critias accordingly suggested on this basis that religion could be justified not for its truth but as a collective expedient to discourage potential lawbreakers. Despite his obvious disbelief, Critias was an active participant in two of Plato's dialogues, "Charmides" and "Critias," and he later played an aggressive role as a member of Athens' notorious Thirty Tyrants. Unlike other philosophers at the time, he actually died in battle supporting the Tyrants' effort to rule Athens. Quite aside from his politics, his assumption appears credible even today that religion can be useful in encouraging acceptable behavior.

A popular reaction mounted in Athens against disbelief that was intermittent but also both dramatic and predictable. There were public trials, imprisonments, the flight of notorious disbelievers, and most of all the misguided execution of Socrates, perhaps the least culpable freethinker who could have been targeted for this purpose. The collective hostility to skepticism may have led to renewed temple worship, and even the public theater including Aristophanes' comedies used doubt to ridicule skeptics. Classic tragedy served the same purpose through its ritualized enactment of expiation for a tragic flaw that was inevitably the result of disbelief. A protagonist's single inexcusable transgression was indifference to prophecies by the gods as well as their final authority relevant to human affairs. As explained by Aristotle's classic treatise *Poetics*, tragedy depicted the inevitable destiny of a monarch comparable to Pericles whose disdain for holy prophecies guarantees ruination that finally obliges his recognition of his failure. Catharsis thus occurs among the audience as a complex emotional reaction that merges sympathy with a sense of righteous justification.

Sophocles in particular seems to have employed tragedy to challenge Pericles' leadership at the time. Political and religious considerations perhaps merged in his depiction, though Sophocles' effort may have been based upon his sustained hostility to Pericles that lasted most of their lives.[6] In his tragedy, *Antigone*, Sophocles told of the mythical tyrant, Creon, who ignored the edict of gods regarding the burial of the dead. Catharsis occurred as emotional relief shared by the audience upon his discovery of his error in succumbing to the temptation of disbelief. Even more effective was Sophocles' later tragedy, *Oedipus Rex*, which enacted the destruction of an arrogant leader who ignored a sacred prophecy that he was doomed to kill his father. Oedipus' visible limp symbolized his deficiency every step he took, but it also reinforced the myth's relevance to Pericles at the time, since he himself seems to have been slightly crippled. Even suggestive of tragic pride were Pericles' successful public speeches that led to the acquittal of Anaxagoras and Aspasia. In the opinion of many, his effective rhetorical skills in defense of their supposed transgressions displayed undue arrogance that could only have compounded public reaction against Pericles' counterproductive trade policies that led to the Peloponnesian War. In retrospect, the "real" tragedy of Athens was Pericles' death, followed by the defeat of Athens that terminated the most remarkable period of ancient Greek civilization. Yet having lost the Peloponnesian War, Athens would recover well enough to renew at least its intellectual dominance throughout the region. It was still able, for example, to host Plato's Academy, Aristotle's Lyceum, Epicurus's Garden, and the Stoa as a public site for Stoic philosophers. However, the unprecedented Age of Pericles had been brought to a close. Ironically, Athens' later achievement as the highpoint of ancient philosophy supplanted its earlier advantage as the pinnacle of Greek civilization on a more inclusive basis.

II. PROTAGORAS (C. 490-420 BC)

Born in Abdera on the northern coast of the Aegean Sea, Protagoras studied under Democritus and then distinguished himself as a student of grammar. Later, in Athens he became a celebrated educator in public discourse, teaching his disciples how to dissect a stance on any proposition under consideration. He was said to have been the very first teacher to charge fees from his students. In his mature years he distinguished himself as the principal advocate of Sophism in public debate upon a large variety of controversial issues. He offered no particular philosophical theory beyond his insistence that the human mind is the measure of all things and that what is described as the soul is nothing apart from the senses, a proposition later taken up by Aristotle and still later by modern behaviorists. On a practical level, in forensics Protagoras taught how every question can be defended on both sides. He was willing to submit all supposed truths and propositions of philosophy to scrutiny. Contrary to Socrates' famous insistence that all he knew was that he didn't know, Protagoras seems to have been fully confident that he knew enough to be able to expose the errors of others in sorting out the relative validity of their arguments.

Protagoras was famous for having asserted that everything we perceive and try to explain in the world about us is necessarily a projection of our own consciousness. He made this point in his book *On Truth*—in one of only two passages from his entire body of work that survive today: "Of all things the measure is Man, of the things that are, that they are, and of the things that are not, that they are not."[7] Arguably, his final willingness to take into account things that "are not" anticipated the modern dependence on experimental evidence for the purpose of rejecting false hypotheses. Karl Popper, for example, has argued that this negative consideration is an essential aspect of science, since all hypotheses are necessarily susceptible to challenge should later findings prove them false. Protagoras also distinguished between *physis* (freedom) and *nomos* (traditional usage).

What can be described as his final major contribution, his treatise *On the Gods* challenged the ancient Greek gods for belonging to the category of things that are not:

> About the gods, I am not able to know whether they exist or do not exist, nor what they are like in form; for the factors preventing knowledge are many: the obscurity of the subject, and the shortness of human life. [8]

Protagoras did not deny the existence of the gods categorically, but simply argued that he was unable to make such a judgment because of the lack of sufficient credible information as far as he was concerned. To this extent he can be described as having been an agnostic, instead of a hard-core atheist according to Thomas Huxley's distinction in the late nineteenth century. Upon the publication of *On the* Gods, Protagoras was said to have been at the home of the celebrated playwright, Euripides, who was also a good friend of Anaxagoras. Almost immediately afterwards, however, Protagoras was forced to flee from Athens chased by a crowd of enraged religionists who gathered up all of his texts and consigned them to bonfires. During his escape from Athens he unfortunately died in a storm at sea. His indignant compatriots considered this to have been punishment by the gods, because he had suggested the possibility of their non-existence, overlooking the comparable fate of pious individuals on the same boat as later suggested by apologists.

III. SOCRATES (469-339 BC)

Perhaps a dozen years younger than Protagoras, Socrates was born in Athens and began his career as a sculptor. He later served three years as a soldier and was said to have conducted himself with unusual bravery. As recorded by Diogenes Laertius, still later he became a member of the Senate before becoming a disciple of the philosopher Archelaus, himself supposedly a disciple of Anaxagoras. Socrates' role as a Sophist opposed to natural philosophy is stated in his remark "that the study of nature is no concern of ours." At his trial he denied that he " . . . searched into things under the earth and in heaven," obviously suggesting his indifference to materialist philosophy, and when Euripides gave him a copy of Heraclitus' treatise and asked what he thought of it, he replied, "The part I understand is excellent, and so too is, I dare say, the part I do not understand, but it needs a Delian diver to get to the bottom of it.". With obvious reference to the findings of natural philosophy he similarly declared in *Phaedo* that he was "utterly and absolutely incapable of these inquiries."[9] Instead, he explained that he adhered to his own inner voice as a "divine sign" that warned him against accepting ideas he could not fully understand. He conceded his ignorance of materialist inquiry, and instead insisted on his singular commitment to the validity of ideas that could be understood. He also felt that valid knowledge was limited to what he could grasp on a strictly ethical basis, and that what escaped his understanding was not only avoidable but perhaps even evil. His almost total lack of reference to the natural philosophers throughout most of Plato's dialogues would suggest that he relegated their findings to this particular category.

Fellow Athenians eventually tried and convicted Socrates for corrupting his disciples and for having introduced new divinities. Socrates sought acquittal based on the argument that he did in fact accept the possibility of supernatural beings because he considered the universe to consist of a realm of spiritual existence dominated by universal mind as proposed by Anaxagoras, one of the earlier natural philosophers. Socrates went on to defend his religious belief with a question of his own, "Can a man believe in spiritual and divine agencies, and not in spirits or demi-gods?"[10] As quoted by Plato in *Cratylus,* he expressed his full approval of Anaxagoras' assumptions "that mind or soul is the ordering and containing principle of all things," and " . . . that justice is mind, for mind, as they say, has absolute power, and mixes with nothing, and orders all things, and passes through all things."[11] The acceptance of these two principles, he suggested, made irrelevant the particular gods found socially acceptable. In fact, he did believe in the gods if on a different basis from those of his fellow Athenian citizens.

In Plato's dialogue *Phaedo*, Socrates does seem to have abandoned his earlier commitment to disbelief inspired by Protagoras—his simple insistence that he knew he didn't know—in favor of his later confidence that "the best and highest good" was a product of the mind and that supernatural authority somehow exists. On this basis he could continue to adhere to his notion that knowledge is virtue, though it seems to have conflicted with his earlier insistence that he took satisfaction in his ignorance. As transcribed by Plato in *Phaedo*, Socrates' explanation of his spiritual "conversion" just before his execution confirms his emphasis on piety rather than a specific belief in one or more gods:

I heard someone reading from a book of Anaxagoras, that mind was the disposer and cause of all, and I was delighted at this notion . . . mind will dispose all for the best, and put each particular in the best place. Therefore is anyone desired to find out the cause of the generation or destruction or existence of anything, he must find out what state of being or doing or suffering was best for that thing, and therefore a man had only to consider the best for himself and others, and then he would also know the worst, since the same science comprehended both.[12]

Socrates' added that he himself had taken an interest in natural science at an earlier age, but then became "so befogged by these speculations" that he intentionally "unlearned" what he thought he knew. By implication he did not entirely reject the skepticism he had shared with Protagoras and others in the Sophist movement, but turned to Anaxagoras' theory, the single credible pre-Socratic concept of a fully spiritual universe.[13]

It seems that this modest disclosure bore substantial theoretical consequences, for as the principal disciple of Socrates, Plato devised a metaphysics based on the concept of ideal forms. The universe consists of spiritual essence, he insisted, but it also possesses imbedded archetypes with particular relevance to the human soul. Plato more or less emphasized this synthesis the rest of his life without specifying whether these archetypes might have been portions of any binary or quaternary structure such as proposed by Anaximander, Empedocles and others. Within a generation, however, his own principal disciple, Aristotle, inverted this thesis by renewing the materialist inquiry of pre-Socratic materialists on a more sophisticated basis. Just as Plato revived religion at the expense of pre-Socratic materialism, Aristotle revived pre-Socratic materialism in light of his own version of science at the expense of Plato's theory of ideal forms. Since then, the antithetical standoff between Plato and Aristotle's respective philosophies has dominated much of the history of western civilization. In retrospect, Socrates obviously provided the first step in this sequence.

IV. PLATO (427–347 BC)

By many accounts classical Greece's most eminent philosopher, Plato was born in Athens with the name Aristocles. He was a descendent on his mother's side of the legendary Athenian statesman Solon, who was generally credited with having initiated the city's democratic tradition. Little is known about Plato's youth beyond his service as the leader of a choir before his study of gymnastics under the wrestler Ariston, who bestowed on him the nickname Plato ("broad-shouldered") because of his stocky build. Plato also studied natural philosophy, tried to paint, and wrote poetry until he came under the influence of Socrates at the age of twenty, whereupon he supposedly destroyed his poetry and abandoned natural philosophy to become one of Socrates' most loyal disciples as well as his faithful scribe. Nobody knows for sure whose ideas prevailed in the final transcriptions of the dialogues, those of Socrates or Plato, or to what extent Plato might have sought to bridge their differences. Socrates' insistence on his own ignorance seems probably an accurate assessment, while his more complex explanation of theoretical assumptions seems more likely an expression of Plato's arguments.

Along with Socrates, Plato accepted Anaxagoras' theory and would seem to have experienced his own conversion at roughly the same time. Whatever change occurred, the two of them--and probably the rest of Socrates' disciples—advanced from a somewhat moderate level of skepticism inspired by the Sophists to the outright rejection of natural philosophy in favor of spiritual transcendence, which was first suggested by Anaxagoras. Plato and his supporters went on to revive the concept of an ethical transcendent god at a more sophisticated level. Plato argued that Mind plays a major role in the universe as suggested by Anaxagoras when he elevated it to the "finest of all things" and one that "is alone by itself." [14] Plato's concept of universal mind consequently linked godhead with the human soul as advanced manifestations of transcendent achievement. Religion in general and Christianity in particular have continued to employ many of the assumptions that Plato first formulated as an ethical reaction against both natural philosophy and the reliance on skepticism it inspired. This more complex perspective may be suggested by combining sententiae imbedded in various essays by Plato:

- *Timaeus:* God desires that all things should be good and nothing bad, so as far as this was attainable. [15]
- *The Republic:* God is perfectly simple and true both in word and deed. [16]
- *Laws IV:* God ought to be to us the measure of all things and not man. [17]
- *Laws VII:* And God is the natural and worthy object of our most serious and blessed endeavors. [18]
- *Timaeus:* For God only has the knowledge and also the power which are able to combine many things into one and again resolve the one into many. [19]
- *Theaetetus*: If the gods will it so, so be it. [20]

An uncompromisingly pious ethic is present in this sequence of injunctions, and even today devout religionists have had no difficulty in accepting them, quite aside from the particular version of God they choose to worship.

In his famous "Allegory of the Cave" described in Book VII of *The Republic,* Plato offers what might be described as a vivid analogy of religious conversion. The aspiring philosopher crawls through a maze of darkened underground tunnels that symbolize "bastard knowledge" as typified by the philosophy of Democritus in order to gain genuine enlightenment, and once he reaches sunlight the full truth supposedly presents itself in its full glory. By implication this conversion suddenly occurs when nature's remarkable plenitude confirms spiritual inspiration's benefits instead of an incessant materialist analysis beset with earth, stale air, dripping water, etc.. Of course the attainment of this perceived higher "truth" as promised by Plato entailed his own version of religious conversion.[21]

In his dialogue "Theaetetus," probably written at about the age of forty, Plato challenges the skeptical perspective of Protagoras, who had died at sea a few decades earlier. Much had happened over the intervening period, so Plato is able in retrospect to link Protagoras' skeptical epistemology with the materialist cosmology of the earlier natural philosophers. Their assumptions could only take root, Plato suggested, because they had been inspired by tacit skepticism already present, if not yet recognized. Moreover, he argues, if the two principles insisted by Protagoras are true, that "each of us is a measure of what is and of what is not," and that "man is the measure of all things," it becomes obvious that "the truth of Protagoras, being doubted by all, will be true neither to himself nor to any one else."[22] To make his point, Plato quotes Socrates to the effect that this deficiency also necessitates an uncritical acceptance of the contradictory theories proposed by the earlier philosophers.

Both Socrates and Plato rejected pre-Socratic philosophy by focusing on Anaxagoras' tangential insistence that the mind alone both invests and subsumes all existence in its entirety. However, less understandable is how they linked this effort with an ethical pursuit of "the good" at the expense of theoretical adequacy. Often, for example, "the good" turns out not to be particularly beneficial and its advocates lack the analytic skills to recognize the difference. Plato's principal concern was virtue and piety at the expense of cosmology, and toward this end Plato's transcendent archetypes could be featured instead of the supernatural antics of Homer's pantheon of gods and goddesses. Pre-Socratic materialism might have undermined Homeric myth even among the populace, but as interpreted by Plato, Anaxagoras' concept of *nous* came to the rescue, and the social accord of the populace as a whole was effectively restored—or so it seemed. The social customs and prerogatives of religion could be resurrected on a far more sophisticated basis to provide an effective antidote to what seemed materialist dogma that might conceivably dominate philosophy into the indefinite future. What was of primary importance was an acceptable ethics based upon one's belief in the gods, whatever their transcendent manifestation.

The revival of the God concept was far more acceptable to Plato in contrast to the earlier natural philosophers whose interest was focused upon an explanation of the universe as a vast existence with a necessarily complicated arrangement of interactive physical principles. Instead, Plato presented the belief in a world dominated by a God whose existence is both unified and resistant to excessive clarification. As Plato stated elsewhere:

Now that which is created must, as we affirm, of necessity be created by a cause. But the father and maker of all this universe [i.e. God] is past finding out, and even if we found him, to tell of him to all men would be impossible.[23]

Just as pre-Socratic philosophy had advanced from Homeric mythology to a strictly physical analysis of the universe that encouraged both skepticism and social anarchy, Plato introduced spiritual assumptions that had been implicit in many of the earlier religions. If pre-Socratic philosophy had all but eradicated the paramount role of the gods, Plato restored their relevance on a far more persuasive basis, one that could supposedly reunite all portions of society except for inveterate disbelievers.

As a product of his later years, Plato's dialogue *Timaeus* was one of his few attempts to suggest a viable synthesis between religion and certain advances in secular philosophy. Without mentioning any of the pre-Socratic philosophers by name, he paid his respects to earlier concepts such as Heraclitus' theory of fire, Empedocles' cyclical theory of earth, air, fire, and water, and Anaxagoras' version of atomism that featured "smaller particles thrust into the interstices of the larger."[24] He accepted the description of the earth as a globe, a concept first suggested by Pythagoras. However, his analysis had little relevance to the more specific aspects of science and philosophy, and he once again made it plain that his principal concern was the central role of God and the destiny of the human soul. He even described God's manifestation as an "image," in other words a visualized presence whose recognition is essential to the eternal preservation of the soul. God is described in the dialogue's final sentence as: "the sensible God who is the image of the intellectual, the greatest, best, fairest, most perfect—the one only-begotten heaven."[25]

Plato also went so far as to invoke the help of God based on the standard of probability: "I call upon God and beg him to be our savior out of a strange and unwonted enquiry, and bring us to the haven of probability."[26] In *Theaetetus,* Plato had already emphasized the crucial but necessarily loose concept of probability to justify religious belief on the assumption that whatever seems probable can be considered true at least to that extent:

> But in that field I am speaking of—in right and wrong and matters of religion—people are ready to affirm . . . that the public decision becomes true at the moment when it is made and remains true so long as the decision stands.[27]

The reference to "public decision" averted doubts about any particular truth's likelihood if it could be granted validity by a majority of people. Plato also maintained on the same basis that religious doctrine should be accepted at its face value on that basis alone:

> We must accept the traditions of the men of old time who affirm themselves to be the offspring of the gods. . . . How can we doubt the word of the children of the gods? Although they give no probable or certain proofs, still, as they declare that they are speaking of what took place in their own family, we must conform to custom and believe them.[28]

In effect Plato proposed extremely generous constraints in determining the validity of religious convictions acceptable to the public because of their moral necessity as well as their probability. If the populace considered a belief to be probable, this in itself was sufficient justification to concede what amounted to its functional truth. Obviously, this generous acceptance of earlier pagan deities was completely at odds with both the skepticism of Protagoras and the theoretical contributions of earlier materialists! As justified by the admission of "conforming to custom," Plato effectively declared his orthodox belief after having used Socratic doubt to dispense with the secular perspective in his earlier dialogues.

Plato also suggested that if there was any possibility miracles might be true, they can and ought to be considered probable and therefore effectively true:

> [When God] was framing the universe, he put intelligence in soul, and soul in body, that he might be the creator of a work which was by nature fairest and best. Wherefore, using the language of probability, we may say that the world became a living creature truly endowed with soul and intelligence by the providence of God. [29]

Here Plato actually seems to defend the supernatural claims typical of earlier religions based on the consideration of probability. Moreover, he extends this necessity to the acceptance of all mortals able to identify themselves as the children of gods:

Plato encourages a departure from objective philosophical analysis by aging traditionalists who depend on patriarchal authority justified by godhood. Received customs thus take precedence over theory that valorizes truth independent of social and familial authority. [30]

This is completely at odds with both the skepticism and the theoretical contribution of earlier materialists! Here Plato effectively declared his belief to be based on custom after having used Socratic doubt to challenge the secular perspective in his earlier dialogues.

Plato's views upon religion culminated in *Laws X*, apparently his final testament in which he simply described himself as "Athenian." He died while writing *Laws X,* and his disciple, Philippus of Opus, was said to have completed and published it after his death. It is possible that Plato himself may have completed an initial draft, that Philippus substantially revised the text, or that he himself wrote the text based on remarks by Plato that Plato himself would have deleted from the final draft. And of course it could have been brought to completion in any combination of the above. In any case, the text discloses a level of hostility against atheism and natural philosophy more intense than anything he had previously said. Earlier writings certainly displayed aversion, but his anger seems to have predominated toward the end of his life.

Plato's vigorous defense of religion was based on the assumption that his argument was automatically correct if it could not be proven wrong. He proposed an elaborate proof of God's existence in roughly ten pages of text whose essential line of argument was both more vigorous and more questionable than any of his earlier pronouncements.[31] Once again he argued that soul is the dominant stuff of the universe, and that one or more gods can be identified with this more inclusive soul, thus necessitating their worship and the recognition of their final authority in human affairs. He also insisted that natural philosophers had been wrong in their effort to identify physical elements as the original stuff of the universe. Quite the opposite, he argued, the soul alone provides a "motion that can move itself" as well as having serving as the self-movement that initiated the universe:

> . . . soul came first—that it was not fire, nor air, but soul which was there to begin with—it is the existence of soul which is most eminently natural.[32]

Plato insisted that the soul is more "elder-born than all bodies and prime source of all their changes and transformations," and that soul has always been the primary stuff of existence as Anaxagoras had earlier suggested. For if soul both preceded the physical universe and could be identified with God, he maintained, the deduction seemed plain that some kind of a personal God played an essential role in the creation of the universe.

Plato also explained that soul "has *self-movement* as its definition," and therefore, he explained, it may be considered "the source of movement" that is "absolutely complete" as "the first–born of all things," thus giving it a universal role on a strictly ethical basis. Then Plato went on to suggest that the "good soul" effectively steers motion, thereby promoting virtue as an essential feature of existence whereby transition itself manifests its effect. Plato also abandoned any possibility of a natural cosmology by next suggesting conflict between good and evil was strictly a manifestation of soul: "it [soul] controls heaven itself" whether this necessitates either a "single soul" or "more than one." He went on to declare the likelihood of cosmic tension between good and evil supernatural powers: "We must not assume fewer than two, one beneficent, the other capable of the contrary effect."—hence anticipating personification in the conflict between God and the devil later featured in Christian doctrine.[33] And finally Plato expressed his qualified approval of current polytheistic belief:

> Since soul, or souls, and those souls good with perfect goodness, have proved to be the causes of all, these souls we hold to be gods, whether they direct the universe by inhabiting bodies . . . Will any man who shares this belief bear to hear it said that all things are not "full of gods"?[34]

Whatever the quantitative ratio involved, Plato suggested, it is spiritual authority that matters in a universe totally in motion.

In the end, however, it was Plato's indignation that dominated his analysis. At the very beginning of *Laws X*, he insisted, "There is the fact that all mankind, Greeks and non-Greeks alike, believe in the existence of gods."[35] Just a few pages later, however, he warned that young men too readily harbor disbelief which they later abandon: "I can assure you that no one who in early life has adopted this doctrine of the nonexistence of gods has ever persisted to old age constant in that conviction."[36] Presumably young atheists become religious when they mature and become wiser. Then he seems to have contradicted himself by declaring his hostility against older men whose teachings inspire impiety among the youth: "All these views, my friends, come from men who impress the young as wise, prose writers and poets who profess that indefeasible right means whatever a man can carry with the high hand. Hence our epidemics of youthful irreligion."[37] For if all young atheists later become religious, how can there be any older atheists available to misguide young atheists?

In the final three pages of his essay, Plato goes on to complain at greater length about the vices and temptations of atheism among both young and old, suggesting many more atheists than he has indicated only a few paragraphs earlier. He concedes that young atheists might still be virtuous, but also insists that older "men of this class" [atheists] deal in prophecy and jugglery of all kinds, and that they too often become "tyrants and demagogues and generals and hierophants of private mysteries and the Sophists."[38] Again, his assurance that young atheists simply do not retain their misguided assumptions suggests that old and presumably more sophisticated atheists could only have been converted later in life.

Although Socrates had been tried and put to death for similar charges years earlier, Plato, his principal disciple, brought *Laws X* to a close by advocating similar punishment of more recent offenders found guilty of impiety:

> Any person proved guilty of a sin against piety which is the crime of a grown man, not the trivial offense of a child, whether by dedicating a shrine on private ground or by doing sacrifice to any gods whatsoever in public, shall suffer death for doing sacrifice in a state of defilement.[39]

How ironic that such punishment could be advocated by Plato! The reader is left to question what portion of Plato's final text resulted from his mature judgment, what portion from borderline senility.[40] The question also poses itself whether his attitude might have contributed to the otherwise inexplicable choice of Aristotle to leave the Academy just before Plato's death.

Chapter Three

Early Aristotle (384-322 BC)

Aristotle's life was beset with both opportunity and improbability. He was born in Stagira, Macedon, the son of Nicomachus, the court physician of Macedonia's King Amyntus III, who was also the grandfather of Alexander the Great. Alexander later became Aristotle's student and still later, his patron. Aristotle traveled to Athens at the age of seventeen to study in Plato's Academy, and he seems to have become Plato's favorite and most productive disciple, having authored a variety of texts and dialogues more or less supportive of Plato's philosophy. It seems Aristotle left Plato's Academy shortly before Plato's death in 348-47 BC, possibly because of growing theoretical differences as perhaps illustrated for example, by Plato's insistence in *Laws* *X* that elderly atheists be executed despite Socrates' ordeal on similar charges. After Plato's death Aristotle seems to have returned to Athens to compete for the vacant leadership of the Academy, only to find that Plato's nephew Speusippus, had already been selected to serve as its director. Aristotle then severed ties with the Academy and left Athens accompanied by Theophrastus, a fellow student who became his principal disciple for the rest of his life, as later suggested by his final will in which Theophrastus was included along with Aristotle's own family.

Aristotle next taught at Assos, where he enjoyed a close friendship with its dictator, Hermias and his adoptive daughter, Pythias, whom Aristotle married. Within the next year or so he was summoned to Mitylene by King Phillip to tutor his son, Alexander the Great, and he served in this capacity for two years before Alexander became regent of Macedonia during Phillip's military campaign abroad. Aristotle's ties with Alexander remained amicable during Alexander's Asian conquests despite Alexander's execution of Aristotle's nephew Callisthenes for insubordination. On friendly terms with both Alexander and Antipater, Alexander's regent in Greece, Aristotle returned to

63

Athens in 335 BC after an absence of twelve years. Unable to join Plato's Academy despite Speusippus's recent death, he established his own school, the Lyceum, and remained there for the next thirteen years as a scholar and teacher, both gathering a large assortment of scientific data and teaching his students as they strolled among the colonnades (*perapitos*—hence the use of the word "peripatetic" to describe his teachings). This was the most productive phase in his life. With the help of his disciples, he was estimated to have authored as many as four hundred texts, which would roughly be equivalent to long chapters in a modern book.

Among the 150 to 200 texts that can be identified by their titles, not more than thirty or so can be definitively traced to Aristotle's authorship. Some scholars have estimated that he could reliably be identified as the sole author of only four of these texts and that most of the rest were recorded or partially authored by his disciples. However, his unique style that combined precision and complexity seems the same throughout most of them, suggesting that Aristotle's authorship was for the most part his own. A million words of text can be attributed to him, compared to Plato's output of 600,000 words. Unlike Plato, Aristotle more readily took into account alternate possibilities suggested by others, and his analysis displayed this skill in a variety of fields. Whereas Plato could expatiate at length in response to relatively short questions posed by his disciples, Aristotle put effort into summarizing credible analysis by others before launching into his own more conclusive findings in such fields as physics, biology, aesthetics, metaphysics, rhetoric, government, politics, and, not least, deductive logic. He formalized ethics based on the so-called Golden Mean as the pursuit of moderation relevant to all aspects of human behavior. Similarly, his *Politics* suggested appropriate roles in society, and his *Poetics* identified the impact of catharsis--i.e. emotional gratification--as the most essential aspect of literary achievement. Altogether he played an essential role in establishing all these fields of inquiry and at advanced levels.

Aristotle's intention was the full elucidation of complex issues rather than inspirational effect, but his effort turned out to be successful on both accounts. His methodology alone was a valuable contribution in encouraging the sustained pursuit of a "smaller and finite number of principles" as explained many centuries later by Ockham's famous "razor"--which was also effectively Aristotelian--that the simplest adequate explanation is finally the most likely. Aristotle offered exactly this justification, for example, in *De Caelo* (*On the Heavens*), "Obviously then it would be better to assume a finite number of principles. They should in fact be as few as possible, consistent with proving what has to be proved."[1] In other words, final analysis should be both sufficient and appropriate to the theoretical issues under consideration. Notably, with regard to cosmology his unified explanation of the universe turned out to consist of a basic theory of "mass in sustained motion"—effectively combining two of the three ingredients in Einstein's famous equation. This reductive skill of Aristotle was important to the advancement of both science and philosophy.

As for Aristotle's secular perspective, a major difficulty is that much of his analysis was in conflict with one or more orthodoxies, and censorship too often became a factor either through the destruction of texts or through their textual modification. The outright eradication of ancient secular texts was commonplace throughout ancient and medieval history, and today's almost total absence of extant writings by Strato, Theophrastus, and Clitomachus suggests a similar fate, as does the absence of Democritus' theory of atomism, including Aristotle's single essay on Democritus.

To avoid censorship and the possibility of prosecution by the citizens of Athens, Aristotle reserved the full examination of his theories for his students and disciples, while his less offensive writings were made available to the public. Plutarch records a letter to Aristotle from Alexander the Great that obviously refers to this distinction:

> Alexander to Aristotle greeting. You have *not* done well to publish your books of oral doctrine [i.e. information exclusively for the benefit of students]; for what is there now that we excel others in, if those things which we have been particularly instructed to be laid open to all? For my part, I assure you, I had rather excel others in the knowledge of what is excellent, than in the extent of my power and dominion. Farewell.[2]

Here Alexander asserted his presumed right as an ex-student to have access to Aristotle's theories that were to be kept unavailable to the public at large. By publishing his ideas, Aristotle had disregarded this supposed convention. Alexander's complaint discloses the distinction at the time between "exoteric" public knowledge and "esoteric" oral doctrine or "knowledge of what is excellent," the latter reserved for colleagues and disciples as opposed to fellow citizens at large.[3] The right to examine this information was restricted to these privileged individuals, and whatever was later preserved was recorded only in the so-called "acroamatic" transcripts in the possession of Aristotle himself. Quite by accident it was the strictly esoteric texts that became available for publication many centuries later. The texts available to the public at large at the time have all been lost, whereas those kept confidential were later salvaged and continue to exist today.

Arguably, Aristotle's grand theoretical synthesis was the most remarkable achievement of ancient Greek philosophy. While Plato's unified concept of transcendent mind, as earlier suggested by Anaxagoras, provided a substantial philosophical advance upon the scattered assortment of theories by pre-Socratic natural philosophers, Aristotle provided a more challenging theoretical perspective that effectively reformulated these theories on a more defensible basis. By doing so he paradoxically laid the groundwork for both religious orthodoxy and the many fields of scientific inquiry taken for granted today. His encyclopedic achievements included the invention of both biology and deductive logic as independent disciplines, and his later theoretical contributions anticipated Ockham's Razor, Bacon's induction, Spinoza's pantheism, Locke's behavioral psychology, Hegel's negative dialectics, Darwin's evolutionism, Dewey's functionalism, and, not least, modern psychology.

I. COMPARISON WITH PLATO

Whereas Plato can be credited with having invented modern idealism, Aristotle's inductive analysis effectively set the stage for the secular achievement of the Renaissance almost twenty centuries later. As opposed to Plato's invention of "ideal forms" within a spiritual universe, Aristotle employed empirical analysis applied to the physical universe. His dialectical confrontation with Plato had been anticipated by the earlier standoff between Anaxagoras' theory of soul and the various concepts of materialism advanced by pre-Socratic natural philosophers culminating with Democritus. In the beginning Aristotle served as a loyal advocate of Plato's spiritual teleology, but he later pursued a materialist alternative with an emphasis on the "intrinsic order of nature" as confirmed by empirical evidence. This choice can be illustrated by his explanation in *Generation of Animals* on the study of bees:

> Such appears to be the truth about the generation of bees, judging from theory and from what are believed to be the facts about them; the facts, however, have not yet been sufficiently grasped; if ever they are, then credit must be given rather to observation than to theories, and to theories only if what they affirm agrees with the observed facts. [4]

Aristotle's emphasis on confirmation by factual data elevated speculative inquiry to a new and more sophisticated level, since it rested upon the close examination of inductive evidence as opposed to supposedly fixed "truths" that were otherwise unsubstantiated.

One can only speculate how long it took for Aristotle to realize that he preferred the various assumptions of pre-Socratic philosophers to Plato's concept of transcendence. By the time he wrote *Physics* Aristotle seems to have almost entirely abandoned Platonism, but at this point his use of pre-Socratic natural philosophy might not have yet reached its final stage, as suggested by his later choice to accept Melissus' concept of spatial and temporal infinitude, a stance entirely different from his earlier hostility. [5]

Plato's successful invention of metaphysics rested on Anaxagoras' theory of universal mind which was in turn inspired by Parmenides as well as Heraclitus' concept of *Logos*. In contrast, Aristotle sought what amounted to a more inclusive synthesis of pre-Socratic philosophy. His materialist perspective benefitted from the theoretical achievement of the Milesian school as well as the holistic perspective of the Eleatic school that included Melissus. Other influences to be found in *Physics* were (1) the concept of conflict in process inspired by Heraclitus; (2) the holistic concepts of matter and incessant motion inspired by Anaximander, Anaximenes and Diogenes Apollonius: (3) the concept of spheres inspired by Pythagoras and Xenophanes, (4) the concept of cyclical inertia inspired by both Heraclitus and Empedocles; and even (5) the reluctant acceptance of atomism featured by Leucippus and Democritus. Aristotle's variety of sources might seem to have been unabashedly eclectic, yet in the end he achieved an unprecedented synthesis in the simple--even stark--concept of mass in motion, a far more functional explanation of the universe than anything yet proposed. Whereas Plato had featured the perpetual motion of soul in *Laws X*, Aristotle featured "mass in perpetual motion," a concept more amenable to modern science.

That Aristotle emphasized pre-Socratic materialism to a much greater extent than Plato is also indicated by comparing citations in their respective standard editions both on an absolute and relative basis. For example, once the number of Aristotle's indexed citations are compared with those of Plato, a considerable imbalance in references becomes obvious pertaining to Anaximander (7 vs. 0), Anaximenes (8 vs. 1), Xenophanes (11 vs. 0), Pythagoras and the Pythagoreans (73 vs. 7), Zeno (21 vs. 5), Empedocles (98 vs. 2), Melissus (18 vs. 2), Leucippus (13 vs. 0), Diogenes of Apollonia (5 vs. 0). Aristotle's total exceeds that of Plato even for Anaxagoras (64 vs.17), and, as to be expected, Democritus (55 vs. 0) and reveal a considerable imbalance. Plato's citations turn out to be more plentiful only for Thales (7 vs. 7), Parmenides (23 vs. 22), and Heraclitus (32 vs. 22). Altogether, the disparity between their totals, Aristotle's 430 citations as opposed to Plato's 86 citations, involves roughly a 5-1 ratio. In addition, natural philosophers who were Plato's contemporaries—including Melissus, Democritus, and Diogenes of Apollonia—were virtually ignored in his dialogues. In contrast, Aristotle referred to Plato himself 119 times and Plato's mentor Socrates 45 times. Aristotle was willing to take their assumptions into account but without overlooking pre-Socratic natural philosophy. In effect, Plato ignored most of the earlier philosophers except for Anaxagoras and his suggestion of the transcendent concept of soul, whereas Aristotle "resurrected" the other major pre-Socratic natural philosophers by advocating a broad functional concept of the universe on a strictly physical basis.

Even Aristotle and Plato's respective modes of thought and expression suggest the difference between their philosophies. Aristotle's inductive persistence necessitated a prose style more specific and intricate than that of most of the ancient poets and prophets who depended on broad repetitive epithets as well as an almost endless conjunctive sequence such as "and then, and then," or "Yes, oh Socrates." In contrast, Aristotle's sentences feature lucid complexity taken to its appropriate limit and sometimes beyond. This may be observed, for example, in his explanation of the earth as a sphere with weight (or gravity) based upon Melissus' theory of mass in light of Pythagoras' emphasis on mathematical exactitude:

> [The earth's] shape must necessarily be spherical. For every portion of earth has weight until it reaches the centre, and the jostling of parts greater and smaller would bring about not a waved surface, but rather compression and convergence of part and part until the centre is reached. . . . If, on the one hand, there were a similar movement from each quarter of the extremity to the single centre, it is obvious that the resulting mass would be similar on every side. For if an equal amount is added on every side the extremity of the mass will be equidistant from its centre, i.e. the figure will be spherical.[6]

In translation this brief passage is held together by the connecting words, (1) *necessarily, (2) For, (3) not, (4) but rather, (5) If, . . . it is obvious that,* and (6) *For if . . . will be.* Apparently aware of speculative inquiry by Eudoxus, Heraclides, and other contemporary naturalists whose astronomical findings undoubtedly superseded the philosophical assumptions of Pythagoras and Melissus, Aristotle was nevertheless able to propose a credible explanation of the physical forces as well as taking into account the concepts of mass, gravity, and the spherical structure of heavenly bodies that anticipated and were later confirmed by Newtonian physics.

In contrast, Plato's explanation of the earth's spherical shape a few decades earlier certainly provided a picturesque but far more speculative explanation:

> There are many hollow places all round the earth, places of every shape and size, into which the water and mist and air have collected. But the earth itself is as pure as the starry heaven in which it lies, and which is called aether by most of our authorities. The water, mist, and air are the dregs of this aether, and they are continually draining into the hollow places in the earth.[7]

Plato accepted the Pythagorean assumption that the earth has a spherical shape, but his simplistic description was almost irrelevant to any explanation of the physical formation of the earth. Aristotle's analysis provided a precise description of the earth's shape and matter, while Plato's description leaves open the possibility of a celestial origin of its water supply. With considerable serendipity, Plato accidentally may have been partly right, as recent scientific research indicates that clouds of ice specks from outer space may have produced a significant amount of the earth's water. Still, Aristotle's explanation involved careful analysis as confirmed by both logic and modern geology. To this extent, at least, their two styles may be compared, though they exemplify two entirely different visions of cosmology.

Substantial differences between Plato and Aristotle's texts and respective audiences also bear an impact on their modern interpretations. First since ancient times, there has been a far more continuous history of the acceptance of Plato's texts. Their indicated order might not exactly duplicate the chronological sequence of their composition by Plato, but over the centuries there seems consensus on their general unity, and their ideas were later deemed acceptable by the Catholic ecumenical councils at Nicaea, Ephesus, and Constantinople. In contrast, Aristotle's ideas seem to have become more complicated as he grew older, especially pertaining to the issue of religion. *Physics,* for example, provided his first sustained analysis on cosmology, followed by *Metaphysics,* which seems to have been compiled as a loose collection of essays in response to issues raised in *Physics.* Ironically, the book's title seems to have been intended to indicate this intention—*beyond* (or additional to) the topic of physics—rather than a new and different field of inquiry on transcendental matters. In fact, the title seems to have invented the field, not the other way around. Other dislocations become obvious in exploring the separate chapters, some of which are important. Moreover, there are substantial variations among the chapters. Aristotle both formulated theory and seems to have sought out additional sources in doing this, and the overall effect suggests continuous modification on his part until his flight from Athens.

A brief and often overlooked two-sentence summary by Plutarch of Aristotle's cosmology helps in sorting out the sequence of his texts. Plutarch identified exactly two texts by Aristotle, *De Caelo* and *De Anima,* as primary sources on cosmology as a field of inquiry. Plutarch then went on to supplement these with comparable works by Aristotle's followers and disciples connected with the Lyceum. He specifically identified four disciples who could be linked with Aristotle's cosmology--Theophrastus, Strato, Heracleides, and Dicaearchus. Like Aristotle, according to Plutarch, these disciples "constantly challenged Plato's transcendental philosophy, contradicting him about the most fundamental and far-reaching questions relevant to natural philosophy."[8] Unfortunately, their texts no longer exist, so Aristotle's perspective stands alone today in its commitment to secular cosmology. In effect an entire field of inquiry dedicated to the holistic investigation of the physical universe on a secular basis was eradicated except for the writings of Aristotle.[9] Why, one asks, did Plutarch omit both *Physics* and *Metaphysics* from his list? The most obvious explanation would be that they consisted of complex preliminary assessments superseded by more outspoken secular analysis.

II. CHRISTIAN INTERPOLATIONS

For modern readers a second difficulty in the interpretation of Aristotle's writings is the presence throughout his works of forged passages—interpolations—especially in texts that might otherwise express a secular viewpoint. Unlike Plato's dialogues that were generally compatible both with contemporary beliefs and with Christian theology, Aristotle's theory necessitated the effort to obscure or eliminate secular passages at odds with received religious assumptions. Offending secular passages could be eradicated, as many undoubtedly were (for example Aristotle's essay upon Democritus), but scribes also salvaged other texts of possible value to their beliefs by adding brief segments of their own to render Aristotle compatible with Christian doctrine. There is little or no evidence available today how and why this happened, but this expedient seems to have primarily been undertaken when Aristotle's works were finally translated into Latin during the thirteenth and fourteenth centuries. With their added interpolations, these texts ceased to be treated as unacceptable ventures in impiety. Today, these editorial modifications often are obvious, especially those that refer to a single god with a capital "G" or that become exultant in their declarations of piety. Most can be recognized by careful readers, but others will probably continue to go unnoticed until a statistical analysis of Aristotle's style is sufficiently advanced to identify and eliminate them. As a measure of Aristotle's importance, no other author in western tradition has been saddled with so many counterfeit inclusions to prevent the destruction of his writings.

Today these anachronistic pronouncements often stand out. An example is this interpolation from *Nicomachean Ethics*:

> We assume the gods to be above all other beings blessed and happy. . . .
> Therefore the activity of God, which surpasses all others in blessedness, must
> be contemplative; and of human activities, therefore, that which is most akin to
> this must be most of the nature of happiness."[10]

Who is we? Also, the repeated conjunction of "blessed" and "happy," the praise of contemplative behavior, the mixed reference to God and gods, the singular reference to God's "activity," and the notion of such an activity "surpassing" another in "blessedness" suggest an anachronistic expression of an entirely different and more orthodox religious perspective.

The same problem arises in *Eudemian Ethics*, in which three references to god are polytheistic, two are monotheistic, and the sixth seems to have been Platonic in suggesting the soul as God. The logic of one particular interpolation, for example, is entirely at odds with Aristotle's earlier description in *De Anima* of mind and intelligence as opposed to a transcendent vision of god(s) that primarily involves the soul:

The object of our search is this—what is the commencement of movement in the soul? The answer is clear: as in the universe, so in the soul, it is god. For in a sense the divine element in us moves everything. The starting-point of reasoning is not reasoning, but something greater. What, then, could be greater even than knowledge and intellect but god? [11]

Almost completely at odds with Aristotle's philosophy, this passage consists of an abrupt sequence of five short sentences with an average of twelve words apiece that differs from Aristotle's more convoluted analytic style. Moreover, the concept of soul in this passage might be both compact and even persuasive, but it completely deviates from Aristotle's explanation throughout *De Anima*, where the soul [i.e. consciousness] is often identified not with any kind of a god, but instead with consciousness shared by animals as well as human beings. [12]

Another example, an even more blatant interpolation is the following passage steeped in monotheistic certitude:

Moreover, life belongs to God. For the actuality of thought is life, and God is that actuality; and the essential actuality of God is most good and eternal. We hold, then, that God is a living being, eternal, most good; and therefore life and a continuous external existence belong to God; for that is what God is. [13]

Once again both the syntax and strained piety in combination clearly deviate from the articulate complexity to be expected of Aristotle. Moreover, the anachronistic reference to a monotheistic "God," with a capital "G," is repeated five times for rhetorical effect, and the inverted noun phrase, "life most good and eternal," is followed by another rhetorical flourish that is even more noticeably inverted, "eternal, most good." "Most" indeed! This emphatic effect is then redoubled by a final righteous deduction, "for this is what God is." Also, the rhetorical emphasis terminating with the word "God" closely resembles the wording of the passage already quoted from *Eudemian Ethics*—"What, then, could be greater even than knowledge and intellect but god?"[14] It seems likely that Christian scribes were responsible for these interpolations. Such liberties might well have been useful in preserving Aristotle's philosophy during the late Middle Ages, but they pose difficulties for thoughtful modern readers. Still, the very fact that medieval scribes resorted to this intrusiveness confirms their recognition that Aristotle's perspective might otherwise be interpreted as blasphemy. We can be grateful for their success in preventing the destruction of Aristotle's works, but their changes should be recognized.

Other interpolations suggest miracles, an afterlife, and other modes of intervention by God (or gods) in addition to the concept of initial creationism. Quite the opposite, however, Aristotle featured in his mature cosmological writings an infinite physical universe devoid of supernatural intervention.

He might have considered the possibility of an unmoved mover in Books VII and VIII of *Physics* and later in Book XII of *Metaphysics,* but his later arguments suggest otherwise, especially in his final texts upon cosmology. For the close reader the detection of interpolations becomes almost a sport. They seem to crop up wherever Aristotle's argument suggests secular possibilities, as for example in *De Caelo, On Generation and Corruption,* and *De Anima.* They may be found most often at the beginning of such texts and within the proximity of especially controversial passages.

III. *PHYSICS*

Aristotle's first major work pertaining to cosmology and supernatural authority was undoubtedly *Physics,* a text in which he confirmed his abandonment of Platonic doctrine while formulating his own. His basic arguments appear in the first chapter of Book I, in which the second sentence simply declares, "For we do not think that we know a thing until we are acquainted with its primary causes or first principles, and have carried our analysis as far as its elements." In his second chapter he summarizes a variety of theories of the pre-Socratic philosophers, and finally suggests his own, "We . . . must take for granted that the things that exist by nature are, either all or some of them in motion—which is indeed made plain by induction."[15] As suggested by this sentence alone, Aristotle's concept of "things in motion" anticipated his full explanation in *De Caelo* and *On Generation and Corruption.* He mostly ignores Plato in the chapter and seems to refer to him as having been among "the later [or more recent] of the ancient thinkers" who were bothered by the comparison between "one and the many." Also, his oxymoronic implications of "the more recent of the ancient thinkers" suggests the possibility of irony at the expense of Plato.[16] In Book III of *Physics* Aristotle concedes the seemingly harmless abstract definition of the whole as "the whole that from which nothing is wanting."[17] However, he attributes the principle to the physical universe in its entirety rather than the spiritual dimension emphasized by Plato.

Aristotle criticizes the static limitations of both Parmenides and Melissus' respective models of the universe for emphasizing undifferentiated spiritual and material infinitude. "We physicists on the other hand," he insists, "must take for granted that the things that exist by nature are, either all or some of them, in motion—which is indeed made plain by induction."[18] This aspect of Aristotle's theory becomes the central consideration in his later text, *De Caelo,* where his concept of motion is expanded to apply to all aspects of the universe and linked with the concept of matter. Aristotle traces this emphasis to the earlier theories of so-called "physicists"—or "natural philosophers"-- such as Heraclitus, Anaximenes, Empedocles, and even Anaxagoras. He also suggests a fundamental aspect they share, which is that whatever predominates in its early manifestation is more likely to produce an alternative that somehow occurs as its opposite. These before-and-after phases can be identified as sequential "contraries:" Suggestive of Heraclitus (as well as Hegel many centuries later), Aristotle explains that, "Everything, therefore, that comes to be by a natural process is either a contrary or a product of contraries."[19] He specifies, however, that this strictly relates to process, and he goes on to illustrate this dynamic with his abstract definition of evolution, "that there must always be an underlying something, namely that which becomes . . ."[20] Process effectively involves transition from one stage to another, necessarily its successor, and essential to this transition is difference that somehow amounts to negation.

In Book II, Aristotle mentions the possibility of a first cause of the whole universe, and he links its origin with spontaneity and chance as earlier suggested by Hesiod. However, he also suggests the possibility that intelligence was a later product of the universe. Aristotle goes on to propose four materialist categories: (1) matter, (2) form, (3) mover, and (4) final outcome ("that for the sake of which").[21] The second, third, and fourth of these categories possibly suggests the influence of a God or gods, but Aristotle does not venture to offer such an explanation. Instead, he mentions organized spontaneity "in a fitting way" as selective intelligence imbedded in nature rather than from outside by supernatural authority. If anything, the concept of matter in motion combines form's organization of matter with motion as the agent of change, and with a result stable enough that change has been controlled. There is a plateau effect afterwards that persists until change catches up with possibilities once again. As suggested by David Sedley, author of *Creationism and its Critics in Antiquity*, and others, this portion of Book II effectively sets the stage for the more specific analysis of Book VIII relevant to metaphysical considerations.

Aristotle explores the likelihood of infinitude in greater depth in Book III. He accepts the received concept of endlessness as "uncreatable" and indestructible, and he goes on to propose the existence of an imperishable universe as a necessary consequence of infinity. However, he also proposes that the physical attraction which is now identified as gravity resists the effect of infinitude, since a body "has a natural locomotion towards the center if it is heavy, and upwards if it is light."[22] Things of more weight displace things of less weight, and these get thrust upwards as a result--just as water fills the sea and air exists above water.

In Book IV Aristotle challenges the concept of atoms suspended in a void as proposed by Democritus, but he does so without mentioning atomism or its proponent by name. Instead, he rejects the possible existence of a void by insisting on the necessity that "everything which is, is body." [*sic*] The supposed non-existence of air, for example, involves relatively low density as opposed to Democritus' notion of empty space that separates atoms. Aristotle's emphasis on mass in motion accordingly depends on the concept of spatial continuity as opposed to Democritus' concept of atomism that was based on the assumption that atoms are suspended in space, which itself was basically—effectively "a place with nothing in it."[23] Toward the end of his argument, however, Aristotle seems to concede the possibility of synthesis based on the assumption of movement among bodies that make room for one another.[24]

Books IV through VI of *Physics* concern such issues as void, motion, time, matter, and the immovable with little obvious relevance to the question whether God or gods play any transcendent role in human affairs. Book IV Section 6 is certainly useful in helping to explain the presumably godless concepts of the void by the atomists Leucippus and Democritus as well as Melissus and the Pythagoreans. Also possibly relevant is the discussion linking soul with time in *Physics,* Book V Section 14. However, it is not until Book VI Section 6 that Aristotle returns to the task of showing that motion in the universe could never have had a full beginning and so, as suggested by Parmenides, there was no need for a prime mover for creation to take place. In modern terms, of course, the concept of a so-called Big Bang might seem to justify the notion of creationism on a strictly material basis, but this possibility supposedly occurs in a far bigger celestial realm in which countless similar cosmic events take place on a more inclusive scale. Thus Aristotle's assumption, perhaps inspired by Anaximander and Heraclitus still remains credible, that everything in motion "must have been in motion before . . . so a thing cannot be becoming without having become or have become without having been becoming."[25] Excluded from this paradox is religious creationism, the concept of an abrupt initial transition from total void to sudden existence produced by an agent that always existed without becoming. Such a concept of privileged creation is excluded from Aristotle's list of credible alternatives.

It seems accepted among modern scholars that Book VII is probably inauthentic, and in fact its arguments differ significantly from most everything Aristotle says elsewhere in *Physics.*

On the other hand, Book VIII, the final and longest book in *Physics,* culminates with a paradoxical summary that can be interpreted any number of ways. The basic choice, however, is between (a) accepting the initial creation of the universe by a God or gods and (b) rejecting this possibility in favor of the universe's eternal existence without the need for any kind of a creator as already suggested by Melissus. The first paragraph of Book VIII declares this essential choice with full clarity but makes no effort to identify a creator able to initiate motion. The basic question, Aristotle suggests, is simply whether existence preceded motion:

Was there ever a becoming of motion before which it had no being, and is it perishing again so as to leave nothing in motion? Or are we to say that it never had any becoming and is not perishing, but always was and always will be? Is it in fact an immortal never-failing property of things that are, a sort of life as it were to all naturally constituted things?[26]

Aristotle cites the pre-Socratic philosophers Empedocles and Anaxagoras as having accepted the premise of eternal existence, and he later suggests he could have easily added all the rest of the philosophers preceeding Plato to the list, since he had exclusively featured initial creation as a necessary aspect of the physical universe. Moreover, Aristotle explained, "Plato alone asserts the creation of time," on the assumption that it began when the universe did.[27] This seemingly harmless concept suggests the need to renew pre-Socratic natural philosophy after its rejection by Socrates and Plato, who themselves sought a credible alternative to the dubious multitude of gods and goddesses featured by Homer and Hesiod. While Plato seems to have been tolerant of creationism, early natural philosophers as well as Aristotle rejected this. As implied by Aristotle, the alternative to perpetual existence depends on the simple assumption that "before this first change [whatever it might consist of] there will be a previous change."[28] Thus, endless time both before and after predominates, as emphasized by Parmenides, and therefore perpetual motion without an absolute beginning becomes credible.

At this juncture in the text, Aristotle declares his intention to refute all seemingly valid arguments at odds with his own: "The arguments that may be advanced against this position [an endless universe without a creator] are not difficult to dispose of."[29] However, Aristotle's analysis becomes quite confusing at this point, perhaps intentionally so. He mounts credible alternative arguments in explaining motion relevant to the existence of God (or gods), and it becomes difficult, if not impossible, to determine what he himself believes beyond his earlier assurance that he concurs with pre-Socratic physicists.

Among his arguments, Aristotle turns to the more specific hypothetical concept of a first mover, one of the primary traits often assigned to godhead:

And here it is sufficient to assume only one "movent," the first of unmoved things, which being eternal will be the principle of motion in everything else.[30]

On this basis the involvement of a single God might seem credible in explaining motion at every level of manifestation. However, Aristotle complicates his analysis by once again emphasizing the involvement of cyclical motion:

> Rotatory locomotion is prior to rectilinear locomotion, because it is more
> simple and complete. . . . Rotatory motion can be external; but no other
> motion, whether locomotion or motion of any other kind, can be so, since in all
> of them rest must occur, and with the occurrence of rest the motion has per-
> ished.[31]

Based on the unavoidable necessity of circularity, Aristotle reduces the
function and identity of an unmoved first mover to a disposable agent that
otherwise lacks physical existence. According to Aristotle, the seemingly
contradictory explanation of such a supernatural agent devoid of motion (e.g.
the received concept of God or gods) turns out to depend on two basic
principles mentioned in adjacent sentences that are easily overlooked: "Nothing finite can possess an infinite force. So it is also impossible for a finite
force to reside in an infinite magnitude."[32] Here one might object that all
finite forces in fact do occupy at least a portion of infinitude as well as
exerting a miniscule portion of infinite force. On the other hand, this con-
straint would seem to eliminate any kind of finite authority for a supposedly
infinite God. Simply enough, whatever God can be identified as "all" is
neither visible nor effective in interceding in human affairs.

Aristotle concludes his analysis—and the text of *Physics* in its entirety--
by suggesting the likelihood of a perpetual universe lacking both a beginning
and an end, and therefore necessarily without the authority of godhead identified as "the mover." This he maintains in an involuted deductive argument—effectively a loose version of sorites that brings *Physics* to a close:

> We have now already proved that it is impossible for a finite magnitude to
> have an infinite force, and also that it is impossible for a thing to be moved by
> a finite magnitude during an infinite time. But the first "movent" causes a
> motion that is eternal and does cause it during an infinite time. It is clear,
> therefore, that the first "movent" is indivisible and is without parts and without
> magnitude.[33]

Finally, he concedes that godhead might exist, but only if its indivisible
lack of magnitude does not manifest itself. As a result, at least by implication, it does not play an active role in human affairs. Aristotle's elaborate use
of logic obviously serves two purposes: first in declaring the improbability of
the god concept in light of cosmic circumstances he has already described,
and second in obscuring his necessarily controversial assumption with ex-
traordinary effectiveness. He both excludes from consideration the concept
of a personal God who created the universe in its entirety and rejects the
more abstract concept of a first (or primary) motion that initiates and then
dominates existence. Instead he suggests the infinite physical determinism of
an endless self-sufficient universe as taken for granted in his later texts, *De
Caelo*, *On Generation and Corruption,* and *De Anima.*

IV. *METAPHYSICS*

Metaphysics is often considered Aristotle's major effort to link religion with philosophy. It was undoubtedly written after *Physics* as indicated by at least three internal references to *Physics*.[34] Moreover, as far as can be determined, Aristotle's first editor, Andronicus of Rhodes, invented the title *Metaphysics* in order to indicate an assortment of issues pertaining to physics rather than "above" or "beyond" it, and the prefix "meta" apparently meant "additional to," not "transcendent." Aristotle himself used the words "divine science" when referring to the study of spiritual matters. Moreover, Andronicus omitted a portion of the text that specifically dealt with the explanation of God's existence in the original edition of Book 12 (described as "Lamda"). This chapter's later insertion might well have been performed by somebody else.

In Book I of *Metaphysics,* Aristotle characterizes his inquiry as a divine science about the power of God—notably a single God rather than a polytheistic assortment of gods. However, his argument in this passage is so convoluted that it requires close analysis to disclose its secular implications. The Ross translation reads as follows:

> For the science which it would be most meet for God to have is a divine science, and so is any science that deals with divine objects . . . for God is thought to be among the causes of all things and to be a first principle, and such a science either God alone can have, or God above all others. All the sciences, indeed are more necessary than this, but none is better.[35]

Here Aristotle seems to have resorted to irony. A monotheistic God is mentioned four times with a capital "G," and the remark, "God is thought to be, etc." suggests possible disagreement about such a likelihood. Moreover, the word *better* might signify superior knowledge, but it could also suggest an entirely different meaning, "more useful among religious believers." The Tredennick translation of this passage in the Loeb classics contains several modifications that convey this ambivalence. For example, the wording of "all believe that God is one of the causes . . . " supplants "God is thought to be among the causes . . ." Tredennick's version also suggests shared certitude about the existence of gods, whereas Ross's version suggests the possibility of doubt. This difference bears significant implications. In both translations Aristotle also compares poetry with divine science (his wording for metaphysics) as two acceptable modes of expression because they serve a purpose at least as important as the truth—on one hand as heightened poetic experience, and on the other as moral improvement through religious belief. Both translations acknowledge transcendent poetic liberties that Aristotle ascribes to poets, "bards tell many a lie," followed by his quick assurance that divine science is "most honourable" (or "precious") and therefore perhaps a better and more valuable distortion of truth than poetry. But Aristotle seems unclear in explaining himself, letting the reader extend its application to divine science as well as poetry in the sense that both exemplify his much later suggestion in *De Anima* that men "often act contrary to knowledge in obedience to their imaginings."[36]

Aristotle brings the passage to a close by contrasting metaphysics with "more necessary" sciences, presumably including the various fields of inquiry that he himself encouraged at the time. On this basis he apparently feels justified in differentiating divine science from the pursuit of verifiable truth. This entire passage seems cluttered with ambiguity because of his effort to be both accurate and socially acceptable in the same context.

Aristotle's respect for the study of religion also seems questionable in Book III when he characterizes believers, " . . . the people who said there are gods, but in human form . . . were positing nothing but eternal men."[37] Also, he suggests in Book VI of *Metaphysics* a necessary choice between science and metaphysics as one's "first philosophy." He argues that natural science would be the "first science" if nature entirely consists of substance, but as suggested later by Simplicius, he concedes the possible transcendent existence of an "immovable substance" such as the soul, whereby divine science would necessarily predominate.[38]

According to Simplicius, Aristotle considers God to be either mind (i.e. Plato's version of existence) or something beyond mind (for example the physical universe itself).[39] Aristotle does not explore this choice in depth in *Metaphysics,* but he does acknowledges the possibility of a strictly physical realm "beyond mind," in other words *different from* mind as explained by his later treatises *De Caelo, Generation and Corruption*, and *De Anima.*

In Book XII, Aristotle more specifically concedes the value of popular religion as a sincere tradition "in the form of a myth" worthy of esteem on this basis alone. He describes early pantheistic assumptions with obvious disdain but suggests his own willingness to accommodate the "persuasion of the multitude" relevant to its needs:

> Our forefathers in the most remote ages have handed down to us their posterity a tradition, in the form of a myth, that these bodies are gods and that the divine encloses the whole of nature. The rest of the tradition has been added later in mythical forms with a view to the persuasion of the multitude . . . [But] these opinions, with others, have been preserved until the present like relics. [40]

The word "multitude" seems to have been the preferred translation of *anthropopoedeis,* the word he specifically used in ancient Greek, but at least one translation, by Tredennick, goes so far as to substitute the more pejorative epithet, "the vulgar."[41] The implied disdain for the populace apparently reflects Aristotle's attitude toward its customary religious belief.

Aristotle also contrasts Plato's doctrine of an unmoved mover with his own assumption that he shared with most pre-Socratic natural philosophers: "That nothing comes to be out of that which is not, but everything out of that which is, is a dogma common to nearly all the natural philosophers."[42] This assumption about a universe without beginning had already been proposed by Parmenides, Melissus, and even Aristotle himself. Aside from the question of its validity, what is important in this context is that Aristotle himself assumed its validity and by doing so reaffirmed his willingness as a natural philosopher able to accept the notion of temporal infinitude.

Book XII provides Aristotle's "only systematic essay in theology" in his entire writings, and its analysis of religion seems to bear little relevance to any other portion of his work as acknowledged by David Ross, the editor-in-chief of the Aristotle's standard Oxford edition.[43] Moreover, Aristotle's specific arguments on religion can be found in sections 6-10 of Book XII, where a substantially different level of interpretation seems to prevail.[44] What appears to be his sole concern at this point, the possibility of God's existence, occupies not more than about eight pages, and his principal three arguments may be listed according to their apparently unresolved contradictions:

> So the unmovable first mover is one both in definition and in number; so too, therefore is that which is moved always and continuously; therefore there is one heaven [i.e. transcendent space] alone.[45]

> We must consider also in which of two ways the nature of the universe contains the good and the highest good, whether as something separate and by itself, or as the order of the parts. . . . And all things are ordered together somehow, but not all alike . . . [46]

> In all things the good is in the highest degree a principle. The school we first mentioned [Platonism?] is right in saying that it is a principle, but *how* the good is a principle they do not say—whether as end or as mover or as form.[47]

In their implications, all three of these passages essential to Aristotle's supposed proof of God's existence in *Metaphysics* seem contradictory, and now and again their cumbersome wording suggests heavy interpolation. Aristotle also appears to revert to Platonism in his effort to explain the actual governance of the universe based on religion, and seemingly in accord with Plato, he suggests God's sacred role as the ultimate agent of all thought dependent on the effectively tautological assumption, "Throughout eternity is the thought which has *itself* for its object."[48] Aristotle also suggests Plato's cosmology when he identifies transcendent virtue with God, "In all things the good is in the highest degree a principle." Here Aristotle's agreement seems a later interpolation. Its prose is simplistic and steeped in Platonic idealism essential to Christian cosmology not to be found elsewhere in Aristotle's texts.

In Section 10, the final portion of Book 12, Aristotle ends his brief treatment of religion by listing what seems a variety of issues that remain unsolved. In regard to the concept of the soul he suggests the need to explain the "motive principle" as something different from thought itself. He asks why some things perish and others do not, but also how there can be an infinite process of becoming as later featured by his theory of motion in *De Caelo*. Moreover, he questions how wisdom can be the highest knowledge if we are not particularly wise or well-informed, and he almost seems willing to jettison the primary assumptions of *Metaphysics* in light of natural philosophy: "If besides sensible things no others exist, there will be no first principle, no order, no becoming, no heavenly bodies."[49] It turns out that nonsensible "things" might exist at what seems a spiritual level, but strictly pertaining to the physical universe including human behavior as suggested by Aristotle's later analysis in *De Anima*. That the last chapter of *Metaphysics* culminates with a list of mixed considerations presumably deserving of further inquiry almost seems intended to suggest Aristotle's relative indifference about the assumptions he took into account throughout *Metaphysics*.

Chapter Four

Late Aristotle

I. *DE CAELO (ON THE HEAVENS)*

What confuses modern readers about Aristotle's final and essentially atheistic stance in *De Caelo* is a result as much as anything of the title's misleading English translation as *On the Heavens*, a cosmic site usually considered the abode of one or more gods. However, the original title of the text in Greek, *ouranos,* bore a broad reference to the heavens more or less as the sky, the cosmos, and/or the entire physical universe much as already described by Plato in *Timaeus* 34ab and *Laws X,* 893. The translators and scholars committed to a religious interpretation may prefer the English equivalent, *heavens*, but its secular implications as suggested by both *ouranos* and the Latin translation, *De Caelo,* indicate the universe in its entirety. In *Physics* Aristotle himself had already sought to clarify this distinction:

> In one sense, we apply the word *ouranos* to the substance of the outermost circumference of the world, or to the natural body which is at the outermost circumference of the world . . . especially to the outmost and uppermost region, in which also we believe all divinity to have its seat. [Secondly] to the outermost circumference . . . in which are the moon and sun and stars . . . And yet in another sense . . . give the name of *ouranos* to the world as a whole. [1]

Aristotle conceded, perhaps for the benefit of his religious contemporaries, that a small portion of this celestial region is customarily understood to be the domain that "we take to be the seat of all that is divine."[2] But he also suggested that he himself did not necessarily share this belief despite his rhetorical use of "we." In the very next sentence he declared his own perspective with a secular argument that applies to cosmic cycles at all levels:

It is too in unceasing motion, as is reasonable; for things only cease moving
when they arrive at their proper places, and for the body whose motion is
circular the place where it ends is also the place where it begins. [3]

In effect he rejected the apocalyptic assumptions of religion in favor of a
cyclical theory of the universe that featured endless motion as earlier suggested by Heraclitus. Like the motion of stars, he suggested, life itself perpet-
uates itself into the indefinite future by means of sustained reproduction from
one generation to the next rather than temporary individual experience on
earth before eternal existence in some kind of an afterlife.

In his three texts upon cosmology, *De Caelo* (*On the Heavens*), *On Generation and Corruption,* and *De Anima* (*On the Soul*), Aristotle seems to
reexamine his assumptions on a more radical basis yet. Possibly in response
to the theories of Heraclitus and Empedocles, he maintains that the unlimited
perfection of the universe is only possible through "continuous circular motion" as to be observed in the motion of stars and planets at night. Of course
the cause of this perceived effect results from the rotation of the earth rather
than the circular orbit of stars across the sky, but astronomical motion does
occur as perceived by Aristotle, and all cycles, including the cycle of life can
be compared with it. Aristotle suggests a simpler and more functional cyclical model than Empedocles' theory of four basic elements in motion, and in
doing so he advanced his own version of what amounted to a "unified field
theory." Indeed, cycles do occur in the sky, as well as with biological reproduction, and perhaps numerous other modes of passage as well, and although
Aristotle seldom declares this in such obvious terms, it is implicit throughout
his text.

The obvious problem with this self-sufficient materialist cosmology is
that it gives divine authority a diminished role, if any at all. A strictly cyclical
theory of cosmology can be construed as a recipe for atheism, reducing the
god concept to little more than a redundant hypothesis of a God primarily
concerned with cosmic cycles. Aristotle's willingness to risk this supposition
seems implied, and so it is not surprising that sympathetic theologians many
centuries later sought to impose the modifications needed to render Aristotle's theory more compatible with orthodox religion. Undoubtedly this effort
included deletions that cannot be detected today. However, scribes also seem
to have been willing to add a number of orthodox Christian interpolations
that can still be detected. As a result, the task of modern readers sympathetic
with Aristotle's secular viewpoint is to salvage his original analysis as well
as possible despite these earlier efforts to obscure it. An unusual number of
such modifications occur toward the beginning of *De Caelo,* in which the
likelihood of atheism is suggested as effectively as anywhere in his writings.
The reader is thus confronted with the task of isolating his cosmology. For

example his initial effort to explain circular motion as a basic aspect of nature is abruptly interrupted by the passage:

> These premises clearly give the conclusion that there is in nature some bodily substance other than the formations we know, prior to them all and more divine than they.[4]

The prose seems appropriate except for the assurance, "clearly give the conclusion" as well as the adjectival modifier, "prior to them all and more divine than they," which bears obvious religious implications contrary to Aristotle's thesis as explained elsewhere in the text. More obvious yet is a later passage that displays cumbersome pontification entirely at odds with Aristotle's style and conceptual assumptions:

> For all men have some conception of the nature of the gods, and all who believe in the existence of gods at all, whether barbarian or Greek, agree in allotting the highest place to the deity, surely because they suppose that immortal is linked with immortal and regard any other supposition as impossible. If then there is, as there certainly is, anything divine, what we have just said about the primary bodily substance was well said. The mere evidence of the senses is enough to convince us of this, at least with human certainty.[5]

This rambling assertion is simply not Aristotle speaking. The author declares with awkwardness that "all men" do somehow believe in "the deity"--itself an obvious anachronism. Moreover, his righteous wording, "What we have just said," "was well said," and "the mere evidence of the senses" seems entirely atypical of Aristotle. What is intended, for example, by the implications of "mere"? That such pontification clutters Aristotle's prose at the very beginning of *De Caelo* suggests that whoever inserted it felt compelled to go to this extreme as a preliminary measure to justify the text's existence despite its implicit incompatibility with Christian doctrine at the time. It seems likely there were too many remarkable insights for the text to be destroyed, so textual modifications were inserted to justify its retention.

Once initial additions supportive of Christian orthodoxy have been discounted, Aristotle's sustained analysis is almost totally oblivious to a spiritual God or gods. If sublime authority exists, it is described as a function of the entire universe as mass in motion. There seems little effort on Aristotle's part to reconcile the contrast between Plato's concept of transcendent mind equivalent to godhead and his own alternative explanation of the physical universe in perpetual motion. He instead suggests his own version of materialism that is a synthesis of pre-Socratic secular cosmologies of Anaximander, Anaximenes, Heraclitus, Empedocles, and even Melissus. Missing from his synthesis, on the other hand, are transcendental alternatives suggested by Parmenides and the limited portion of Anaxagoras' theory featured by Plato's version of metaphysics.

As compared to his stance in earlier texts, Aristotle's increased support of materialism in *De Caelo* is also indicated by his obvious shift in attitude toward Melissus' concept of infinite space. In his much earlier text, *Sophistical Refutations,* he had obviously opposed Melissus' theory as a corollary of Parmenides' theory of temporal infinitude:

> The argument of Melissus that the universe is infinite assumes that the universe has not come into being (for nothing could come into being from what does not exist) and that everything which has come into being has come from a beginning; if, therefore, the universe has not come into being, it has no beginning and therefore is infinite. But this does not necessarily follow; for even if what has come into being always has a beginning, anything that has a beginning need not have come to be, any more than it follows that a man which is hot must be in a fever because who is in fever is hot. [6]

Obviously, the analogy does not hold, since eternal existence and the lack of a beginning are effectively identical, whereas heat and fever are often linked but not identical. Also, Aristotle seems to have overlooked that it was Parmenides who first emphasized temporal infinitude, and in fact that Melissus' principal contribution was in having both accepted and enlarged Parmenides' thesis to include spatial infinitude as well. In any case, Aristotle concluded his analysis:

> . . . for he [Melissus] claims that if that which has come to be has a beginning, that which has not come to be has no beginning, and so if the heaven has not come to be, it is also eternal. But this is not true; for the sequence is the reverse. [7]

"But that is not so," Aristotle actually insisted. Later, in his first pages of *Physics* he accused both Melissus and Parmenides of harboring false principles relevant to time and space as opposed to his own assumption that "things of Nature. . . some of them do move and change" As yet unaware that these concepts could be linked, he declared that Melissus' analysis was simplistic, and that he made "unsound assumptions" and argued "unsoundly from them." [8] Nowhere else in his writings did Aristotle criticize a natural philosopher as aggressively as in this brief diatribe attacking Melissus. Still later, in *Metaphysics* he once again criticized both Parmenides and Melissus for having proposed cosmic unity that he himself would later concede, and in particular he specifically rejected Melissus' emphasis on "materially one" as a dubious variant of Parmenides' concept of "the Unity" as one in definition." To this extent, he suggested, Melissus could be compared with Xenophanes and "may be completely ignored" and both having been "somewhat too crude in their views."[9] How could anybody believe in the concept of one in matter, he asked? This would later become an essential aspect of his own concept of matter in motion, but at the time he was obviously still unaware of such a possibility.

Only in *De Caelo* does Aristotle finally express a more generous assessment of the shared cosmology of both Melissus and Parmenides, one based on metaphysical analysis justified by astronomical observation. In fact he seems in almost full agreement:

> Nothing that is, . . . is generated or destroyed, and our conviction to the contrary is an illusion. So maintained the school of Melissus and Parmenides. But however excellent their theories may be, anyhow they cannot be held to speak as students of nature. There may be things not subject to generation or any kind of movement, but if so they belong to another and a higher inquiry than the study of nature.[10]

By "higher" Aristotle apparently implies "more inclusive," and he thereupon suggests his own concept of a transcendent cosmology whereby cyclical motion occurs as indicated by several of Heraclitus' paradoxes to this effect.[11] Finally in what seems his most advanced cosmology as explained in *De Caelo,* Aristotle suggests what seems a defensible supposition—holistic stasis effectively based on endless mass in perpetual motion that is visible at night. Parmenides and Melissus had already proposed their respective holistic theories, Leucippus and Democritus had proposed the concept of mass (i.e. atoms in combination) immersed in a cosmic vacuum, and finally Aristotle seems to have fully recognized the possibility of infinite unity of what seems endless mass in motion.[12] This strictly physical metaphysics seemed to justify the abandonment of Plato's holistic concept of a spiritual universe for an enlarged and more credible holistic concept based on the principle of mass in motion. In short, just as Anaxagoras, followed by Plato adopted Parmenides' assumptions regarding spiritual unity relevant to the whole, as already suggested by Heraclitus' concept of *Logos*, Aristotle adopted Melissus' version of a strictly physical universe first suggested by Anaximander and Anaximenes based on cyclical motion, later featured by Heraclitus and Empedocles.

In effect, Aristotle's holistic secular perspective seems confirmed by his concept of the universe as an infinite self-sufficient cyclical system. It can be self-sufficient because it is physical, and it can be cyclical because it is self-sufficient. Moreover, the need for any particular god's supportive role becomes irrelevant if the universe never had a beginning and therefore was not the product of supernatural intervention—also if there is no possibility for transcendent space outside the universe. Physical and temporal continuity accordingly predominate based on the unstoppable cyclical motion of stars and planets. On this basis Aristotle was able to maintain the radical (but

credible) assumption that the cyclical movement of planets is somewhat
similar to that of animals and plants at least as a manifestation of regularity. [13]
While Aristotle proposed the ultimate necessity of an immutable universe, he
also defended the more inclusive paradox that this cosmic necessity sustains
itself at all levels. Life itself plays its role, as does human behavior from one
generation to the next.

In addition Aristotle proposed three radical secular assumptions regarding
the holistic composition of the universe on a dialectic basis. In doing so he
mentioned the gods, but without suggesting any kind of a functional role.
These included first the total rejection of any separate realm—heaven for
example—that might seem to exist beyond the physical universe; second, the
rejection of original creation except as the result of change from an earlier
existence, and third, the rejection of the possibility of existence beyond death
as suggested by "ancient beliefs." Aristotle effectively framed these negative
principles in abstract terms and on a positive basis:

> It is evident not only that there is not, but also that there could never come to
> be, any bodily mass whatever outside the circumference. The world as a
> whole, therefore, includes *all* its appropriate matter, which is, as we saw,
> natural perceptible body. [14]

> A limit is a thing which contains; and this motion, being perfect, contains
> those imperfect motions which have a limit and a goal, having itself no begin-
> ning or end, but unceasing through the infinity of time, and of other move-
> ments, to some cause of their beginning, to others offering the goal. [15]

In combination these passages again tend to confirm Aristotle's belief that
we do in fact inhabit a godless universe, and that its combined spatial and/or
temporal aspect cannot be acknowledged on a religious basis except in pantheistic terms that identify God's existence with the universe itself. Only an
explanation of the universe itself as a manifestation of God is acceptable
much as insisted by Spinoza many centuries later.

Entirely in accord with Melissus, Aristotle insists in Part I, Chapter 9, on
the existence of a single universe without any outlying region such as the
remote domain of one or more gods as already suggested by Melissus. [16]
Aristotle also argues that "all the worlds must be composed of the same
bodies, being similar in nature," thereby rejecting both transcendent existence and the existence of a unique spiritual realm. [17] To describe the universe as a self-sufficient realm he once again resorts to the concept of an
enormous cosmic cycle unique unto itself. [18] As suggested by modern astronomy, this assumption seems valid if Aristotle's reference to "the world" takes
into account the universe in its entirety including countless stars within
countless galaxies. Aristotle also rejects Greek tradition's legendary explanation of creation first suggested by Hesiod and later in *Genesis* that chaos

came first. This supposition was unacceptable to Aristotle, because it implies a privileged cosmic site where God could dispense his authority over all things and events. With obvious irony he declares, "and if such a thing should really exist well might we contemplate it with wonder.[19]

Instead, Aristotle insists that stasis occurs through sustained repetition. This is also suggested by Heraclitus' fragments that beginning and end are "general" in a circle, and that wisdom consists of understanding this final "purpose which steers all things through all things."[20] As before, Aristotle resorts to a broad universal concept to explain all instances of incessant motion including the seasons, the passage of life from birth to death, from hunger to satiation, etc. His explanation rests upon the paradox that celestial regularity is nevertheless comparable to the irregular and often seemingly chaotic interplay among things and events in human behavior. Whatever its outward complexity, life depends on biological replication--once again mass in motion, if at a more immediate level as Aristotle later suggests in *De Anima.*

In Book II of *De Caelo,* Aristotle expands this argument by demonstrating that all stasis is necessarily temporary and that transition inevitably brings negation into play. Locked in cyclical transition, each stage somehow takes effect as the opposite of an earlier stage much as Heraclitus had proposed and as Hegel would much later adopt in his version of metaphysics. To this extent, all cyclical change relating to earthly matters replicates celestial motion, and the inevitability of transition pertains to all behavior, however erratic. Whatever its circumstances, its outcome somehow is a rejection of an earlier state of affairs. In his final two sentences of Book I, Aristotle declared the abstract basis for this paradox first suggested by Heraclitus:

> Whatever is destructible or generated is always alterable. Now alteration is due to contraries, and the things which compose the natural body are the very same that destroy it.[21]

Just as fire burns wood to produce ashes, all process occurs as an act of denial preliminary to the later existence of its agent, if nothing more than a pile of ashes. On a much larger scale in biological history, a reduction in sunlight several million years ago seems likely to have first made life possible on earth as compared to Mars, but continued reductions into the indefinite future can be expected to make life difficult, then impossible.

In his introductory sentence of Book II, Aristotle once again concurs with Parmenides that the universe as a whole possesses neither a beginning nor an end. By doing so he suggests the lack of any role by a God or gods in having created the universe or provided any kind of an eternal afterlife. Aristotle also mentions how early idolatry—including Homeric worship--took for granted the ability of its particular assortment of gods to exist forever without suggesting such a possibility for humanity or even the universe itself.[22] He implies in contrast that the divine capacity for movement turns out to be movement itself. God consists of the universe in motion, and vice versa. If such exists, the unique authority of transcendent godhead entails the universe in its entirety.

Of course Aristotle lived three centuries before Christ, so his attitude toward religion was colored by Homeric mythology rather than Biblical tradition, but his attitude toward popular religious belief at the time was hostile. To illustrate his disdain for Homeric mythology, he described with irony the concept of Atlas as a muscular deity who holds up the universe—a mythical belief among the Greek populace that supposedly explained how upright beings owe their safety to Atlas in thwarting the principle of gravity.[23] Similarly, Aristotle expressed his disdain for Plato's assumption: "that it [the universe] should persist eternally by the necessitation of a soul."[24] Aristotle suggested in response that such infinitude might turn out to be surprisingly unpleasant if typified by the fate of Ixion, a mythical figure tied to a fiery spinning wheel forever. To the extent that supernatural power might be involved, he contends, it entails nothing more than an eternal process of things in motion. His analysis was admittedly simplistic, but for his time he proposed a remarkable theory pertaining to the universe as a whole.

In the final two books of *De Caelo*—respectively Books III and IV—Aristotle repeated his sympathetic response to Empedocles' cyclical analysis and Democritus' concept of a void among atoms. He somewhat anticipated the theory of gravity with his brief comparative assessment of weight as an abstract concept but did not extend his analysis. In Book III, Chapter 2, he actually suggested the possibility of a more cohesive original unity before "separation" occurs as the result of cosmic interaction [perhaps a "Big Bang"?] that ultimately "proceeded from unity and combination" at an even more cohesive level: "The elements of the cosmos *are* in a state of separation, so that its formation must have proceeded from unity and combination." Lucretius later proposed that this transition suggests that such possible modifications may result in catastrophic impact.[25] In Chapter 4 of Book III, Aristotle shifted his focus to the concept of atomism, advancing from macroscopic infinitude to microscopic spatial considerations by suggesting that the number of elements is finite, not infinite as suggested by both Democritus and Anaxagoras.[26] In Chapters 5-8 he offered the dubious paradox that atoms as "primary masses" cannot be "infinite in number and indivisible in mass," since this would somehow necessitate their being more minutely differentiated.

In Chapter 2 he returned to Democritus' concept of void in light of Heraclitus and Empedocles' respective theories of fire and the impact of weight. He concluded by exploring the distinction between these two antithetical components of existence—mass and the void—as an explanation of motion.[27] These somewhat random considerations inspired by Democritus effectively bring *De Caelo* to an end, setting the stage for the later theoretical pursuits of both Theophrastus and Strato, his two principal disciples who would later succeed him as leaders of the Lyceum. Both were fully as productive as Aristotle himself, but unlike Aristotle's writings, theirs were later almost entirely lost. Both later sought a synthesis between Aristotle's assumptions based on continuity and Democritus' dichotomy between atomic particles and the void that presumably surrounds them.

It should finally be noted that Aristotle paid little attention in *De Caelo* to Plato's version of cosmology as featured in *Timaeus*. He mentioned his contribution only six times throughout the text in almost dismissive asides perhaps indicating there was no need for further discussion pertaining to his own argument.[28] In contrast, he referred in generally positive terms to Empedocles twelve times, Democritus and Leucippus nine times, and both Anaxagoras and the Pythagoreans six times apiece. It would be a mistake to consider Aristotle's text as evidence of his sustained adherence to Platonism, for quite the opposite, his arguments demonstrate the extent to which he instead used pre-Socratic assumptions to propose a seemingly better and more credible explanation of the universe.

II. *ON GENERATION AND CORRUPTION*

Aristotle seems to have written *On Generation and Corruption* soon after *De Caelo*, and their sequence is strongly suggested by the link between their last and first sentences. *De Caelo* ends with the assertion, "We have now finished our examination of the heavy and the light and of the properties connected with them," and *On Generation and Corruption* begins with what seems a continuation, "Our next task is to study coming-to-be and passing-away."[29] Whereas mass in motion is featured in the first text, the second specifically addresses questions related to motion and transition. Both texts differentiate religion and secular philosophy, but *On Generation and Corruption* seems to introduce more rigorous concerns about religion. Moreover, it further confirms Aristotle's renewed appreciation for pre-Socratic assumptions. Also, because of its brevity, it offers the most vigorous defense of Aristotle's secular cosmology.

Perhaps the most significant theoretical contribution of *On Generation and Corruption,* is Aristotle's explanation of causation as a "coming to be" that might be able to persist forever because of infinite cyclical motion. Manifestation serves as change—what "does" necessarily takes place in sequence, and its circular pattern becomes almost a central theme that anticipates the cyclical implications of human reproduction later discussed in *De Anima*, again helping to confirm the sequence of Aristotle's books from

Physics to *Metaphysics* followed by *De Caelo, Generation and Corruption,* and finally *De Anima.* The large assortment of concepts featured in *On Generation and Corruption* is noteworthy to this particular stage in the overall progress of his theoretical assumptions as illustrated by his cyclical explanation of multiplicity as the outcome of simple causes:

> But if there is to be movement there must be something which initiates it; if there is to be movement always, there must always be something which initiates it; if the movement is to be continuous, what initiates it must be single, unmoved, ungenerated, and incapable of 'alteration'; and if the circular movements are more than one their necessitating causes must all of them, in spite of their plurality, be in some way subordinated to a single originative source.[30]

Some version of supernatural authority, most obviously a monotheistic God, might be construed to provide this "single principle," but Aristotle seems to attribute this circularity instead to the inertia of the material universe itself:

> But among continuous bodies which are moved, only that which is moved in a circle is continuous in such a way that it preserves its continuity with itself throughout the movement. The conclusion is that *this* is what produces continuous movement, viz. the body which is being moved in a circle; and its movement makes time continuous.[31]

By means of continuous cyclical motion celestial formation governs itself as anticipated by Empedocles' simpler model of cosmic sequence. However, Aristotle proposes the likelihood of circular momentum free of the cumbersome fourfold sequence of reversals described by Empedocles. Also, without identifying himself as an atheist, Aristotle is more willing to dispence with the possibility of an external creator of the universe.

Many of Aristotle's sentences in *On Generation and Corruption* can be quoted as fragments to help clarify his version of materialism. He discusses Platonism in perhaps twenty contexts. In contrast he does the same with Empedocles two dozen times, and Democritus and Leucippus at least two dozen times. Moreover, the aphoristic vitality of many of his theoretical pronouncements seems almost a parody of fragments by pre-Socratic natural philosophers:

> A single matter must always be assumed as underlying the contrary 'poles' of any change—whether change of place, or growth and diminution or 'alteration.'[32]

> In so far as the One results from *composition* (by a consilience of the Many), whereas they result from *disintegration,* the Many are more elementary than the One, and prior to it in their nature.[33]

But now it is obvious that a body is in fact divided into separable magnitudes which are smaller at each division—into magnitudes which fall apart from one another and are actually separated. . . . But there is a limit beyond which the "breaking up" cannot proceed. The necessary consequence—especially if coming-to-be and passing-away are to take place by association and dissociation respectively—is that a body must contain atomic magnitudes which are invisible.[34]

Why, then, is this form of change necessarily ceaseless? Is it because the passing-away of *this* is a coming-to-be of *something else*, and the coming-to-be of *this* a passing away of *something else?*[35]

The substratum is the material cause of the continuous occurrence of coming-to-be, because it is such as to change from contrary to contrary and because, in substances, the coming-to-be of one thing is always a passing away of another, and the passing-away of one thing is always another's coming-to be.[36]

It is evident, therefore that the coming-to-be of the 'simple' bodies will be cyclical; and that this cyclical method of transformation is the easiest, because the *consecutive* elements contain interchangeable complementary factors.[37]

Since the elements are transformed into one another, it is impossible for any one of them—whether it be at the end or in the middle—to be an 'originative source' of the rest.[38]

Every addition of a new 'element' will carry with it the attachment of a new contrariety to the preceding element. Consequently, if the 'elements' are infinitely many, there will also belong to the single element an infinite number of contrarieties.[39]

What, then, is the first mover and the cause of motion? Presumably not Love and Strife: on the contrary, these are causes of a *particular* motion, if at least we assume that the first mover to be an originative source.[40]

An additional absurdity is that the soul [i.e., conscious behavior] should consist of the "elements," or that it should be one of them.[41]

The rival treatments of the subject now before us will serve to illustrate how great is the difference between a 'scientific' and a 'dialectical' method of inquiry.[42]

All of the fragments listed here can be compared to pre-Socratic assumptions, especially those of Anaximander, Heraclitus, and Empedocles. Only one of them, the very last, leaves open the possibility of Plato's stance (dialectic) as opposed to that of Democritus (scientific).

Aristotle specifically suggests the possibility of God in only one passage, and it occurs in an awkward sentence toward the end of the text that seems an interpolation at odds with everything that is discussed elsewhere. A conventional vision of God is specifically taken into account for the first time:

> For in all things, as we affirm, Nature always strives after 'the better.' Now 'being' . . . is better than 'not-being;' but not all things can possess 'being,' since they are too far removed from the 'originative source'. God therefore adopted the remaining alternative, and fulfilled the perfection of the universe by making coming-to-be uninterrupted: for the greatest possible coherence would thus be secured to existence, because that 'coming to be should itself come-to-be perpetually' the closest approximation to eternal being.[43]

Perhaps Aristotle authored this, but probably not. This is the only passage in which a monotheistic deity is linked to the terms "eternal being" and "perfection of the universe." The passage is located near one in which Aristotle has begun declaring his own argument, and its very wording seems awkward even as quoted in translation. Moreover, why is this unique God featured with a capital "G" as opposed to the custom at the time to refer to one or more gods with a small "g"?

In contrast, Aristotle suggests just a few sentences later suggests a strictly material explanation of the role of motion as the single basic principle at the root of the universe:

> But if there is to be movement . . . there must be something which initiates it; if there is to be movement always, there must always be something which initiates it; if the movement is to be always, what initiates it must be single, unmoved, ungenerated, and incapable of alteration; and if the circular movements are more than one, they must all of them, in spite of their plurality, be in some way subordinated to a single originative source.[44]

Aristotle's argument is sufficiently abstract that both Christians and modern secularists would find it acceptable since the identity of the single originative source is left unidentified by Aristotle--whether the authority of one or more gods or the basic matrix of a strictly physical universe. Aristotle seems to describe this sustained primal force as a cosmic function imbedded in the universe, possibly suggesting pantheism or a limited mode of godhead. However, he then links this function with circularity similar to the so-called cycle of life on earth. In the context of Aristotle's explanation God's contribution effectively minimizes any kind of authority beyond the task of governing infinite recurrence.

In the last chapter of Book II, Aristotle reiterates his basic assumption, "Since what is infinite has no beginning, neither will there be any primary member that will make it necessary for the remaining members to come-to-be."[45] In other words, if there is no beginning, there is no need for any kind of a God to initiate it. In contrast, the simpler designation "principle" limits governing law to a useful function through incessant cyclical motion.

Aristotle concludes *On Generation and Corruption* by contrasting cyclical permanence with the so-called "rectilinear" outcome of human experience that culminates in death without the possibility of resurrection. An individual's life is linear only in the sense that it consists of a relatively small arc in a much bigger cycle of life. For any species in its entirety, he argued, such a cyclical process necessarily repeats itself on a larger scale through reproduction by a sufficient portion of the species participating in the task:

> Now it is evident that those things, whose substance—that which is undergoing the process—is imperishable, will be numerically the same for the character of the process is determined by the character of that which undergoes it. Those things on the other hand, whose substance is perishable (not imperishable) must return upon themselves specifically, not numerically. . . . at any rate this does not happen with things whose substance comes-to-be—whose substance is such that it is capable of not-being.[46]

Here Aristotle resorts to tortuous abstraction, at least in translation, to suggest that individuals do expire when their deaths finally occur, whereas the species as a whole continues to survive from one generation to the next thanks to the so-called "character of the process," Aristotle's genteel term for sexual reproduction from one generation to the next. Otherwise, the perishable fate of individuals could be described as rectilinear instead of cyclical as it is destined to end because its "substance" upon death has achieved nonexistence. Instead, individuals do effectively renew their species despite their own deaths if their descendants live on. Humanity thus sustains itself without the need for heavenly rewards by a hypothetical God or gods.

III. *DE ANIMA (ON THE SOUL)*

Just as the ancient Greek wording of "On the Heavens" is more accurately translated to English as "On the Physical Universe," the wording of "On the Soul" refers to conscious behavior rather than transcendental experience. In effect, mental performance is the basic topic rather than the pursuit of heavenly rewards. The two titles in sequence, *On the Heavens* and *On the Soul,* feature the words *heaven* and *soul,* and necessarily suggest a Christian version of Platonism, but the word combination is a misleading reflection of Aristotle's theoretical stance. For just as the word *caelo* represents sky or outer space in its entirety, the word *anima* represented mind, consciousness, and even animal consciousness as a biological necessity. Thus, the title *De Anima* presents human thought as the keystone of Aristotle's mature philosophical perspective—perhaps less grandiose than Plato's universal soul, but the mental ability that both supports life and is able to discern basic truths. Just as Aristotle explains sky as endless space in *De Anima,* he explains the human mind as a unique product of biological existence that is also cyclical but without immortality except by means of reproduction. Otherwise, he ignores the concept of human immortality. The species as a whole might survive into the indefinite future, he suggests, but individual human beings live and die without later access into a transcendental realm identified as heaven. Aristotle makes this inevitability plain in two passages: " . . How comes it that it [the soul] is destroyed simultaneously with the disappearance of the quiddity of the flesh and of other parts of the animal?" and, more specifically " . . . the soul seems rather to hold the body together; at all events, when it has departed, the body disperses in air and rots away."[47] Of course such a departure might suggest passage to a better world, but Aristotle ignores this possibility.

As opposed to the Platonic vision of mind as a final and transcendent manifestation of spiritual achievement, Aristotle limits its function to the purposefulness of nature and the task of survival at every level of physical existence:

> For the soul [*anima*] is the cause of animate bodies as being in itself the origin of motion, as the final cause, and as substance. . . . And for living things existence means life, and it is the [soul] which is the cause and origin of life. . . . Manifestly, too, the [soul] is final cause. For nature, like intelligence, acts for a purpose, and this purpose is for it an end.[48]

Motivation is accordingly an essential feature of mental performance, but so also are perception, ideation, and every other dimension of mental behavior.

Also noteworthy is the lack of reference to gods except for having told of Thales' belief in them, and elsewhere in *De Anima* he concedes Plato's suggestion in *Timaeus* that God created cosmic cycles. However, he also attributes a striking impiety to Empedocles that "God is quite the most unintelligent of beings" because of His seeming ignorance of strife (i.e. much of what happens in the universe).[49] As explained by modern psychiatry, Aristotle seems to have projected onto a philosopher he respected a sacrilege he preferred not to acknowledge as his own.

Roughly half the length of *De Caelo, De Anima* enlarges Aristotle's secular perspective by explaining mental activity as an aspect of human behavior important to individual and genetic perpetuation that can be compared to the cyclical motion of stars and planets in the sky: "For when mind moves it thinks; when a circle moves it revolves. If then thought is a revolution, the circle which has such a revolution must be mind."[50] Essential to his analogy is the crucial role that mind (or "soul") plays in the realm of biology, for human behavior is steered by sensation linked with cognition, and thought serves at a higher level yet in promoting the survival of both the individual and the species. This relationship has already been suggested in Book II of *De Caelo*:

> We must, then, think of the action of the lower stars as similar to that of animals and plants. For on our earth it is man that has the greatest variety of actions.[51]

On the other hand, Aristotle mentions the importance of procreation with the vague wording, "actions . . . various and directed to ends," but he refers to this dependence more specifically in *De Caelo* and *On Generation and Corruption*, as well as providing a brief but more lucid explanation in an entirely different text, *Generation of Animals*:

> For since it is impossible that such a class of things as animals should be of an eternal nature, therefore that which comes into being is eternal in the only way possible. Now it is impossible for it to be eternal as an individual—the substance of the things that are is in the particular; and if it were such as it would be eternal—but it is possible for it as a species.[52]

This explanation of reproduction "possible for it as a species" might have been deleted from *de Anima* by censors but overlooked in *Generation of Animals*.

Aristotle effectively reverses Plato's theoretical stance by subsuming all aspects of mental behavior to the continuation of mankind based on the advance from one generation to the next as one particular demonstration of mass in sustained motion. Instead of accepting Plato's concept of soul as elevated transcendence that exceeds animal behavior, he focuses on all mental behavior conducive to survival, the dominant purpose of biological existence. Even the limited capabilities of a roundworm's brain, estimated to comprise 302 neurons, justify Aristotle's analysis of effective mental performance relevant to intentional motion. As he explains on what seems an evolutionary basis,

> Now there are two points especially wherein that which is animate is held to differ from the inanimate, namely, motion and the act of sensation, and these are approximately the two characteristics of [soul] handed down to us by our predecessors.[53]

On this doubled reductive basis, all thought pertaining to all aspects of life at every level of performance is crucial to "the whole domain of truth and, more particularly, to the study of nature, the soul [*anima*] being virtually the principle of all animal life."[54] Perception guides behavior, and behavior just as inevitably takes action according to what is perceived. Even at this simplest level of response the concept of *anima* is applicable as the most essential function of consciousness--the sustained perpetuation of life, a goal more or less compatible with the larger momentum of the whole physical universe. Not accidentally, both stimulus and response play roles in cyclical recurrence, each in its own way.

Aristotle also suggests what seems a sophisticated pre-Darwinian similarity between human and animal consciousness despite the difference between their respective levels of cognitive performance. He explains mind not simply as a material feature of the body, but as a neural system of functions that serves the whole body according to its needs:

> Now the soul [i.e. mental performance] is that whereby primarily we live, perceive, and have understanding: therefore it will be a species of notion or form, not matter or substratum. . . . It is not body, but something belonging to body, and therefore resides in body, and what is more, in such and such a body.[55]

Unlike Plato, Aristotle offers a broad definition that includes the consciousness of anything alive with legs, wings, or even fins as opposed to the nebulous transcendence of "mind" at the highest spiritual level suggested by Anaxagoras and featured by Plato. This principle even applies to insects, oysters, and possibly even vegetables that turn their leaves to gain better access to sunlight. Aristotle extends his analysis of intelligence from humans to apply to the mental and pre-mental performance of all life remotely capable of purposeful behavior. On the other hand, he explains human consciousness as pragmatic behavior relevant to abstract issues as well as to needed change.

Aristotle also proposes that the union of body and thought is based on a close relationship in which each acts upon the other. He even goes so far as to propose a cyclical interaction--a physical need affects the soul [or mind], and in turn the mind guides the body according to its circumstances—for example by eating food, building a house, or simply by changing where one sits. Aristotle summarizes a variety of other relevant behavioral theories but obviously holds little regard for those that explain body and soul without taking into account biological need: "Most theories about the soul [consciousness] . . . join the soul to body, or place it in a body, without adding any specification of the reason for their union, or of the bodily conditions required for it."[56] Without mentioning Plato as an example, he suggests that such theories bear little if any connection to functional consciousness whereby body and mind interact in a harmonious manner.

In the second book of *De Anima*, Aristotle links the concept of soul with the capacities of sensation, thought, appetite, touch, motion, and in general the desire for pleasure. Both the imagination and "reasoning faculty" remain essential components of soul as functional aspects of mental behavior, but at the most basic level the soul is ultimately the final agent of sustenance, and to this extent the body is the principal beneficiary of choices imposed by the soul. Nothing beyond can be anticipated. Upon one's death this partnership ceases to function altogether, for neither can exist without the other.

In the third and final book of *De Anima*, Aristotle once again bases human experience on sustained interaction between body and soul (or consciousness): "The soul is the first actuality of a natural body having in it the capacity of life."[57] However, interaction between physical and mental performance is entirely interdependent: "So that there is an analogy between the soul and the hand; for, as the hand is an instrument of instruments, so the intellect is the form of forms, and sensation the form of sensibles."[58] Just as the body acts to satisfy its needs as interpreted by the brain (i.e., soul), Aristotle suggests, the brain directs the body to satisfy these needs in such a manner that consciousness and physical existence both control and depend on each other. This is perhaps best exemplified by the experience of hunger followed by its satisfaction. Consciousness enlists the body to fulfill its need by eating food to eliminate hunger. However, the body has already played an equally important role by inducing the sensation of hunger in the first place. Here at least, Aristotle describes mental performance in response to need much as explained by modern behavioral psychology.

The binary distinctions Aristotle proposes suggest any number of modern variations: mind and body, thought and action, perception and belief, restraint and behavior, and so on. Perhaps the most controversial example would be Freud's neglected dichotomy between the so-called reality and pleasure principles, the inescapable difference between understanding and desire, between thought and belief. In the words of Aristotle:

> Imagination, in fact, is something different both from perception and from thought, and is never found by itself apart from perception, any more than is belief apart from imagination. Clearly thinking is not the same thing as believing.[59]

Aristotle concedes the benefit of imagination as a source of emotional gratification, but he also maintains that its accuracy is susceptible to distortion by means of skillful creativity whereby untruths are rendered to seem valid. He accordingly identifies imagination's capacity to "think falsely" as an often useful function of intellect for the acceptance of hypothetical supposition. He has already suggested such a possibility in Book I of *Metaphysics*, to the effect that "bards tell many a lie." Here with obvious irony he seems to grant this category of self-delusion a much larger role relevant to the shared assumptions of society as a whole: For men often act contrary to knowledge in obedience to their imaginings, while in the other animals there is no process of thinking or reasoning, but solely imagination.[60] But of course exactly the opposite can be argued, that animal consciousness falls short of imagination. Perception and a relatively primitive logic are possible, but not the ability to pursue suppositions to any extent. On the other hand, similar if less constrictive limitations also apply to the level of imagination among most of humanity—for example Aristotle's fellow citizens in Athens were able to applaud a tragedy by Sophocles but lacked the ability to take into account abstract formulations to any extent. Aristotle extends this discrepancy to explain all false thought relevant to politics, religion, and the many popular assumptions that typically cloud the public mind. And literature sometimes succeeds in configuring imagination on a presumably useful basis whereby the reader or playgoer emerges from vicarious experience a better or more enlightened individual, quite aside from questions of factual accuracy. However, difficulties arise when the "suspension of disbelief" typical of fictive imagination as later described by Coleridge obstructs accurate analysis of the most important aspects of life.

Aristotle seems to extend this consideration to both religion and philosophy itself. He identifies the satisfaction of belief as a particular version of the imagination that deviates from conceptual integrity. At least by implication he includes religious belief typified by Greek mythology as an obvious mode of imagination with hypothetical benefits. On the second page of Book I, for example, he offers a variety of definitions of god [with a small "g"] based on the distinction between levels "either as nonexistent or, if existent, as logically posterior."[61] He seems to concede the emotional benefits of religion as a useful agent of satisfaction for those with questionable deductive skills.

Then again, Aristotle suggests, philosophy itself, for example as illustrated by Plato's concept of the transcendent soul might serve the same purpose as both poetry and the arts in general as already explained in Book I of *Metaphysics*.[62] But of course this level of conceptual risk often clouds objective inquiry as well as received belief, each in its own way. As a result, systematic analysis is more valuable whenever truth is exclusively the final concern. Toward the end of *De Anima,* Aristotle suggests his rejection of Plato's transcendent assumptions on this basis by contrasting objective judgment based on empirical evidence with optimistic creative innovation already mentioned in Book I of *Metaphysics*. For just as fiction and religion too easily lapse into obvious wish fulfillment that defies true verification, theory supportive of questionable assumptions, no matter how complex, can be prone to error through the subordination of meaning to belief:

> For perception of the objects of the special senses is always true and is found
> in all animals, while thinking may be false as well as true and is found in none
> which [do] not reason also. . . . Clearly thinking is not the same as believing.[63]

Whereas belief can be beneficial in bringing thought into play, productive thought based on thorough analysis nevertheless supersedes the immediate rewards of credulousness. There is obvious appeal in Plato's concept of the human soul as a unique agent of transcendent godhead, but Aristotle rejects this possibility by excluding it from consideration just as he ignores Plato's assumptions throughout most of the text. Significantly, he identifies Plato by name not more than twice in an entire text supposedly relevant to Plato's primary thesis, the dominance of the soul. In contrast, he mentions such pre-Socratic philosophers as Anaxagoras (six times), Democritus (eight times), and Empedocles as many as nine times. His primary consideration throughout *De Anima* is human consciousness, and, simply enough, Plato's theory of soul has little to do with it.

In light of philosophy's difficulties in the sustained pursuit of the truth, philosophy becomes Aristotle's culminating issue discussed in *De Anima*. His approach anticipates the later and more advanced distinction between idea and perception offered by the seventeenth-century English philosopher John Locke. According to Aristotle, for example, thought and perception necessarily differ in their respective levels of accuracy:

> Perception of the objects of the special senses is true, or subject to the mini-
> mum of error. Next comes the perception that they are attributes; and at this
> point error may come in. . . . Thirdly, there is perception of the common
> attributes, that is, the concomitants of the things to which the special attributes
> belong: I mean, for example motion and magnitude, which are attributes of
> sensibles. And it is concerning them that sense is most apt to be deceived.[64]

The binarism "motion and magnitude"—roughly comparable to mass and motion--also suggests pre-Socratic naturalist assumptions about tangible existence, and the alternative proposed by Aristotle once again entails the role of imagination too often in conflict with this truth. Obviously the hierarchy he proposes here has higher levels yet. He takes it for granted that truth exists, but he also warns that imagination—including unsubstantiated belief--necessarily distorts the truth, and he believes that philosophers should be fully aware of this likelihood. As for the link between idea and perception complicated by the imagination, Aristotle proposes the obvious paradox that the human mind can often be the most prone to error at its most advanced level of analysis. The more elaborate our thinking, the more likely our ideas go wrong—hence by implication the greater the necessity to exercise our cognitive skills to the best of our ability:

> Now it is clear that perception and intelligence are not the same thing. For all animals share in the one, but only a few in the other. And when we come to thinking, which includes right thinking and wrong thinking, right thinking being intelligence, knowledge, and true opinion, and wrong thinking the opposites, neither is this identical with perception. [65]

In their relatively simple pursuit of food and shelter, small rodents with simpler minds might lapse into error fewer times than Plato, Aristotle, and other philosophers whose more difficult task is to formulate their various philosophies with conceptual adequacy. At least by implication, Aristotle suggests that the philosopher's ability to unravel complexity at a second and higher level is more likely to depend on a strictly cognitive function, the valid analysis of empirical evidence. This seems to have been his final assessment of philosophy as the most advanced mental achievement, one necessarily dependent on thorough research.

IV. NICOMACHEAN ETHICS

Aristotle extended his deterministic assessment of life to personal conduct and social behavior as explained in *Nicomachean Ethics,* much as he did for institutions and social practices in *Politics.* His basic recommendation in these two texts was that the health and prosperity of individuals and society as a whole depend on the collective adherence to sustained moderation according to the golden mean, a healthy intermediate position between extremes of all voluntary behavior. For all individual and social behavior, there are two possible extremes--of excess and deficiency--and the best and most useful choice in all instances is to choose the intermediate possibility. Of course there will be circumstances when this cannot be done, but here again the best choice is to not let these circumstances become habitual.

The origin of the concept golden mean seems to have preceded Aristotle by many centuries. Carved on a temple at Delphi, "Nothing in Excess" (*Medan Agan*), was said to have originated with Theano, wife of Pythagoras. Later, Heraclitus declared its benefits in fragment 116, "All men have the capacity of knowing themselves and acting with moderation," and both Socrates, and Plato likewise advocated moderation. However, Aristotle featured its central importance to effective human behavior in *De Anima.* In *Nicomachean Ethics*, he made this assumption even plainer:

> . . . both fear and confidence and appetite and anger and pity and in general pleasure and pain may be felt both too much and too little, and in both cases not well; but to feel them at the right times, with reference to the right objects, towards the right people, with the right aim, and in the right way, is what is both intermediate and best, and this is characteristic of virtue. Similarly with regard to actions also there is excess, defect, and the intermediate. Now virtue

is concerned with passions and actions, in which excess is a form of failure, and so is defect, while the intermediate is praised and is a form of success; and both these things are characteristics of virtue. Therefore virtue is a kind of mean, since it aims at what is intermediate.[66]

Since human behavior almost inevitably benefits by maintaining a benign middle course between antithetical excesses, Aristotle advocated the pursuit of moderation in all aspects of behavior. He linked every mode of human performance with the need for moderation. For if moderate behavior is the best agent of survival, the golden mean turns out to be the most suitable standard of conduct toward such a result. Just as life enacts mass in motion, human behavior best serves this purpose by sustaining life the most effectively.

V. AFTERWORD

Aristotle played a substantial role in the history of ancient philosophy—perhaps the most influential of all--but the disordered history of his influence was beset by difficulties that were unique. Not more than forty-seven of the two hundred treatises he was said to have authored have survived, yet on the whole their theoretical contribution has been even more influential than the output of Plato or anyone else. No history of an author's productivity has ever been as chaotic and beset with difficulties, yet his dominance, compounded by the additions of Theophrastus and Strato has been without parallel despite the misinterpretation of many of his ideas that has been almost as universal. Written while he was a disciple of Plato, most of his early dialogues were lost and forgotten within a few generations, and the recovery of his mature writings was accidental as already indicated in this book's Introduction. More specifically, Theophrastus, his friend and chosen successor as the director of the Lyceum, bequeathed his collection of Aristotle's original manuscripts to his disciple, Neleus of Scepsis, on the assumption that he would become the Lyceum's next director. When Strato was chosen instead, Neleus apparently refused to give up Aristotle's entire collection that he felt was his rightful inheritance, and subsequently bequeathed them to his family, who stored them in their cellar for almost two centuries without recognizing their importance. Much later a collector, Apellicon of Teos, bought and published them in an unedited version, but which had few if any readers. In effect Aristotle was all but forgotten at that point. In 86 BC the Roman general Sulla took possession of the collection, and two years later, in 84 BC, he transported it to Rome, where the scholar Andronicus of Rhodes edited and published it somewhere between 70 to 60 BC, two and a half centuries after Aristotle's death.[67] Such authors as Cicero, Plutarch, Sextus Empiricus, and Diogenes Laertius were impressed by his philosophy, but there is no clear evidence to what extent the Roman public at large might have been acquainted with his ideas.

Early medieval Christian philosophers initially limited their exploration of Aristotle's texts to those upon logic, which were translated by Victorinus and Boethius. His philosophy was preserved by such figures as Philoponus, Alexander of Aphrodisias, and Simplicius. In response to their effort to integrate his arguments with Christian doctrine, the Emperor Justinian actually took the remarkable step in 529 of banning the teaching of Greek philosophy in Athens. Although all philosophy was banned, the philosopher who was targeted seems to have been Aristotle. Except for his invention of logic, his philosophy seems to have been widely censored.

Aristotle's influence was then limited to Arab civilization until the twelfth century, culminating with the analyses of Avicenna and Averroes that inspired such figures in Europe as Siger of Brabant and Albert the Great to promote an acceptable synthesis between Aristotle and Christianity. Once justified by appropriate interpolations, the original Latin translation of *De Anima* seems to have been available by the twelfth century, and a second translation, perhaps by Michael Scott, was available by the third decade of the thirteenth century. Full Latin translations became available of all of Aristotle's major texts by Gerard of Cremona and, most important, by William of Moerbeke, a close friend of St. Thomas Aquinas. By 1300, Aquinas' *Summa Theologica* provided a grand synthesis that integrated Aristotle's philosophy with Catholic doctrine. Aquinas actually quoted Aristotle 3,500 times to document his analysis, and within a century all of Aristotle's extant theories were taught at the University of Paris, Europe's dominant university in philosophy at the time. For a few centuries Aristotelian cosmology effectively supplanted Platonism as the dominant synthesis between religion and philosophy.

However, by the turn of the seventeenth century such figures as Bacon, Descartes, Hobbes, and Gassendi went on to promote their own versions of empirical philosophy that featured experimentation to an even greater extent.

The rejection of Aristotelian assumptions also played an important role in the division between Catholic and Protestant theology. Ironically, Protestants rejected Catholicism based on its adherence to nominalism, an emphasis on universals they linked with Aristotle's version of materialism. This was despite the fact that Ockham's famous "razor" proposed by the Catholic theologian William of Ockham that the simplest explanation is the usually the best had first been suggested by Strato who was inspired by Aristotle. Since then, Catholicism has sustained its adherence to Aristotle's perspective despite ample evidence of his secular assumptions to be found in such texts as *De Caelo* and *De Anima*. Few if any of the obvious interpolations have been deleted, and respectable classicists have effectively ignored them in their necessarily biased analysis of his arguments as a result. On the other hand, modern scientists almost entirely depend on data collection as initiated by Aristotle as well as the use of experimentation as initiated by his disciple Strato. Despite this remarkable paradox in western civilization's intellectual history (but also perhaps because of it), Bertrand Russell, modern philosophy's most eminent advocate of secularism, has been able to declare in the mid-twentieth century, " . . . after [Aristotle's] death it was two thousand years before the world produced any philosopher who could be regarded as approximately his equal."[68]

Chapter Five

The Lyceum after Aristotle

The Hellenistic age lasted three centuries, extending from the deaths of Aristotle and Alexander the Great to the establishment of the Roman Empire under Augustus. During this period the city of Alexandria in Egypt supplanted Athens as both the dominant port city in the eastern Mediterranean region and its cultural epicenter, except for the sustained pursuit of philosophy in Athens. Scientific investigation in Alexandria included the fields of physics, biology, geology, medicine, mathematics, astronomy, and philology; and its prestigious library, the Bibliotheca Alexandrina, contained at its peak as many as 700,000 scrolls, the equivalent of perhaps 100,000 modern books. The large number of astronomers and mathematicians who lived in Alexandria included Aristarchus, Eratosthenes, Euclid, Hipparchus, Callimachus, and Apollonius of Perga as well as the inventor, Hero. On the other hand Plato's Academy remained active in Athens, and almost as influential were the newly established schools of Epicurus' so-called Garden and the Stoa of Zeno where he and his disciples sought a credible synthesis of Platonism and religion. In Aristotle's Lyceum, Theophrastus and then Strato sustained a high level of achievement in both science and secular cosmology, but unlike the theoretical writings of Aristotle, theirs were later almost entirely lost, leaving little documentation of their mature theoretical assumptions.

Over time, economic and political trends became more hostile to secular philosophy. Populist collective needs prevailed at the expense of the seemingly indifferent secular philosophical speculation at odds with religion.[1] Once Rome attained victory in the Punic Wars, it became the dominant military presence in the region, and an empire emerged that tolerated various religions and fertility cults brought to Rome by the many immigrants from captured territory throughout the Mediterranean region and beyond. A concomitant decline seems to have occurred in secular philosophy except for the contribution of such figures as Lucretius, Posidonius, Cicero, Plutarch, and a diminishing assortment of their contemporaries preceding the emergence of Christianity. In effect, the unique ideological achievement of ancient natural philosophy seems to have undergone a gradual rise and fall that both anticipated and somewhat overlapped with the later and more famous rise and fall of the Roman Empire.

Not that philosophy had yet displayed signs of severe decline. The materialist perspective of Aristotle's two remarkable disciples--Theophrastus followed by Strato--remained at a high level. The many inhabitants of Epicurus' controversial Gardens continued to link religion with hedonism supposedly justified by Democritus' theory of atomism, and Pyrrho's version of skepticism more or less encouraged the pursuit of religion. In contrast, Arcesilaus, the sixth head of Plato's Academy, abandoned Plato's doctrine of ideal forms, instead featuring systematic disbelief based on sustained common sense (*eulogon*). A century later his successor Carneades went even further by proposing sustained analysis dependent on the question of probability. Platonists and Stoic philosophers continued to stress transcendent assumptions, but the Aristotelians, Epicureans and Academic skeptics beginning with Arcesilaus remained secularists, and both Strato and Carneades in particular came to be recognized as militant atheists. Carneades took disbelief to an extreme that was arguably more aggressive than that of anyone else either before or since.

As with Epicurus, almost the entire theoretical productivity that Theophrastus and Strato sustained at a high level throughout their lives was to be lost to posterity. As a result there is little record of their ideas in their own words. They may paradoxically be said to have provided the most sophisticated but least influential analysis identified with ancient secularism. Fortunately, Diogenes Laertius compiled extended bibliographies for both of them that were even more inclusive than Aristotle's extant writings, but with little textual evidence of their content relevant to science and cosmology.

The seven outstanding figures in secular philosophy who played significant roles during the three-century Hellenistic phase include Theophrastus and Strato of Aristotle's Lyceum, Epicurus followed much later by Lucretius among the so-called Epicureans, Arcesilaus and Carneades among the so-called Academic skeptics, and finally Cicero because of his early education by tutors linked with a variety of philosophical schools, as well as his pivotal role in history of Rome. His two remarkable dialogues, *Academica* and *Nature of the Gods*, together provide an excellent picture of secular philosophy as a whole up to that time.

I. THEOPHRASTUS (CA. 371-287 BC)

For roughly fifty years after Aristotle's death the Lyceum continued to exist as a major school of philosophy under the leadership of Theophrastus, followed by Strato as his disciple. Both were exceptionally talented, and the school's theoretical predominance diminished only after the death of Strato. Born with the name Tyrtamus, Theophrastus was said to have been given his nickname by Aristotle because of his graceful style. Fourteen years younger than Aristotle, he first studied at Plato's Academy, then seems to have left Athens with Aristotle following Plato's death. He later joined Aristotle's Lyceum at its inception, and when Aristotle fled from Athens to avoid prosecution, he replaced him as director of the Lyceum and retained this role for the next thirty-six years until he himself died at the age of eighty-five. Altogether, as many as 2,000 students were said to have attended his lectures, and unlike Aristotle, he also seems to have enjoyed a high level of popularity among his fellow citizens in Athens throughout his life. When he was tried for atheism, apparently for opposing animal sacrifice, he was declared innocent of the charges and became even more popular among Athenians.

Theophrastus extended Aristotle's research on a basis that Aristotle himself would have fully supported. In particular Theophrastus' prolonged studies in botany justified his later status as the so-called father of botany, despite Aristotle's earlier findings. He also continued to expand his inquiries into many areas as suggested by his enormous bibliography of 741 texts, 490 of them listed by Diogenes Laertius. According to their titles he published at least fifty texts pertaining to science, thirty-five on human behavior, thirty on logic, ten on religion, and at least a dozen relevant to philosophy in general, and he authored specific studies of Anaxagoras, Anaximenes, Archelaus, Diogenes, Empedocles, and two apiece on Democritus and Plato. Unfortunately, all of these philosophical texts were lost except for his brief essay, *Metaphysics.* This seems to have been found among Aristotle's lecture notes when they were discovered and his *Metaphysics* is quite useful as a summary in helping to clarify his version of cosmology as compared to Aristotle's earlier perspective.

A single easily overlooked citation in Sextus Empiricus' biography of Parmenides discloses that among his twenty-nine lost scrolls upon physics, Theophrastus published what amounted to a standard history of ancient theories about the connection between the soul and the body, in other words between mind and conscious behavior.[2] Relevant to the concepts of Parmenides, Anaxagoras, Plato, Aristotle, and probably Theophrastus himself, it seems a major split continued to exist between theories that featured transcendent consciousness and those that emphasized mental performance linked with physical behavior. That Theophrastus authored such a history suggests the continuation of secular analysis, but also that he felt obliged to acknowledge the concept of transcendent soul in the very effort to discourage its implications. Theophrastus summarized Aristotle's perspective with relative objectivity and displayed his ability to present controversial analysis without provoking a hostile reaction.

Not more than eighteen pages long, *Metaphysics* offers a broad summary in response to Aristotle's theories in *De Anima* and other late writings. There is no hard evidence that Theophrastus wrote the text only its strong likelihood, since he alone was uniquely qualified having discussed the relevant issues. The text's final perspective seems quite compatible with Aristotle's assumptions, but is based on less stringent analysis. Obviously Theophrastus wrote it in an effort to clarify Aristotle's complex arguments and present them in a simpler and more accessible form for the general reader. In addition, he was able to perform such a task while mentioning a variety of tangential issues far more elusive than Aristotle might have been willing to concede. Many of Theophrastus' ideas seem retrospective, effectively the reconsideration of arguments more closely elaborated in earlier works, but there is also the sense that much remained to be ascertained on a more inclusive basis.

At the beginning of Theophrastus' text several early portions seem to promote a monotheistic version of godhead that might have been acceptable to Plato. For example, he writes:

> It is necessary, presumably, to recognize [realities] by some power and some superiority to other things, as if it were God that we were apprehending; for the ruling principle of all things, through which all things both are and endure, *is divine.*[3]

The use of italics suggests the possibility of interpolation, especially with the additional wording, " . . . for the ruling principle of all things . . . *is divine.*" Here his insistence seems plain that a higher power dominates the universe, and it can be most readily described as God. However, word play in later passages suggests a pantheistic equation between the god concept and the universe itself as a substitute for deity.

Elsewhere Theophrastus concedes that Plato had been able to apply ruling principles to ideas, numbers, and "the things we have names [for]," but complains of Plato having sought to "treat of the ruling principles only." How much better, he argues, is the scientific approach he shared with Aristotle that featured the discovery and interpretation of such principles without implying their imposition by any kind of a higher power. As opposed to metaphysics, science should feature empirical analysis to determine the validity of ruling principles quite aside from whether they have any link with godhead. Theophrastus emphasizes the variable freedom of the universe and actually praises Heraclitus' startling fragment to the effect that the universe "is like a rubbish-heap of things thrown anyhow."[4] The standard translation of Heraclitus' sentence features dust rather than rubbish, but the word "rubbish" bears useful connotations pertaining to a jumbled anarchy that too often defies simplistic cause-and-effect analysis.

Just a page later, Theophrastus points out the pantheistic dilemma that occurs if God is both the moved and mover:

> And even sense-perception seems in a way to join in proclaiming that the mover need not always, because the one acts and the other is acted on, be different from what it moves; the same result follows if we apply the question to reason itself and to God.[5]

The emphasis here is decidedly pantheistic. If the universe, like God, is both moved and the mover, it possesses comparable authority, so the two are in effect identical at least to this extent. If one is nothing less than the product of itself, so is the other. But the only God that can be the product of itself would be the universe, and the only universe that can be a product of itself would be God.

Early on in the text Theophrastus expresses doubts he shared with Aristotle about the use of binary combinations in explaining the dynamics of existence. However, he concedes on the final page that heavenly bodies "possess order" that suggest mathematics, and he declares both that the "whole of reality . . . consists of contraries" including the Manichaean standoff between good and evil, virtue and vice, heaven and hell, and benevolent and hostile gods. He also seems to concede the validity of physical binarisms between heat and cold as suggested by Anaximander, between fire and *logos* as suggested by Heraclitus, and between atoms and void as suggested by Democritus. Even more basic, Theophrastus suggests, are binarisms between what "is" and what is "not," between truth and error, and between existence worthy of analysis and transcendent suppositions. Theophrastus softens his wording, but the phrase, "transcendent sort of wisdom," seems obvious and almost prophetic of the later convergence between Platonism and religious revelation.

In Chapter VII, Theophrastus points out the important linkage between Aristotle's texts, *De Caelo* and *De Anima*, by defining philosophy as a comprehensive explanation of both celestial motion and animal life:

> It is clear that the celestial system also in its rotation . . . is a sort of life of the universe. Surely, then, if the life in animals does not need explanation or is to be explained only in this way, may it not be the case that in the heavens too, and in the heavenly bodies, movement does not need explanation or is to be explained in a special way?[6]

Here Theophrastus seems to imply the Aristotelian cosmology that all existence partakes of cyclical infinitude in addition to the interaction among contraries that do not need to be explained by transcendent authority. Sustained existence accordingly predominates both in the sky as demonstrated by the endless orbits of stars and planets, and on earth by endless procreation of life from one generation to the next as Aristotle suggested in *De Anima*.

In Chapter IX, the final chapter of the treatise, Theophrastus discusses the possibility of evolution earlier suggested by both Anaximander and Aristotle:

> In the case of plants and still more of inanimate things that have a nature which is determinate, . . . there seems to be some plausibility in the view that after all it is fortuitously and by the rotation of the universe that these things acquire certain forms or differences from one another."[7]

Implicit in this somewhat confusing sentence is Darwin's notion of both genetic variation and the improved chances of survival among variant species. Also implicit is the suggestion that all of nature very likely occurs without the intervention of one or more gods.

Theophrastus concludes his short essay by suggesting both the modest role of human life in the universe and the importance of the ethical distinction between good and evil in the universe:

> For what is animate is a small part of the universe, and what is inanimate is infinite; and of animate things themselves there is only a minute part whose existence is actually better than its non-existence would be. But to say that *in general* the good is something rare and found only in few things, . . . is the act of a most ignorant person. . . . Rather, reality in fact is and always has been good.[8]

As far as he is concerned, human ethics that depend on religion are inconsequential compared to the benign indifference of the universe as a whole. He also asserts that even the one or more deities worshipped by believers "cannot guide everything to what is best."[9]

Theophrastus makes an abrupt transition at the very end of *Metaphysics* to what seemed the theoretical incompatibility between Aristotle and Democritus' respective cosmologies. This transition is admittedly sudden, as the topic has no obvious relevance to the issues under discussion. However, it is significant in the history of science, for Theophrastus apparently suggests the necessity of obtaining a synthesis between Aristotle's cyclical model of the universe as a whole and Democritus' concept of atomism at a microscopic level. Theophrastus himself seems to have already proposed the tentative concept of a "micro-void" as a possible compromise between the two competitive theories of natural philosophy. Thus, he abruptly shifts his topic to the need for sustained investigation in order to obtain a viable synthesis between the two seemingly incompatible perspectives. The enormous task he proposed was obscured by his bland wording, "But at any rate these are the questions we must inquire into."[10] Apparently he sought what would have amounted to an ancient unified field theory and in fact, Strato did attempt reconcile the two theories for example, by conducting experiments using a relatively crude version of a vacuum jar he invented. His effort was doomed to failure because of the inadequacy of his equipment, but, more significantly, his primitive effort initiated the dependence on experimentation in order to confirm the validity of one or more theories. To this extent, at least, Theophrastus can be said to have inspired Strato's effort as a major step toward the remarkable achievement of modern science later reinvented by Sir Francis Bacon.

II. STRATO OF LAMPSACUS (CA. 335-287 BC)

Strato was born in Lampsacus and was the tutor of Ptolemy II in Alexandria, where he also played a central role in secular philosophy. He was the mentor of several of Alexandria's most important scientists as well as the friend and mentor of Arcesilaus, the dominant Academic skeptic in Athens at the time. After Theophrastus' death, Strato became the third director of the Lyceum in Athens and served in that capacity until his own death eighteen years later. During this period he published upon a large variety of topics including physics, ethics, cosmology, logic, psychology, and zoology among many others. Diogenes Laertius lists specific titles of some of his lost papers including "On Chance," "On Definition," "On Justice," "On Happiness," and "On Modes of Life." Only in recent times has Strato's extant corpus of fragments and segments been gathered, consisting of 150 fragments and paraphrastic summaries by as many as fifty ancient and medieval authors.[11] Simplicius salvaged seventeen of these fragments, the early doxographer Aetius obtained sixteen, Plutarch fourteen, Sextus Empiricus seven, and Cicero four.

It can be assumed that Strato's name was stricken from the record and that his works were all but eradicated because of his outspoken arguments supportive of atheism. Throughout his lifetime he seems to have freely acknowledged his atheism, and it seems without threat of prosecution. However, by the late Middle Ages his contributions in both philosophy and natural science had been almost totally erased from the history of ancient philosophy. The choice among scholars at the time appears to have been to preserve Aristotle's contribution through a few appropriate deletions and editorial modifications; to acknowledge Theophrastus' contribution without preserving his papers on cosmology, with the exception of *Metaphysics*; and finally to ignore Strato's contribution in its entirety. He seems to have been erased from the record of both science and philosophy, and this omission persists today. This is even true, for example, for two recent histories of ancient secular philosophy, Jennifer Hecht's *Doubt: A History*, published in 2003, and Tim Whitmarsh's *Battling the Gods: Atheism in the Ancient World*, published in 2015. Neither mentions Strato despite the significant role he played in the advance of secularism during the Hellenistic period. The unusual convergence at the time between the two schools, Plato's Academy under the leadership of the skeptic Arcesilaus, and Aristotle's Lyceum under the leadership of Strato, was itself evidence of the central role Strato played in the history of philosophy.

As documented in Diogenes Laertius's biography, Strato's last will and testament discloses his close friendship with Arcesilaus. Both the wording and provisions of the will indicate strong rapport between the two, suggesting the extent to which Arcesilaus' version of Academic skepticism dominant at the time was in fact compatible with Strato's outright atheism. If true, the earlier standoff between Plato and Aristotle's antithetical philosophies seems to have been resolved by Strato and Arcesilaus, the two famous philosophical schools' directors, with Strato's insistence on rigorous scientific methodology and Arcesilaus' theory of *epoche* as relentless skeptical inquiry.

Strato's atheism was undoubtedly linked with his effort as a scientist to discover an inclusive theory of the physical universe that was independent of supernatural authority. He was quoted as having boasted that he "did not make use of the gods in explaining the origin of the world," and according to Cicero, he further insisted, "The sole repository of divine power is nature, which constrains in itself the causes of birth, growth, and decay, but is entirely devoid of sensation and of form."[12] Strato promoted two basic concepts that later became standard assumptions of scientific materialism, the first, the so-called "Stratonician Presumption" as named by the contemporary English philosopher, Anthony Flew. Formulated as an axiom, it declared that any idea or supposition including the god concept must be fully substantiated in order to be accepted as a probable truth. Implicit was the concept that the universe is nothing more or less than its own cause and therefore provides its own explanation:

"Whatever characteristics we think ourselves able to discern in the universe as a whole are "underivative" [sic] characteristics of the universe itself."[13]

The second concept entailed the insistence that all observable phenomena can be explained as imminent forces of nature, much as Aristotle and Theophrastus had already implied or stated as qualified by the role of probability:

. . . and he [Strato] says in the end that the universe itself is not animate and that nature is subsequent to chance, for the spontaneous initiates the motion, and only then are the various natural processes brought to pass."[14]

A strictly physical universe could then be described based on principles of determinism. Perhaps unexpectedly, the theologian Lactantius, an advisor of the Emperor Constantine, later took this argument even further on the assumption either that "first-principles came together at random" or that the universe "was brought into existence by nature in an unlooked for way":

Nature . . . has in itself a power of producing generation, growth and decay, but it has no consciousness or shape, so that we may understand that all things have . . . been produced spontaneously, not by any craftsman or originator.[15]

Lactantius insisted both alternatives—"random" and "unlooked for"-- were "idle and impossible." However, as suggested by Plutarch, who quoted the passage, their connection seems possible. According to Cicero in *Academica*, Strato insisted on the existence of a unique but explicable godless universe:

He [Strato] declares that he [himself] does not make use of divine activity for constructing the world. Instead, his doctrine is "that all existing things of whatever sort have been produced by natural causes . . . dependent on the "natural forces of gravitation and motion.[16]

He implied that the universe is susceptible to scientific analysis devoid of religious implications.

Strato also proposed that the underlying structure of matter is "particulate," and that there are only two primary qualities, hot and cold--a notion first suggested by Anaximander. At a comparable level of abstraction, Strato went on to explain that all existence "has been caused by natural forces of gravitation and motion."[17] Thus, Strato was able to reduce Aristotle's explanation of motion to just two impersonal cosmic forces, the attraction of matter and the numerous transitional displacements produced by this attraction. There was no role for any kind of a god or gods in the physical universe proposed by Strato, and an entirely different unifying physical force was needed. Aristotle had already mentioned gravity in both *De Caelo* and *Metaphysics*, and Strato tried to identify it more specifically and to measure its force.[18]

Strato's most important contribution to natural philosophy was his invention of scientific experimentation to confirm the function of physical attraction and measure it as described by Aristotle. Encouraged by Theophrastus, he apparently sought to obtain a valid synthesis between Aristotle and Democritus' respective macro- and micro-cosmic theories of physics. This methodology seems to have been the first of its kind to test a basic theory. Earlier novelties such as the so-called Baghdad Battery might have been devised to exhibit the presumed mysteries of both magnetism and static electricity, but the use of experimentation to measure the impact of a physical force had never been attempted before. As to be expected, the experiment was only partially successful. However, as explained by G.E.R. Lloyd, the importance of Strato's theory of gravity was "not so much in what [he] was trying to prove [e.g. the fact that acceleration occurs or that falling objects tend to cause other objects to rise] as in the way he sought to prove it."[19] On this basis Strato seems to have invented scientific experiments, and, however primitive his effort, it turned out to be an even more important step than Aristotle's earlier emphasis on the accumulation of data. Aristotle had already established the importance of collected data relevant to biological sciences, but it was Strato who enlarged the scope of science to include physics and astronomy and employed the experimental principle of "falsifiability by observation," as explained by the twentieth century philosopher Karl Popper. To confirm any particular explanation of the physical universe, for example the relationship between gravitation and velocity, the experimental scientist needs to measure evidence on a controlled basis in experimental situations designed for exactly this purpose. The success of an experiment demonstrated the validity of a particular theory, and its failure could be just as useful in demonstrating the need to explore possible alternatives.

Strato sought, for example, to measure the effect of gravity by dropping an object from two different heights—less than an inch and a hundred feet—in order to compare the relative effects of their impact. However crude, the measurement of comparative differences helped to justify his seemingly obvious conclusion that acceleration occurs when anything falls and that it is a result of gravity, ergo gravity exists to the extent that it can be measured. As explained by Strato, "The weight of the object does not increase, the object itself has not become greater, it does not strike a greater space of ground, nor is it impelled by a greater [external force]; nevertheless, it moves more quickly, thereby producing a greater impact."[20] Having dispensed with four alternative hypotheses, Strato demonstrated the likelihood that acceleration was influenced by "attraction" as anticipated by Aristotle and much later as explained by Galileo. Strato confirmed this principle in his essay, "On Motion," as quoted by Simplicius. To confirm the principle of acceleration, he also measured a falling stream of water that breaks into drops toward the bottom of its fall, supporting the likelihood that water particles as well as objects gather speed when they fall.

> For if one observes water pouring down from a roof and falling from a considerable height, the flow at the top is seen to be continuous, but the water at the

bottom falls to the ground in discontinuous parts. This would never happen unless the water traversed each successive space more swiftly.[21]

Lower portions of the stream accelerate to such an extent that they can be observed to break loose from higher portions. As can be observed of fountains, the water speeds up while falling such that the lower portions of water separate as drops from higher portions.

One step further, Strato demonstrated weight's essential role by demonstrating the more basic principle that comparative weight increases the greater downward thrust of some things (e.g. iron) as compared to others (e.g. dirt), resulting in the upward thrust of much lighter substances (notably both water and fire):

> . . . every body possesses heaviness and moves towards the center [of the world], but because the heavier ones settle at the bottom the less heavy ones are forcibly squeezed out upwards by them, so that, if someone removed the earth, water would go to the centre, and if the water, air, and if the air, fire.[22]

Strato accordingly revised Aristotle's distinction between opposite forces, one downward and the other upward, by proposing a simpler distinction between various downward forces, some of them sufficient to force the compensatory upward thrust of others. Strato's findings based on this experimentation were substantial. Again, his experimental analysis was later unfortunately lost or destroyed.

Aristotle and various contemporaries had already suggested numerous valid concepts and suppositions, but none had turned to the use of experimental evidence to confirm their validity. Aristotle himself completely overlooked such an approach, with the possible exception of a brief passage in *De Caelo* that mentioned different effects to be observed in a jar, and Plato actually suggested such a mode of investigation in *Timaeus* only to warn against what seemed the misguided effort to determine probability based on powers that are limited to God. His advice may be quoted in its entirety:

> There will be no difficulty in seeing how and by what mixtures the colors derived from these are made according to the rules of probability. He, however, who should attempt to verify all this by experiment, would forget the difference of human and divine nature. For God only has the knowledge and also the power which are able to combine many things into one and again resolve the one into many. But no man either is or ever will be able to accomplish either the one or the other operation.[23]

Plato emphasized the limits of human intelligence compared to divine intelligence in the ability to dispense and interpret particular truths, quite aside from the future benefits of experimentation for almost all fields of scientific inquiry.

Also important in the advance of natural philosophy was Strato's text, "On the Void," which seems to have explored in depth the possibility of resolving what seemed a basic contradiction between Democritus and Aristotle's versions of natural philosophy. Democritus had featured discontinuity resulting from the universal existence of void to explain the possibility of motion, and Aristotle had featured the necessity of continuity throughout the universe whereby all such voids are impossible. In *Physics* 4.6-9, he seems to have been confident of his stance except at the very end in 217b-20-28, where his analysis becomes confused. For Strato, however, the question was whether some kind of a synthesis could be found on an experimental basis to resolve this question. Theophrastus had suggested the necessity to address this question in his last paragraph of *Metaphysics*; and in "On the Void" Strato sought an acceptable theoretical synthesis by withdrawing air from a drum in order to measure a sufficient vacuum for the purposes of analysis. His equipment, a simple vacuum jar, was far too primitive to clarify the question, but his ingenuity was unprecedented.

In light of modern physics there is no insurmountable contradiction between the seemingly divergent theoretical perspectives of Democritus and Aristotle. In one sense all space is occupied by an infinite assortment of atoms and particles, as proposed by Democritus, but, as proposed by Aristotle, these atoms and particles can also be treated as concentrations of energy vastly smaller than the distances among them in any medium more concentrated than a perfect vacuum. Indeed, visible things do exist as "bound" collections of atomic particles that can travel in space, but in doing so they displace other things less tightly bound as collections of particles. To this extent a rock necessarily displaces a loose assortment of water particles as it drops to the bottom of a tank full of water, and in fact similar displacements occur at a microscopic level for every motion, every manifestation of displacement.

Strato's task was to obtain a synthesis that salvaged both options and reconciled their seemingly contradictory theories of the physical universe. As later explained by his protegé, Hero, he proposed that the exterior space of mass consisting of atoms includes micro-voids, effectively "pockets of emptiness" that exist both within atoms and among them as well. With specific reference to water penetrated by light, Hero went on to quote Strato's suggestion that the void inside atoms can be penetrated without obvious impact.[24] Temporary micro-voids that comprise intermittent empty space could also be explained within objects or atoms, if not among them.[25] Again, this is evidence of Strato's effort to obtain a synthesis between Democritus and Aristotle. According to Hero, Strato's conclusion was necessarily simplistic, but more important, his effort anticipated modern scientific analysis totally beyond both metaphysics and ancient mythology.[26] For who else in the ancient pursuit of "truth" resorted to experimentation preceding Strato except perhaps Aristotle? In fact, Aristotle mentions such a possibility almost incidentally at the very end of *De Caelo*, but there is no evidence he turned to this level of observation on a systematic basis.[27] Moreover, Strato's relatively awkward synthesis set a precedent for similar inductive determinations much later in the history of science. Two such examples are the eighteenth century discrepancy between Newton and Huygens' respective theories of light (as particles and/or waves), and, more recently, the early twentieth century discrepancy between quantum mechanics and Einstein's theory of relativity. Though at a far more sophisticated level of analysis, Einstein's effort in his later years to reconcile these seemingly incompatible theories into a unified field theory was comparable to Strato's effort to integrate Aristotle and Democritus' theories of space.

Strato explored many additional questions on a strictly empirical basis, including the theories of light, displacement, condensation, rarefaction, and elasticity. Without mentioning Strato by name, Bacon drew upon his example at the turn of the seventeenth century, and with sufficient success that experimental science has become standard since then.[28] Strato had other insights and hypotheses that called for experimental confirmation. These included the likelihood that hot and cold repel each other, that change is just as unpredictable as stasis, that time is a measure of both change and rest, that the human personality changes with age, that every living creature is capable of thought, and that the seat of thought—thus by implication the soul itself— is located in the middle of the brain. Even today most of these issues remain worthy of investigation.

Strato's two successors as directors of the Lyceum, Lyco followed by Aristo, can be considered to have been relatively inconsequential, and Aristotle's Lyceum fell into obscurity within the next few generations. However, at the time Strato seems to have borne a substantial influence upon the scientists who gathered in Alexandria at the time. Most notably he served as the mentor of such major astronomers and scientists in Alexandria as Aristarchus, Hipparchus, and Eratosthenes, and, as already indicated, he had been a friend and mentor of Arcesilaus in Athens. Through Aristarchus, Strato was also said to have had at least an indirect influence on Archimedes of Syracuse. The achievement of scientists influenced by Strato was also impressive. In the field of astronomy, for example, Aristarchus, Eratosthenes and Hipparchus established the earth to be a sphere located in a heliocentric universe, and among other findings they demonstrated that the sun is larger than the earth, that the earth rotates on its axis, causing day and night, and that it slightly tilts on its axis, resulting in the seasons. Hipparchus alone calculated the accurate length of the year as well as the accurate sizes of the sun and moon, and he also charted the stars. In turn, Eratosthenes successfully measured the size of the earth and suggested the possible expansion of continents, the position of mountain chains, the geological submergence of lands (already a topic of keen interest to Strato), and the elevation of ancient sea-beds.[29]

A loyal student of Strato, the mathematician and inventor Hero explored such phenomena as the flow of water in pipes and the reflection of light rays in short paths, and he invented a number of ingenious devices, including siphons, fountains, an air pump, a water organ, a thermoscope, and, most notably, the first steam engine that almost worked. In turn these scientific and technological achievements inspired almost three hundred years of medieval Arab scientific inquiry from the ninth to the twelfth century and finally the scientific inquiry of modern European civilization beginning with Bacon, Galileo, and their contemporaries in the sixteenth century. Certainly Strato was not the unique source of all these achievements, but he played a pivotal role in linking ancient Greek materialism and modern science.

Last but not least, Strato's outspoken atheism probably helped to inspire Carneades' later atheistic stance that was also influential. During their lifetimes, both were dominant in their respective fields. Strato was the last major natural philosopher in the ancient tradition extending from Thales to Aristotle's Lyceum and beyond, and more than a century later Carneades in his role as the director of Plato's Third Academy was the single most persuasive skeptic opposed to religious belief since Strato. Not surprisingly, historians supportive of organized religion have disregarded both of them. Everything they produced has been lost except for fragments that are only beginning to receive examination based on their theoretical merits.

Chapter Six

The Epicureans

I. EPICURUS (341-270 BC)

At the beginning of the Hellenistic period the most notable accomplishment in secular philosophy, aside from Aristotle's Lyceum, was the successful effort of Epicurus to reconcile natural philosophy with hedonistic ethics. Epicurus was born of Athenian heritage and raised on the Island of Samos, where he became interested in philosophy at the age of twelve. When he reached eighteen, he went to Athens to study at Plato's Academy under Xenocrates, and his arrival occurred at almost the same time as Aristotle fled the city to avoid prosecution on the charge of atheism. Two years later he himself was exiled from Athens along with a random selection of emigrants at the orders of the dictator Antipater. Once relocated in Colophon, he studied philosophy under Nausiphanes, a former disciple of both Democritus and the skeptic Pyrrho. By the age of thirty-two he started his own school in Mytilene on the Isle of Lesbos followed by a second school in Lampsacus. Finally, in 307 he was able to return to Athens, where he purchased property described as "the Garden," located within a mile of Plato's Academy. At this site he both taught and practiced his version of philosophy among friends and disciples until his death at the age of seventy-two. His motto on the front gate to his garden was, "Here our highest good is pleasure." He attracted a large number of disciples and was supposedly a generous patron, but his relationship with philosophers beyond his inner circle was mostly hostile. There is no evidence of a friendly interaction with the Lyceum, even though he was a contemporary of Theophrastus and Strato, who seems to have lived just a few miles away.

Epicurus' total output as an author was supposedly unmatched in size throughout ancient history except for the transcription of Carneades' lectures by Clitomachus. Many contemporaries considered his arguments to be clumsy and unworthy of serious consideration, but he retained a large number of disciples who lived both within his community and elsewhere. The ancient library at Herculaneum that was destroyed by Mt. Vesuvius in 79 AD seems to have included many papyri by and about Epicurus, and there has been an effort to recover their texts, but as yet without success. Today, his extant texts include three elongated letters, one of which seems a manifesto, "Letter to Herodotus." All three are available as supplements in an appendix to Diogenes Laertius' *Lives of Eminent Philosophers*. Fortunately, Lucretius based his remarkable philosophical epic on Epicurus' arguments, and during the Renaissance modern philosophers such as Ariosto, Gassendi, Hobbes, and Sir William Temple proposed natural theories inspired by these arguments as well as Lucretius' interpretation.

Epicurus was criticized during his lifetime for not documenting his sources, and to justify his self-designated role as a prophet he repeatedly insisted that his ideas were entirely his own, not acquired from anybody else.[1] Most obvious among the sources he neglected to credit was the atomism of Democritus, whose writings he "filched word for word" according to Plutarch.[2] In any case he seems to have accepted Democritus' concept of atomism without having entirely rejected the possibility of godhead. To a certain extent his emphasis on atomism might have been linked with his hostility to Aristotle's Lyceum located nearby in Athens. As an ethicist he also seems to have deviated from the ethical principle of moderation advocated by Aristotle's *Nicomachean Ethics* by emphasizing the maximization of pleasure short of harmful consequences.

Epicurus also rejected the teachings of his single mentor Nausiphanes, a Democritean philosopher, calling him among other things, "a jelly-fish, an illiterate, a fraud, and a trollop." With obvious sarcasm he called Plato the "golden Plato," and he called Plato's disciples, "the toadies of Dionysius" as well as having described Socrates as nothing more than a buffoon. Aristotle he dismissed as "a profligate who after devouring his patrimony took to soldiering and sold drugs," and he similarly dispensed with Protagoras as a "pack-carrier," Heraclitus as a "muddler," and Pyrrho as an "ignorant boor."[3]

Epicurus was suspected of atheism. However, he seems to have escaped prosecution by avoiding any discussion that would suggest the possibility. As a result there is no clear evidence of his feelings comparable to the outspoken atheism of such earlier figures as Diagoras and Critias as well as the candid agnosticism of Protagoras and Simonides. Later in *De Natura Deorum*, Cicero nevertheless described him as a skeptic hostile to the concept of a benevolent personal God.

To justify his religious convictions, Epicurus reinvented Homeric gods as a host of deities who supposedly occupied a transcendent garden of their own in a separate and inaccessible realm perhaps suggestive of his own such garden. Such an implied analogy could only have attracted a variety of disciples to reside in his garden. Cicero and Posidonius (one of Cicero's eminent teachers) later suggested that Epicurus took this approach primarily in order to avoid the fate of Socrates, Aristotle, and many others. Significantly, the later expulsion of Epicurean disciples from other sites identified with Epicurean philosophy in Rome, Messene, Lyttus, and Phalana was always based on hedonistic grounds rather than the charge of atheism.

The primary evidence available today regarding the materialist emphasis of Epicurus can be found in his summary *Epitome* that was attached to Diogenes' text upon Greek philosophers. This remnant of his numerous writings includes a 24-page explanation of his theory of atomism addressed to Herodotus, an 18-page explanation of astronomy addressed to Pythocles, and finally a short discussion of ethics and religion addressed to Menoeceus. Epicurus' provocative advice, limited to two separate paragraphs, seems unique in its radical departure from the secular perspective in the rest of his text. The initial wording reads as follows in its translation by Cyril Bailey:

> First of all believe that god is a being immortal and blessed, even as the common idea of a god is engraved on men's minds, and do not assign to him anything alien to his immortality or ill-suited to his blessedness: but believe about him everything that can uphold his blessedness and immortality. For gods there are, since the knowledge of them is by clear vision. But they are not such as the many believe them to be . . . For the statements of the many about the gods are . . . false suppositions, according to which the greatest misfortunes befall the wicked and the greatest blessings the good by the gifts of the gods. For men being accustomed always to their own virtues welcome those like themselves, but regard all that is not of their nature as alien.[4]

Three pages later, however, Epicurus concluded his "Letter to Menoeceus" and included a passage that specifically rejects natural philosophy and seems to recommend the advantage of unexamined belief suggestive of Pyrrhonian skepticism's principle of *hmartia*:

> For, indeed, it were better to follow the myths about the gods than to become a slave to the destiny of the natural philosophers: for the former suggests a hope of placating the gods by worship, whereas the latter involves a necessity which knows no placation.[5]

Accept the necessity of received legends, he recommended, since the pursuit of scientific accuracy too easily becomes an endless obligation that only natural philosophers can be expected to endure.

In his final sentence Epicurus also suggested such blessings can be enjoyed while alive based on the expectation of their continuance during an afterlife. Moreover, he emphasized the value of "legends" telling of what might have happened once upon a time as opposed to their more likely

designation as "myths." On the other hand, he mentioned how "natural philosophers" risk their peace of mind by denying the likelihood of life after
death:

> It were better, indeed, to accept the legends of the gods than to bow beneath
> that yoke of destiny which the natural philosophers have imposed. The one
> holds out some faint hope that we may escape if we honour the gods, while the
> necessity of the naturalists is deaf to all entreaties.[6]

However, Epicurus explained, a second and more credible destiny becomes possible, a different version of heaven provided by a "true" God:

> For life has no terrors for him who has thoroughly apprehended that there are
> no terrors for him in ceasing to live. . . .Death, therefore, the most awful of
> evils, is nothing to us, seeing that, when we are, death is not come, and, when
> death is come, we are not.[7]

If heaven does not exist, death simply consists of non-existence, which is
nothing to be afraid of. As later explained by Sextus Empiricus, this second
alternative—the absence of life after death—consists of total obliteration and
therefore by implication the total absence of negative experience:

> Death is nothing to us; for what is dissolved is senseless, and what is senseless
> is nothing to us. Inasmuch as we are compounded of soul and body, and death
> is a dissolution of soul and body, when we exist death does not exist (for we
> are not being dissolved), and when death exists we do not exist, for through the
> cessation of the compound of soul and body we too cease to exist.[8]

The Roman historian Pliny later described this symmetrical principle in
even simpler terms: "All men are in the same state from their last day onward
as they were before their first day, and neither body nor mind possesses any
sensation after death, any more than it did before birth."[9]

In the debate he constructs in, *De Natura Deorum*, written perhaps 250
years later, Cicero specifically addressed the issue of Epicurus' insincerity
pertaining to religious belief. Delegated by Cicero as the debate's spokesman
of skepticism, the individual identified as Cotta insisted that Epicurus did not
really believe in the gods, and for the most part that he argued otherwise to
avoid ostracism.[10] Cotta also suggested that Epicurus featured the indifference of gods to human destiny in order to encourage their rejection among
his followers. In response to Cotta, Cicero conceded his own doubts about
Epicurus' religious belief by mentioning that he did not seem particularly
vigorous in his defense of their existence. What Cicero also found bothersome about the gods described by Epicurus was their utter indifference to
everything else that seemed to matter.[11] Perhaps two hundred years after
Cicero's debate, Sextus Empiricus likewise mentioned a contradiction. Epi-

curus seems to have affirmed the existence of a God but without at all exploring its supposed relationship with the universe.[12] The possibility of sustained hypocrisy on the part of Epicurus, as both Cicero and Sextus Empiricus suggested, seems justified in light of circumstances at the time. Socrates had already been martyred for his supposed atheism; both Anaxagoras and Pericles' mistress, Aspasia, had barely escaped the same fate only because of Pericles' impassioned defense in the public forum; and the sculptor Phidias had been imprisoned for impiety only to die soon afterwards, Theophrastus had been tried and acquitted for impiety, the hedonist philosopher Theodorus had been banished for impiety, both Diagoras and Aristotle had fled Athens for their lives on similar charges, and Protagoras had taken flight only to die at sea. Epicurus could hardly be blamed for his effort to avoid a comparable fate, nor can it be forgotten that even the venerable Plato, disciple of Socrates, had recommended the execution of all mature atheists in the final paragraph of his final text in *Laws X*.

Relevant to cosmology, Epicurus supported Melissus' thesis as explained by Aristotle that "the sum of things is infinite," and that infinitude characterizes the physical universe in all of its dimensions. He also agreed with Parmenides that the entire physical universe always existed and always shall. He rejected creation stories and the notion of a judgment day, his own version of the conservation of matter having been strictly in agreement with Parmenides' argument that there is no possibility of either initial creation or any kind of termination:

> The sum total of things was always such as it is now, and such it will ever remain. For there is nothing into which it can change. For outside the sum of things there is nothing which could enter into it and bring about the change.[13]

Here in three sentences Epicurus summarized with forceful clarity the Eleatic stance of both Parmenides and Melissus as well as Aristotle's basic assumption in *Physics*, *Metaphysics*, and *De Caelo*. Moreover, Epicurus' insistence that "nothing" that exists outside "the sum total of things" would seem to have referred to the existence of heaven beyond the physical universe. By implication there could be no edge to the universe beyond which an independent realm of God, heaven, or hell might be located. Epicurus accordingly reiterated Melissus' most basic principle already accepted by Aristotle:

> Now the sum of things [i.e. the universe] is not discerned to comparison with anything else: hence, since it has no extremity, it has no limit; and since it has no limit, it must be unlimited or infinite.[14]

This shared assumption seems in full accord with contemporary estimates by astronomers that our particular galaxy, containing many billions of stars, is but one among an infinity of others and that all stars in the sky--and possibly all stars in other galaxies as well--average one planet apiece. The remarkable infinitude suggested by Epicurus seems to have been confirmed by modern astronomy.

Epicurus' principal deviation from Aristotle's version of physics was that he fully accepted Leucippus and Democritus' theory of the atom as the very smallest component of the universe without any kind of void within it.[15] Therefore, he argued that further divisions of particles smaller than the atom are impossible if atoms lack the space (or void) in which these smaller particles can exist. Epicurus went even further by maintaining that without exception all material differences result from the interaction among fast and slow atoms and big and small atoms, but that nothing exists smaller than atoms, and that the space that separates them is necessarily empty.

In order to explain random motion and the freedom of the will, Epicurus might have suggested elsewhere, if not in his texts that have survived, that falling atoms swerve slightly to one side at the bottom of their fall, providing microscopic impetus with unpredictable results. For if atoms swerve, if ever so slightly, variation becomes possible that defies predictability at all levels of existence. Even free will could be explained as an aspect of consciousness that was ultimately derivative of the swerve of atoms. The modern reader knows of this hierarchic theory of variation supposedly proposed by Epicurus only because Lucretius later submitted it to his own analysis identified as a *clinamen*. In *De Rerum Natura*, however, Cicero criticized the concept as an extravagant supposition, in fact more absurd than anything else suggested by Democritus. Why would Epicurus have proposed this? It seems he wanted to transcend the stark inevitability of determinism at the expense of freedom at every level beginning with the interaction of atoms. According to Cicero, however, the concept of such a "swerve" was effective in discrediting Epicurus' version of atomism more than if he had simply abandoned his effort in defense of free will.[16] However, Epicurus himself did not address the topic in his *Epitome*, and Cicero insisted that Democritus had never suggested such a possibility.

Over the centuries, however, the swerve has continued to intrigue many supporters and detractors of both Epicurus and Lucretius. Jonathan Swift resurrected the concept to ridicule the atomism of Gassendi as scientific nonsense, but Karl Marx more favorably explored its implications in his doctoral dissertation, and the prestigious early twentieth-century quantum physicist, Niels Bohr, still later suggested its relevance to modern laws of chance. Whatever its validity, the concept effectively demonstrates Epicurus' willingness to explore theoretical possibilities beyond Democritus' basic atomist concept.

Like Aristotle, Epicurus can be identified as having been a behaviorist in his analysis of human consciousness. He described visual perception as the interpretation of "outlines" or "films" that emanate from surfaces, producing an image, or "presentation," which can be interpreted by the brain. All such sensations are both "true" and "quick as thought" in the sense that they are instantaneously perceived. Then again, he insisted that feelings and preconceptions can also be valid, and that various assortments of these may contradict each other now and again, justifying the effort to determine their respective truth. He also proposed that both falsehood and error are the inevitable results of "the intrusion of opinion," and that scientific method is needed to minimize this threat, for "it is upon sensation that reason must rely when it attempts to infer the unknown from the known."[17] Here again, as suggested by Aristotle throughout *De Anima*, inductive observation confirms its own truths despite the possibility of contradiction with the observations of others or even with one's own observation at other times. When such disparity arises, it becomes necessary to renew investigation on an even more systematic basis.

It was the concept of soul (or *psyche*) that determined Epicurus' theoretical preference for Aristotle's secularism rather than the god concept advocated by Plato. Without mentioning either Plato or Aristotle by name, Epicurus supported Aristotle's assumptions based on what seems to have been an anatomical explanation, "that the soul is a corporeal thing, composed of fine articles, dispersed all over the frame." Because of the fineness of its particles Epicurus argued that the soul "keeps in touch with the rest of the frame" and "has the greatest share in causing sensation."[18] This explanation suggested the need to explore the full complexity of brain physiology, though Epicurus obviously risked absurdity in explaining the unique status of soul as a portion of the body "composed of the smoothest and roundest of atoms, far superior in both respects to those of fire."[19]

Epicurus also proposed a general analysis of mental behavior as a manifestation of soul that was based on neural interactivity without any suggestion of transcendent spiritual implications:

An empty space cannot itself either act or be acted upon, but simply allows body to move through it. Hence those who call soul incorporeal speak foolishly. For if it were so, it could neither act nor be acted upon. But, as it is, both these properties, you see, plainly belong to the soul.[20]

We could say today that mental behavior depends on interaction among cranial "atoms" (i.e. brain cells) as well as the empty space that separates these cells. As opposed to Plato, who had treated soul as an incorporeal substance that both subsumes and transcends the physical universe, Epicurus maintained that consciousness is a product of biology that provides an organized response to external agents, for example perception of danger and the appetite for food. Like Aristotle, he identified consciousness as primarily a function of the body rather than transcendent spirit.

Epicurus also explained the whole body as the product of multiple sensations that "give the body its own permanent nature."--or, more precisely, in the words of Sextus Empiricus, its "stable existence."[21] Epicurus further explained that all modes of consciousness "have their own characteristic modes of being perceived and distinguished, but always along with the whole body in which they inhere and never in separation from it."[22] Behavior as the outcome of holistic physiology was what mattered rather than spiritual purity.

It might well have been the idea of interactive harmony within the body that motivated Epicurus's pursuit of harmony in all aspects of life. He actually mentioned Heraclitus' notion of "globular masses of fire," to warn against disagreeable human relationships, and he added, "[We] must hold that nothing suggestive of conflict or disquiet is compatible with an immortal and blessed nature."[23] His reference to an "immortal" nature might suggest the Eleatic notion of permanent motion without beginning or end, but he seems to have primarily concerned himself with its more immediate manifestation as felt ambivalence regarding conflict and disquiet. And what exactly was the better solution for coping with such problems--religion or secular efficiency? To explain and eliminate difficulties linked with this choice, he argued, "We must hold that to arrive at accurate knowledge of the cause of things of the moment is the business of natural science." Science was essential in determining the truth at least to this extent, but it seems not to have justified his total abandonment of the gods.

II. LUCRETIUS (CA. 99-55 BC)

As secular philosophy's grand epic poet, Lucretius is thought to have been as talented a poet as Homer and Virgil and in addition, expanded his subjects to write about science and human destiny rather than received mythical history. There is little biographical information about his life beyond a brief passage in St. Jerome's chronicle of the fourth century AD, which mentions that he had been poisoned in his youth by a love philter and had spent the rest of his life alternating between insanity and intense creativity while writing his grand epic, *On the Nature of Things* (*De Rerum Natura*). Just before its publication he committed suicide at the age of forty-four, when he was said to have been fully satisfied only with the final draft of Book I. Apparently, Cicero helped him revise *De Rerum Natura* and may also have played a role in obtaining its publication, as a letter from Cicero to his brother after Lucretius' death suggests. Cicero also seems to have expressed ambivalent praise,

"Many brilliant passages of genius, yet much technique."[24] It seems he admired Lucretius' secular vision even more than his poetic skill.

Lucretius achieved a unique synthesis between Homeric inspiration and the empirical perspective of Epicurus and natural science in general. His only predecessor of comparable talent among Latin poets was Quintus Ennius, and except for Cicero's occasional assistance as a copy editor, no other contemporaries seem to have influenced him, with the possible exception of Catullus, a close friend of the decadent aristocrat Memmius, to whom Lucretius dedicated his epic. On the other hand, Lucretius was primarily inspired by the writings of Epicurus that were then still accessible, and it may be assumed that these texts included Epicurus' principal work, *On Nature* (*Peri Physeos*), whose title probably influenced Lucretius' choice of his own title.

As a poet Lucretius' singular accomplishment was in having rendered in unmatched dactylic hexameters his own synthesis of materialist assumptions that Epicurus and various pre-Socratic philosophers had already declared in prose. His sentences were appropriately poetic, but their content was analytical with the purpose of promoting his theory. He addressed a broad range of topics that included sense perception, celestial motion, volcanic eruption, thunderstorms, atomic structure, gravity waves, and finally an apocalyptic depiction of the fifth-century Athenian plague earlier described by Thucydides. Many of the topics he discussed—including the controversial theory of swerving atoms (*clinamen*)--were probably inspired by *On Nature*, though he also seems to have been aware of the major pre-Socratic materialists as well as scientific findings during the two centuries since Epicurus' death.

If there was a single theme of the entire text, it would seem best expressed in his dedication to Book IV, ". . . and I proceed to set free the mind from the fast bonds of religious scruples." Unfortunately, this avowal has been too often ignored in modern translations. The relatively modern Rouse and Smith version, for example, uses the neutral word *superstition*, despite Lucretius himself having used the Latin word *religio*, whose simplest translation seems obvious.[25] In contrast, Karl Marx employed vigorous epithets in quoting the passage, both "the shackles of religion" and "the opium of religion," and Lucretius might have found his translation entirely acceptable. In his dedication of Book I, for example, having promised to explain the inception of the universe as a product of the gods, he shifted to its natural manifestation and soon enough dispensed with the role of gods:

> For I will essay to discourse to you of the most high system of heaven and the gods and will open up the first beginnings of things, out of which nature gives birth to all things and increase and nourishment, and into which nature likewise dissolves them back after their destruction. These we are accustomed in explaining their reason to call matter and begetting bodies of things and to name seeds of things and also to term first bodies, because from them as first elements all things are.[26]

Somehow the topic got reversed, since nature, not the gods, was said to have served as the agent of change. Lucretius then suggested his own epic vision of life and death without resurrection as inspired by Epicurus, who had remained in Athens after its 430 BC plague in order to promote his secular vision:

> . . . a man of Greece [i.e. Epicurus] ventured first to lift up his mortal eyes to her face and first to withstand her to her face. Him neither story of gods nor thunderbolts nor heaven with threatening roar could quell . . . [27]

Lucretius thereupon shifted his topic to nature by introducing the concept of seeds to suggest both an evolutionary and effectively cyclical transition of biological generation throughout the history of the universe, dependent on sustained procreation rather than incessant intervention by one or more gods.

Due to literary convention, Lucretius first dedicated Book I to Venus, the mythical goddess of love, but then he extended his dedication to include his ostensible friend and patron Memmius, supposedly Venus' favorite disciple. However, this allusion may have been insulting, especially in light of Book IV's invocation, in which Lucretius described the pursuit of sexual love as nothing better than "dumb desire." As an exile in Athens at the time, Memmius seems to have responded by purchasing much of the site of Epicurus' Garden and according to some accounts, he even had Epicurus' house torn down to be replaced by his own.

Lucretius finally shifted his dedication to Epicurus, who had lived three centuries earlier. He declared his full agreement with Epicurus' dependence on science and stated that his own first principle was the relative permanence of the physical universe, a position contrary to his later obsession with the likelihood of eventual catastrophe. Lucretius went on to propose several credible assumptions linked with his principle of permanence: (1) . . . that nature sooner or later restores everything to its original components; (2) that nature does not cause the destruction of anything until there is sufficient force to make this happen; (3) that things cannot be destroyed on a separate basis, suggesting the likelihood of more inclusive destruction; (4) that no single thing comes to an end without somehow causing disruption; and (5) that nothing visible totally passes away, since nature somehow compensates for its loss through the creation of something else. [28] Lucretius also offered a sixth corollary, the somewhat ominous principle that "nature takes effect though the manifestation of bodies unseen," with the result that "the initial stage [i.e. creation] cannot be easily observed." [29] The first, fourth and fifth corollaries suggest the influence of Democritus and the third conveys Lucretius' apocalyptic obsession best typified by the Athenian plague earlier described by Thucydides.

Lucretius' second basic principle was based on Epicurus' notion of density inspired by Democritus that nothing is packed in a solid mass. In other words, everything is surrounded by void.[30] He argued, as had both Democritus and Epicurus, that without this void, motion would be impossible. As before, empty space seemed essential to the movement of matter from one site to another, from one level of existence to another. In the words of Lucretius, "Either movement is not possible for all bodies, or void exists intermingled with everything, so each thing is able to initiate movement."[31]

Lucretius' third principle was based upon the essentially binary assumption of Leucippus and Democritus: that the entire universe consists of two entities--bodies and void in which these bodies can move in any direction.[32] In light of this dualism between atoms and the empty space among them, Lucretius excluded the involvement of any additional force or element in nature, presumably including the concepts of transcendent soul and/or supernatural authority.[33] Here, as elsewhere, Lucretius did not mention the role of God or gods, but the holistic limitations of his interpretation again suggested the exclusion of supernatural intervention as an aspect of nature. There was no room for the influence of gods in the universe he described.

Like Democritus and Epicurus, Lucretius identified the atom as the smallest particle of matter with a unity of its own as a "solid singleness."[34] He further expanded the idea by proposing that combinations of atoms occur as a result of a "variety of connexions, weights, blows, concurrences, and motions," and for the most part, he suggested, these are activated by fire, the primary agent of motion suggested much earlier by Heraclitus and Empedocles. However, he expressed his doubt whether fire itself is a basic substance. He conceded that the universe itself consists of fire, but suggested that in the final analysis such a possibility had "gone far astray from the truth."[35] What he overlooked, of course, was the abstract principle of energy symbolized by fire, providing the useful dichotomy between mass and energy in currency since the mid-nineteenth century.

While Lucretius expressed his doubts about Heraclitus' supposedly frivolous philosophy, he accepted the possibility of fire as one of the four basic elements within Empedocles' more inclusive model of a cyclical interaction among earth, air, water, and fire. He also suggested the beginning of the universe as well as its destruction saying that things "go back to heaven and its fires for a beginning," as might be suggested by the contemporary Big Bang theory, since "all things may not return utterly to nothing." [36] He took into account Anaxagoras' notion of *homoemeria* whereby minute particles play an identical role in the overall composition of larger body parts--for example particles within atoms, atoms within molecules, and as well as the countless cells that compose any particular organ.[37] He also accepted Anaxagoras' supposition "that all things are hidden immingling in all things."[38] Copper, he thought, includes all other metals and elements in its atomic structure quite aside from the dominance of its particular substance. "We may be aware that things do not commingle in other things, but seeds shared by many things are somehow able to immingling in things."[39] If the definition of "seeds" [*semina*] can be stretched to refer to protons and electrons in the atomic structure of elements, what might otherwise seem absurd becomes a reasonable supposition.

As already suggested by Aristotle as well as the early pre-Socratic philosophers Anaximander and Anaximenes, Lucretius declared that the entire universe is infinite and exists in incessant motion at every level.[40] He also accepted the existence of void as space adjacent to mass, which permits motion as the most basic function of the universe as explained by both Anaxagoras and Democritus. Of course, he would add the qualification that particular kinds of motion eventually complete themselves when first beginnings end through final destruction--as when Lucretius argues that all things terminate whenever matter has somehow been diverted and can no longer be supplied.[41] It is in the final portion of Book VI that he addresses how this process can be expected to bear a negative impact on human survival itself.

On one hand, Lucretius argued that everything is held together by a principle of weight or attraction as explained by the words "yearning for the middle."[42] Today, this force is identified as gravity but Lucretius suggested that the principle extends to other processes that involve clustering on a much larger scale, for example galaxies and undoubtedly the universe as a whole. However, he specified that there can be no inclusive middle since the universe is infinite, and he suggested that the impact of thrust opposed to gravity might ultimately precipitate a cataclysmic outcome beyond anything that Epicurus was able to suggest in his *Epitome*.

It is mistaken to limit Lucretius' sources to Epicurus' interpretation of Democritus and Leucippus. Their influence was certainly important, but Book I also contains basic concepts linked with other pre-Socratic figures such as Thales, Heraclitus, Parmenides, Melissus, and Empedocles, who was supposedly Lucretius' favorite pre-Socratic philosopher. As to be expected, Lucretius ignored Plato, and he did not mention Aristotle's contribution in his explanation of cosmology despite his expression toward the end of Book I of his indebtedness to Aristotle's theoretical concept of mass in motion. The probable explanation for this omission is that he might not have been aware of Aristotle's texts that seem to have been brought to Rome in unpublished manuscripts during his final years. Of course Aristotle was remembered as a principal disciple of Plato, but his texts on cosmology were not yet available. Thus, it seems likely that Lucretius' knowledge of Aristotle's mature work was superficial, and that he affirmed the concept of mass in eternal motion without fully understanding its implications. Lucretius' first book of his epic accordingly offers a piecemeal cosmology that bridges the gap between the philosophies of Epicurus and Aristotle, but with a sense of cataclysmic decline beyond anything they themselves had proposed. Lucretius accepted their shared versions of cyclical occurrence, but he added the inevitable likelihood of collective destruction, for example, to body parts upon death, the collapse of society, etc. If earlier natural philosophers, with the possible exception of Heraclitus, could be described as cosmic optimists confident of sustained harmony, Lucretius warned of an unavoidable cataclysmic outcome.

Book II begins with a rambling invocation in which Lucretius paid his ironic respects to ancient mythology by describing nature as a mother goddess, a fertile deity of birth and growth. He drew upon prehistoric matriarchal religion to be able to assign to nature itself a generic role that affects all aspects of life. As for the issue of whether gods have personal identities, he declared his preference for supernatural motherhood as a principle of intrinsic growth. Insisting that the world is round, he explained that just as seeds symbolize the vital transition from one generation to the next, the entire earth symbolizes global sustenance through procreation.

The remainder of Book II deals more extensively with topics already mentioned in Book I, for example Lucretius' concern about the unseen motions in matter as well as his concept of "up and down" that implies the force of gravity.[43] He declared his approval of Epicurus' emphasis on both the difference between smooth and hooked atoms and the slight swerve of atoms when they complete their fall as the effect of gravity. As earlier indicated, he suggested the importance of this swerve (*clinamen*) as an agent of freedom linked with atomic structure that provides spontaneity and even the principle of free will. Without this additional factor, he suggested, an otherwise deterministic universe would never have produced anything.[44] The most provocative assertion by Lucretius in Book II, perhaps linked with the swerve, was his suggestion that there is far too much erratic behavior in the universe for it to have been devised by supernatural authority, "so great are the faults it stands endowed with."[45] Lucretius also paid his obligatory respect for Epicurus' notion of gods sequestered in their own garden elsewhere in the universe "far removed and from our affairs."[46] Like Epicurus, he used this heavenly tableau for ironic purposes, in his case by ridiculing the authority of these gods as opposed to the inner power of nature that incessantly recreates itself without the intervention of any force beyond itself.

Lucretius went so far as to predict the existence of life elsewhere in the universe. He argued that if there is endless space in all directions, as first maintained by Melissus, it seems unlikely that our spherical earth is unique unto itself and different from any number of similar bodies in outer space that are also the product of nature and therefore just as likely to have evolved from similar origins. [47] Noteworthy in this passage is Lucretius' confidence that other worlds elsewhere might be similar to our own and that the origin of life perhaps involved some version of the swerve.

Book II ends with another reference to mother earth identified as nature, and Lucretius rejects creationism except as a genetic process of nature that suggests the concept of evolution:

> For it is not true, as I think, that the races of mortal creatures were let down from high heaven by some golden chain upon the fields, nor were they sprung from sea or waves beating upon the rocks, but the same earth generated them which feeds them now from herself. [48]

The allusion in this passage was to Homer's suggestion in Book VIII of *The Iliad* that a golden chain suspended from heaven symbolized Zeus's overwhelming authority, a concept that Lucretius found ridiculous. Instead, he insisted on the inevitability of the growth and decline of both the individual and the species as a whole. In other words, all biological entities feed on their environment as long as they are able to grow, then decline and die "since food sooner or later fails advanced age." [49]

Book III begins by linking spirit with mind as a function of the body just as Aristotle had done in *De Anima*. Whereas Plato had identified spirit or soul—or simply mind--as a universal principle dominant across the universe, Lucretius assigned it to the biological realm as conscious behavior essential for the purposes of survival. Lucretius more explicitly claimed that thought plays a comparable role with the function of hands, feet, and eyes, in the composition of the human being. He also suggested that intelligence and spirit merge and coexist in the unique realm of the mind, though he located this function within the chest near the heart rather than the skull.

Lucretius explained death as the departure of both heat and breath (a "vital wind"), and suggested (in light of Anaximenes) that death occurs when the heart no longer pumps oxygen as a "vital wind" needed to produce "heat mixed with air" throughout the body. He also insisted that death results in the complete cessation of life. Like Epicurus he argued that there is no afterlife—that upon death "heat and wind abandon our frame." [50] Moreover, he repeatedly asserted in particular that the notion of an afterlife whereby the mind (i.e. the "soul") can somehow be prolonged is not possible: "When we shall no longer be, then sure enough nothing at all will be able to happen to us, who will then no longer be . . ." [51] He concluded Book III with the bothersome paradox that in the end the elongation of life has no impact on the eternity of death." [52] Whereas the passage of life can be subjected to temporal measurement, lifelessness persists forever, both before we are born and after we die.

In Book IV, Lucretius shifted his argument to explore the body's senses in greater detail, particularly visual perception. He explained the senses are the primary source of the truth and argued that they cannot be refuted. [53] His insistence might seem arguable today, but science necessarily depends on the collection and analysis of observable data. Any hypothesis, the God concept included, can only be accepted on a tentative basis until adequate supportive evidence provides confirmation. Lucretius accordingly proposed an effective analogy between sloppy science and the design and construction of a house by incompetent architects and carpenters:

> As in a building, if the rule first applied is warped, and the square is untrue and deviates from its straight lines, and if there is the slightest flaw in any part of the level, all the construction must be faulty, . . . so too all reason of things must needs prove to you, distorted and false, which is founded on false senses.[54]

The analogy between "false senses" and bad carpentry has possible applications to religion and any conceptual system that might favor a loose assortment of assumptions on a flawed holistic basis. Whatever system of thought depends on unverifiable assumptions is just as vulnerable to collapse as the unstable building produced by hasty architects and their ineffectual carpenters.

In Book V, Lucretius offered a history of the earth from its first origins to its anticipated final cataclysmic annihilation. Comparable to the process of growth and decay at every level of existence, he argued, the earth itself is confronted with the same fate. He challenged the accepted religious assumption among his contemporaries that the earth and sky will exist forever. Instead, he offered a totally different prediction as suggested in the *Bible's* Book of Revelation that the entire world is vulnerable to cataclysmic destruction. He suggested the possibility of earthquakes, and even warned of a heat wave comparable to global warming as a possible source of destruction.[55] Today his prognostication seems at least possible. Contrary to Christ's prediction of a judgment day within the lifetime of his disciples, Lucretius reassured his readers that a final cataclysmic outcome is inevitable but can be expected in the distant future, since "the world is young and new, and it is not long since its beginning."[56]

Lucretius proposed that meanwhile tumultuous destruction happens on a limited basis throughout history, as a result of countless circumstances. As for human destiny, he argued, its future is necessarily limited to the span of history with which we are familiar. He then shifted his emphasis to such human issues as wealth, royalty, clothes, labor, language, the use of fire, and even the arts. In an eighty-line segment he explained the institution of religion as a manifestation of collective behavior and proposed that humanity invented anthropomorphic worship of polytheistic gods to cope with its ignorance of natural phenomenon.[57] He also identified worship as a product of fear, especially fear of wholesale destruction, exactly the collective destination he predicted. Here a major transition occurred in Lucretius' text, as if he intended to suggest that nothing was left to be said about religion.

Lucretius begins his final segment, Book VI, by renewing Epicurus' insistence on the acceptance of the laws of nature rather than the possibility of intervention by the gods. Through ignorance and blind reasoning, he insists, did people "abase their spirits" because of the fear of the gods. In effect, their ignorance of physical causes compels them to depend on the authority of the gods for what they cannot otherwise understand. To whatever extent the gods might exist, he declares, nature's destructive impact should be attributed to nature itself rather than supernatural interference. Lucretius goes on to furnish an exhaustive analysis of thunder, lightning, wind, fire, waves, tornados, earthquakes, volcanoes, landslides, floods, and other such natural threats in order to demonstrate that their occurrence is entirely a product of nature and has no relationship to the intentions of hypothetical gods or their relevance to human affairs. He also warns of sulphur, poisons, poisonous plants, the air in gold mines, and even the habit of hot baths after meals.

Lucretius then shifts his discussion to the magnetic attraction between iron bodies as a harmless but inexplicable force, suggesting that its unique powers nevertheless exemplify the necessity for thorough investigation by "exceedingly roundabout ways" to find an explanation. His wording "roundabout ways" perhaps suggests experimentation as a staple of scientific methodology already explored by Strato, but Lucretius made no reference otherwise to Strato's example. Today what seems amazing is that Lucretius' emphasis on the essential role of magnetism would not be adequately explained until Gilbert's findings at the turn of the seventeenth century. With unusual foresight, Lucretius drew upon what seemed the inexplicable example of magnetism to propose the likelihood of "continual flow and discharge" among such phenomena as sounds, odors, heat, and the spray of ocean waves, all of which "disperse in every direction around [such that] there is no delay, no rest to interrupt the flow." Moreover, the porous aspect of matter also seems to apply to stone, wood, gold, etc. as compared to iron, suggesting that the full explanation of these differences might help to explain why iron is the principal agent of magnetism.[58] Even air differs from the absolute void, he argues, since it is "forever buffeting things" and flows towards the void as earlier suggested by Anaximenes.[59] In this instance, he proposes, an invisible current might be possible--much as occurs for electricity. He returns once again to the analogy with seeds. No less undetectable in their flow, he proposes, are biological and non-biological seeds [*semina*] that possess comparable freedom in their passage through space. Lucretius suggests that many seeds are conducive to one's health--even essential to life--but that others can be dangerous, and might even cause plague and pestilence that bring destruction to an entire community.

In bringing his unique epic of natural philosophy to a close, Lucretius provides a vivid description of such a plague that can be expected "like cloud or mist, causing commotion wherever it goes and compelling change." [60] He devotes his final 150 lines to a description of the Plague of Athens from 430 to 426 BC as described by the Greek historian Thucydides, who like Epicurus actually survived the ordeal. It has been estimated that between one-third and two-thirds of the Athenian population died in this catastrophe at the beginning of the Peloponnesian War. Lucretius' graphic description of the plague is both vivid and disturbing, and the question is why he chose this particular catastrophe to culminate his seemingly disinterested natural history of the universe. He had earlier concurred with Epicurus's effort to promote the concept of a benign physical universe without effective godhead. However, he seemed to abandon Epicurus' cosmic optimism when he describes how an entire population was destroyed by an epidemic that was followed by the collapse of Athens, the most advanced city in the world at the time. Lucretius seems to have felt that this particular example effectively predicted the ultimate fate of the entire world sometime in the indefinite future. [61]

Lucretius committed suicide soon after completing his text. His depiction of total catastrophe might have been inspired by his advanced illness and may have encouraged his choice to resort to self-destruction. In any case his apocryphal vision of eventual destruction was far more pessimistic than the indifferent concept of determinism featured in earlier times.

Chapter Seven

Skepticism

Skepticism played a major role in Greek philosophy since its beginning. Pre-Socratic philosophers doubted Homeric myth as well as having entertained doubts about the validity of their respective theories. For an entire generation the Sophists of Athens challenged received assumptions relevant to almost every issue, and even Platonism can be explained as a byproduct of the skepticism taught by Socrates as opposed to versions of disbelief featured by the rest of the Sophists. Within the next century skepticism inevitably split into competitive schools. On one hand Pyrrhonian skeptics featured orthodox belief as a choice just as valid as any other, since no "truth" could be proven to be absolutely valid. In effect they insisted that believers can and ought to depend on the supposed knowledge they find the most acceptable. In contrast, Academic skeptics led by Arcesilaus, the director of Plato's Academy almost a century after Plato, emphasized the uncompromising pursuit of truth based on persistent inquiry. On a systematic basis this approach necessitated the pursuit of the best and most credible explanation as confirmed by valid evidence. Academic skepticism predominated throughout the Hellenistic period until the time of Cicero, perhaps a generation before Pyrrhonian skepticism came to the fore again. Both versions of skepticism, the Pyrrhonian and Academic schools, were later displaced by more affirmative ideological pursuits that included stoicism, the worship of populist deities, and ultimately Christian religious conversion imposed by the Emperor Constantine. Only then was philosophical doubt entirely quashed.

The collective obsession with doubt among an assortment of ancient Greek thinkers deserves closer examination. In its original definition, the word *skeptic* simply referred to one who inquires or investigates, but both Pyrrhonian and Academic skeptics stressed the willing "suspension of assent" *(epoche)* while pursuing better and more acceptable answers. According to Pyrrho and his followers, peace of mind (*ataraxia*) is finally attained through the tentative acceptance of received beliefs based on the assumption that no truth is fully verifiable in the final analysis. Paradoxically, if no truth can be entirely confirmed--perhaps with this single exception that none can be confirmed--the qualified tolerance of all supposed truths, including received belief, is entirely justified. Academic skeptics rejected this conformist logic by imposing more stringent demands in the pursuit of truth, first when Arcesilaus insisted upon the necessity of rigorous common sense (*eulogon*), and almost a century later when Carneades added the more definitive task of establishing the probability of supposed truths, for example by employing Aristotle's deductive logic as well as the use of experimentation introduced by Strato.

Skepticism lost its appeal in later centuries. In his first book, *Against the Academics,* St. Augustine sought to refute ancient Greek philosophy precisely because it put too much emphasis on skepticism, and during the Dark and Middle Ages devout Christians across Europe learned to reject doubt when applied to religious belief, as it became a paramount transgression that could lead to the Inquisition. As an intellectual perspective at odds with belief, skepticism itself came to be considered evil, in fact the worst of all sins because it encouraged the rejection of spiritual devotion. However, the pursuit of skepticism recovered during the Renaissance through the application of a kind of Pyrrhonian double negative. So-called fideists led by Pomponazzi, Pascal, and others promoted the assumption that religious doubt can initiate religious conversion based on renewed discovery that God does in fact rule the universe. More specifically, Descartes used skepticism as a heuristic strategy for this purpose through the acceptance of one seemingly irrefutable axiom, "I think, therefore I am," followed by what seemed its inevitable corollary, "If I exist, so therefore does God." Later fideists such as Pico della Mirandola also exercised doubt to confirm religious faith rather than engaging in the empirical pursuit of knowledge as did such scientists and philosophers as Copernicus, Bruno, Bacon, and Gassendi, who renewed reliance on doubt on essentially the same basis as "ancient" Greek philosophers had done many centuries earlier.[1] Today this version of doubt is almost taken for granted as one scientific theory supplants another almost without public notice from one decade to the next. A year or two ago the public was told that maybe a few billion stars occupy our galaxy, this year that it seems more than a billion galaxies occupy the universe in its entirety, and still later that it seems likely enormous ice clouds in outer space might have furnished at least half the world's water supply.[2]

I. PYRRHO (ca. 360-270 BC)

The first major skeptic later than the Sophist movement was Pyrrho (or Pyrrhon) of Elis, who was perhaps a generation younger than Aristotle. Pyrrho introduced to Greek philosophy his version of skepticism based on his personal knowledge of the moral teachings of India's Magi and Gymnosophists he encountered as a foot soldier during Alexander the Great's invasion of Asia. Pyrrho apparently combined his ethical vision acquired in India with the assumptions of Protagoras, which he had learned from his mentor, Anaxarchus, a follower of Democritus who was also associated with Metrodorus of Chios.[3] If knowledge is unavoidably indeterminate, Pyrrho argued, we must cultivate a suspension of judgment (*epoche*) that lets us emphasize *ataraxia* by living in full harmony with the world that surrounds us. Once *epoche* is achieved, *ataraxia* supposedly follows "like its shadow," or, with more poetic flair, "even as a shadow follows its substance."[4]

According to Diogenes Laertius, Pyrrho first acquired a skeptical viewpoint when he became fascinated with the Gymnosophists' suspension of judgment through quietude (*ataraxia*), and detachment from worldly matters (*apragmosyne*)—principles he later cultivated to guarantee freedom from anxiety resulting from the effort to arrive at a viable choice between contradictory theoretical assumptions. There is no truth whatsoever that cannot be refuted by other truths, he claimed, so their equal likelihood lets us abandon the fruitless pursuit of clear-cut final answers. In light of Gymnosophist principles, he argued as an abstract principle, "no single thing is in itself any more this than that." Moreover, he said that nothing truly predominates in the final analysis except the custom and conventions of society.

Pyrrho listed ten so-called *aporia,* or perplexities, that hinder accurate comparisons in a balanced judgment of experience. These can be summarized as follows: (1) the inevitable confusion of pleasure and pain; (2) variant human idiosyncrasies; (3) sensory differences; (4) the impact of aging; (5) different customs, variable laws, myths, and dogmatic assumptions; (6) mixed environmental influences; (7) differences in visual perspective; (8) variation in quantity; (9) the comparative rarity of events; and (10) paired comparisons (right and left, up and down, etc.). Obviously these categories overlap, but whatever their combination, he suggested, they help to identify numerous distractive effects on one's supposedly objective judgment. The later Pyrrhonian skeptic Agrippa proposed further *aporia* that augment Pyrrho's list: (1) excessive contentiousness based on disagreement; (2) incessant elaboration; (3) unnecessary contextual references; (4) the rushed acceptance of hypotheses; and (5) the dependence on related events that supposedly prove each other.

Pyrrho was the first skeptic to give the term *epoche* a central role as the suspension of judgment in philosophical discourse, but it seems he did so for the purpose of activating *ataraxia,* effectively the comfortable abandonment of further inquiry. In philosophical debate *epoche* might now and again be divisive, but its use was preliminary to the final achievement of *ataraxia* akin to the Zen Buddhist concept of *satori* wherein a full "sense of beyond" supplants analytic thought.[5] Pyrrho suggested that an uncompromising commitment to doubt by means of *epoche* discloses the fallibility of all supposed truths, so one is free to assent to any belief one wants since each is just as valid as another. On this basis religion is fully as credible as any other belief system. The syllogistic implication at the root of this certitude was simple. If everything is potentially false, nothing can be proven true, and one's choice in what to believe finally depends on *ataraxia,* the felt comfort level in accepting its validity. One can therefore be relieved of any sense of shame or hypocrisy in accepting received doctrine. No matter how misguided a religion or belief system might seem, it is no more vulnerable to refutation than another, so it is entirely acceptable to go along with shared assumptions that are acceptable to friends, relatives, and fellow citizens.

As explained by Diogenes Laertius, Pyrrho also argued, "there is nothing really existent, but custom and convention govern human action; for no single thing is in itself any more this than that."[6] Therefore, what predominates must be the full and uncompromising acceptance of conventional assumptions. If everybody who matters in one's life worships Zeus, let it be Zeus who supposedly rules--and the same with Osiris, Mithra, Cybele, or any of the other gods. On this basis it is entirely appropriate to be a Buddhist among Buddhists, and so on. The truth effectively consists of whatever shared concept helps to minimize intellectual discomfort. The most important task in life is the cultivation of intellectual repose through compliance with received opinion without any sense of obligation to justify its assumptions.

Pyrrho did not concern himself with the contradiction that received values are too often dogmatic as defined by earlier skeptics. Nor does he seem to have been bothered that one's full commitment to *ataraxia* makes possible the nominal observance of any number of ideologies including atheism, if they are inoffensive to one's neighbors and fellow citizens. Once the use of skepticism confirms that no proof exists one way or the other about God's existence or any other such consideration, one is free to pursue any belief system that seems even remotely credible as long as it is comfortable.

Pyrrho had only one major pupil, Timon, whose version of skepticism placed an emphasis on the rejection of hypotheses in general. A successful author who apparently wrote satires, Timon was loyal to Pyrrho's version of skepticism, if with little to add to Pyrrho's relatively simple argument. Timon spoke favorably of both Democritus and Protagoras as earlier skeptics, but he despised Arcesilaus, the arrogant and excessively argumentative young leader of the competitive school of Academic skeptics, at least partly because of Academic skepticism's emphasis on sustained uncompromising analysis. Unfortunately, Timon seems to have lacked any productive disciples, so Pyrrhonian skepticism fell into decline soon after his death in 230 B.C. and remained dormant throughout the rest of the Hellenistic period. Only once, for example, did Cicero bother to mention Pyrrho by name. Nevertheless, Pyrrho's version of skepticism regained its popularity during Augustus' reign as Rome's first emperor. Just as Academic skepticism had completely supplanted Pyrrhonian skepticism in the second century BC, the Pyrrhonian approach completely reversed this preference, very likely because it was an ideological stance more compatible with the acquiescence to imperial authority. A young skeptic from Alexandria, Aenesidemus (ca. 90-80 BC), once again codified Pyrrho's arguments, and Sextus Empiricus took them into account in his thorough summary of skeptical theory (ca. 200 AD). Diogenes Laertius also offered a relatively balanced assessment of Pyrrho's influence, though he conceded the ethical difficulties implicit in Pyrrho's approach: "He [Pyrrho] denied that anything was honourable or dishonourable, just or unjust. . . . Universally, there is nothing really existent, but custom and convention govern human action."[7]

Possibly a reflection of the revival of Pyrrhonian skepticism, the poet Virgil wrote *The Aeneid* as requested by Augustus in order to provide Rome with an artificial mythology of its own comparable to Homer's heroic vision of the origins of Greece. Significantly, Virgil asked on his deathbed that the text be destroyed, and of course his request was ignored. Like Lucretius, he wrote consummate poetry, but in obvious contrast with Lucretius he also seems to have become dissatisfied with its propagandistic implications along Homeric lines. In effect he had spent too much of his productive career promoting a misguided imperial destiny as later described by Gibbon and many others. His task had been effectively Pyrrhonian in complying with Augustus' request, but by the end of his life he seems to have recognized that there were better and more useful truths to take into account.

II. ARCESILAUS (CA. 316-241 BC)

The origin of the Academic School of skeptics is usually identified with Arcesilaus, who was roughly a generation younger than Pyrrho. After Plato he was the fifth director of what came to be described as the Old Academy, which had been led in sequence by Speusippus, Xenocrates, Polemon, and Crates during the four decades that followed Plato's death. The influence of the Academy had steadily declined until Arcesilaus assumed its leadership in 247, and under his direction the school recovered its popularity as the Second (or Middle) Academy, effectively the successor to Plato's initial Academy but with an ideological stance that emphasized Socrates' assumption that he

knew he didn't know. Like Socrates, Arcesilaus transcribed none of his ideas, so there is no record of his attitude toward Plato's transcendental idealism
beyond his effort to renew Socrates' original intentions of the pursuit of truth
through sustained analysis. Whereas Plato's version of skepticism had discouraged natural philosophy, Arcesilaus restored its original emphasis on
empirical inquiry. He rejected Pyrrho's stress on intellectual comfort as well
as the theory of Stoicism recently founded by Zeno of Citium, which also
featured ethics dependent on the acceptance of received truths. As opposed to
unsubstantiated collective belief, he instead advocated sustained inquiry to
ascertain valid truth with the full expectation that such a task could never be
fully achieved.

Arcesilaus' principal achievement seems to have been in having detached
Pyrrho's concept of *epoche* from his emphasis on the pursuit of *ataraxia*. The
function of *epoche* was no longer as an effective agent of *ataraxia* and
instead became an uncompromising intellectual commitment whose source
of satisfaction was nothing more than the sense of achievement in having
clarified the issue(s) at least to a certain extent. One did not exercise doubt in
order to believe, but in order to have a better idea of the topic. Like Socrates,
Arcesilaus remained aware that he might stumble on valid assumptions now
and again, but always with the realization that he could only be confident of
its validity on a tentative basis.

The difference between Pyrrho and Arcesilaus' respective uses of the
term *epoche* was of fundamental importance. Whereas Pyrrho featured
epoche as a means to the acceptance of ideas and theories that help to produce the experience of *ataraxia*, the Academic version of skepticism promoted by Arcesilaus was more or less in accord with Aristotle's natural
philosophy as well as Strato's reliance on experimentation. Taken to its
extreme, Pyrrho's skepticism was an anti-intellectual stance that supported
quietude and the status quo, while Academic skepticism encouraged the pursuit of science without the imminent prospect of final answers. [8]

But there were also epistemological issues. If no "truth" is totally verifiable, Arcesilaus suggested, it becomes necessary and appropriate to challenge Stoicism's emphasis on ideas that are supposedly "cataleptic" (or *apo-
dictic*) in the sense that they seem to bear a clear and distinct resemblance to
reality. Indeed, too many of such truths turn out to be false. Instead, he
argued, knowledge (*episteme*) and received opinion (*doxa*) can only be integrated when knowledge is accepted on a tentative basis. In the words of
Cicero, it was Arcesilaus' opinion that "nothing is more disgraceful than for
assent and approval to outstrip knowledge and perception." [9] Since all knowledge is susceptible to error, true wisdom benefits from Socrates' example by
granting one's relative ignorance: "And if all things are non-apprehensible, it
will follow, even according to the Stoics, that the wise man suspends judg-

ment [*epichein ton sophon*], for sustained inquiry is essential to wisdom based on attainable knowledge."[10]

Arcesilaus emphasized the value of obvious ideas toward this presumably more substantial objective. Essential to his argument was the provisional acceptance of common sense (*eulogon*), however risky and beset with mistakes, as the best and most pragmatic initial step, if without confirming any kind of final truth. On the other hand, the uncompromising avoidance of empty suppositions is also likely to justify serious inquiry. Does the concept of Zeus seated on a throne, for example, befit common sense? If not, its likelihood can be doubted at least as a temporary supposition.

Arcesilus apparently felt that common sense is in accord with scientific hypotheses that oblige confirmation as first suggested by Plato's surprisingly advanced use of the word: "I don't know yet whether it fulfills the conditions, but I can propose a *hypothesis*"--in other words a tentative explanation that can be submitted to further examination.[11] For Arcesilaus' friend Strato, the task was one in which a theoretical possibility was framed as a hypothesis followed by one or more experiments to determine its validity. As Strato discovered, every experiment sets the stage for others as well, and as often as not the tentative "truths" they confirm can be accepted or rejected on an enlarged interactive basis. Such freedom in the speculative stages of scientific inquiry gives little role to *ataraxia* beyond Archimedes' "eureka" response that can itself lead to further questions.

Frequently overlooked by classical scholars was Arcesilaus' friendship with Strato, which is indicated by Strato's generous final will that Diogenes Laertius quotes in its entirety. A large number of Strato's possessions were bequeathed to Arcesilaus, so it may be assumed that their personal friendship was matched by their theoretical rapport. It requires no ingenuity, for example, to link Arcesilaus' concept of *epoche* with the Stratonician Presumption that the burden of proof is upon both philosophers and scientists. There is no written evidence of this possibility, but Strato's dependence on testing scientific hypotheses bore a strong affinity to Arcesilaus' concept of *epoche* relevant to philosophical discourse. The suspension of judgment Arcesilaus advocated on an intellectual basis was fully in accord with the use of hypotheses in empirical investigations, and his version of *epoche* can be understood as having been intrinsic to Strato's scientific perspective. In reverse, Strato's effort as a scientist confirmed the value of *epoche* relevant to scientific inquiry. As for the issue of religious belief, their shared doubts reinforce the likelihood that Arcesilaus' radical version of skepticism was compatible with Strato's outspoken atheism. In effect one of them did not believe in God, whereas the other believed that God does not exist. In the same fashion they shared comparable versions of disbelief in the sense that Strato's belief that tentative scientific evidence was nothing more than probable truth until proven otherwise was much the same as Arcesilaus' rigorous suspension of doubt about all topics, both scientific and non-scientific, until proven otherwise.

Arcesilaus' version of *epoche* devoid of *ataraxia* was rejected by Aenisidemus and others during the Emperor Augustus' rule, but the concept again came into vogue much later during the Renaissance. Montaigne himself wrote the word *epoche* on the ceiling above his desk as a reminder of its relevance every time he ventured to look upwards. Also, Montaigne's *locus classicus,* "Apology for Raimond Sebond," featured Arcesilaus' sense of the term throughout its text. He was more inspired by Arcesilaus' concept of doubt rather than Pyrrho' thesis. In effect, his persistent inquiry confirmed his basic discomfort with received assumptions.

Arcesilaus' concept of *epoche* also anticipated various theories of uncertainty that have been proposed since the late nineteenth century by scientists and secular philosophers. The first and perhaps most obvious example would be Charles Sanders Peirce's theory of "abduction" in the sense that "hopeful suggestions" can be entertained in pursuit of ideas that do not immediately or fully present themselves. Also in the same vein was John Dewey's thesis of "warranted assertibility."[12] In the same light Husserl's concept of "bracketing" can be identified as a temporary use of *epoche* to disconnect presumably self-evident ideas from fixed assumptions in order to explore their implications in a new and better light.[13] In effect Arcesilaus' version of skepticism continues to thrive one way or another. Having played a dominant role for many decades during the mid-Hellenistic period, his perspective was later recovered by both science and natural philosophy and remains useful even today.

III. CARNEADES (214-128 BC)

Born at Cyrene in Libya, Carneades traveled to Athens early in life and briefly pursued Stoic philosophy before turning to skepticism. As the head of the Third (or New) Academy, he became the dominant skeptic of the second century BC as well as the fourth director of the Academy in succession after Arcesilaus. Carneades was even more famous than Arcesilaus as a brilliant teacher and consummate polemicist able and willing to debate the merits of any issue. Probably inspired by Strato's example, his outspoken atheistic viewpoint featured the necessary role of probability (*pithanon*) in drawing such a conclusion, a stance that influenced three generations of disciples that included Clitomachus, Philo of Larissa, and finally even Cicero. On his single visit to Rome, Carneades achieved notoriety as a skeptic by giving a public lecture in which he maintained with persuasiveness that those who inflict injustice suffer more than their victims. On the very next day, however, he gave a second lecture in which he argued exactly the opposite position with equal conviction. His purpose was to demonstrate that credible truths can too often be asserted to support contradictory arguments, and more important, he sought to demonstrate the ultimate uncertainty of all such arguments. He continued to emphasize this principle throughout his career, but it was counterproductive at the time, at least in this instance. Shocked by his audacity, Cato the Elder ordered his permanent expulsion from Rome to prevent him from contaminating the morals of its youth. Apparently Carneades never returned.

Like both Socrates and Arcesilaus, Carneades did not transcribe his ideas. Instead, he depended on a scribe--Clitomachus, a disciple from Carthage--to record his dialogues so that he could declare his arguments with relative freedom. It was later estimated that Clitomachus used more than 400 scrolls to contain Carneades' lectures, and according to Diogenes Laertius, without exception he was more productive than all ancient authors. As perhaps to be expected, Clitomachus succeeded Carneades upon his death as the director and principal theoretician of the Third Academy. Unfortunately, however, none of Clitomachus' transcriptions survived, so there is little evidence to document Carneades' pivotal role in the history of skeptical philosophy beyond the historic assessment of Diogenes Laertius, Cicero, and Sextus Empiricus.

Cicero's perspective is particularly useful in the analysis of Carneades, since two of Clitomachus' disciples, Philo and Antiochus, later the directors of the so-called Fourth and Fifth Academies, served as Cicero's teachers at different stages of his youth. Also, Cicero seems to have been familiar with Clitomachus' transcriptions when he wrote *De Natura Deorum* and *Academica*. However, it seems the only portions deleted from Cicero's two remarkable books were those pertaining to Carneades' views. Very likely these passages were eliminated by later scribes in order to preserve Cicero's texts from total destruction. For the most part, today's readers reassemble Carneades' assumptions as well as possible from the fourth portion of *Academica*, in which Cicero seems to have used the persona of Cotta to declare Carneades' ideas without specifically identifying him as their original source.

More useful, however, in reconstructing Carneades' perspective is the summary description by Sextus Empiricus, a Greek philosophical historian who lived two centuries after Cicero. In *Against the Logicians*, Sextus explained with thoroughness Carneades' pursuit of credible truth based on "tested presentations," or accurate "perceived objects" in light of one's ability to grasp their manifestation. Of course any number of suppositions can be recognized as possible truths, but these should be fully conceded if and to what extent they fall short of the whole truth. [14]

At the core of Carneades' skeptical position was an implied epistemology that there is no fully reliable "criterion" (or principle of confirmation) to determine any supposed truth, since each and every mental "presentation" manifests both what it perceives and its own intrinsic limitations as an act of mental perception. Truths do exist, Carneades conceded, but unavoidable mental limitations diminish accuracy except when judged as a matter of probability. The validity of any particular idea turns out to be nothing more than its probable truth (*pithanon*), for we lack the means to achieve any kind of finality in our thinking. Carneades agreed with Protagoras' original assumption that each and every presumed truth can and should be debated on both sides (*in utramque partem*) in order to determine its relative likelihood. Supportive evidence was essential, but the effective rejection of contrary evidence was also needed toward the tentative acceptance as a credible answer. Carneades was also willing to accept Arceilaus' loose concept of reasonableness (*eulogon*) at a preliminary level of inquiry, but he advocated the need for further substantiation at more advanced levels based on painstaking investigation, especially regarding such controversial topics as the existence of one or more gods.

Some modern scholars have sought to minimize the importance of Carneades' theory of probability by treating it as nothing more than a matter of credibility (or *pithanon*) as already explained by Plato and Aristotle, both of whom at least mentioned the need for confirmation based on relevant information. Plato suggested the need for probability in his dialogues *Theatetus* and *Timaeus*, in which he seems to have anticipated Carneades' perspective by remarking, "We may venture to assert that what has been said by us is probable, and will be rendered more probable by investigation."[15] Aristotle also anticipated Carneades' effort by granting probability full status on a scientific basis, but he sought to limit science to a relatively simple determination of "that which is always or . . . that which is for the most part." In *Prior Analytics*, he went so far as to define probability as a "reputable proposition" based on acceptable (or "reputable") knowledge of some event by observers: "What men know to happen or not to happen, to be or not to be, for the most part thus and thus, is a probability."[16] Otherwise Aristotle limited his analysis to "hard" evidence and seems to have restricted the question of probability to what might have seemed relatively soft issues such as he addressed in *Rhetoric* and *Poetics*. Both Plato and Aristotle granted probability a role in their analysis, but with a relatively limited function—almost as an afterthought. In contrast, Carneades emphasized its central importance deserving of methodological confirmation at every stage of analysis. Doubt was no longer an afterthought but in fact a primary feature integral to serious inquiry. Carneades agreed with Arcesilaus in accepting the importance of common sense pertaining to most information, but he also insisted truths be ascertained at three levels of determination: (1) probable in the broadest sense of the word; (2) "irreversible" in the sense that they cannot be disprov-

en by contrary evidence; and (3) confirmation "from all sides," by implication including both logical analysis and scientific verification.[17]

The primary advantage of Carneades' threefold hierarchy was that it necessitated the full confirmation of ideas that might otherwise seem dubious
or even wrong. For just as seemingly wrong ideas often may turn out to be
valid, numerous "right" ideas are just as likely to be wrong.

This possibility had been implicit in Arcesilaus' notion of common sense
(*eulogon*), but Carneades even further liberated speculative inquiry from
orthodox assumptions by upgrading what seemed nothing more than argumentative rigor to systematic application. No longer was the sage (or "wise
man") fettered by received truisms. Carneades addressed this necessity with
unusual vigor, most notably pertaining to religious belief, which he felt
lacked sufficient confirmation to justify it. In retrospect it was this issue that
established his notoriety in the record of ancient conceptual history available
to modern readers. Such figures as Democritus and Aristotle had tested limits, but Carneades actually declared his atheism.

Effectively buried in three of his four published volumes, Sextus Empiricus both summarizes and illustrates Carneades' defense of atheism through
his use of logic to stretch the concepts underlying religious belief to total
absurdity. In *Outlines of Pyrrhonism,* he devotes four pages to a brief explanation of Carneades' version of atheism, which is dependent on the assumption that "the existence of God is not pre-evident." He expresses his agreement with Arcesilaus on what might seem a tentative basis, "we cannot
apprehend whether God exists," but the implication is clear that such a possibility is not likely.[18] He maintains, for example, that a truly omniscient and
omnipotent God able to anticipate the future inclusive of human behavior
should have no difficulty in preventing evil and/or misfortune. If such a
presumably sympathetic deity cannot perform this simple task, Carneades
insists, he necessarily lacks (a) omnipotence, (b) omniscience, or (c) both,
thus justifying doubts about his benevolence as well as his supreme authority. As summarized by Sextus Empiricus:

> But if he [God] had forethought for all, there would have been nothing bad and
> no badness in the world; yet all things, they say, are full of badness; hence it
> shall not be said that God forethinks all things. . . . And if, again, he has the
> power but not the will to have forethought for all, he will be held to be
> malignant; while if he has neither the will nor the power, he is both malignant
> and weak—an impious thing to say about God. . . . Therefore God has no
> forethought for the things in the universe. . . . So for these reasons we cannot
> apprehend whether God exists.[19]

In other words, God can be either omniscient or omnipotent, but can't play
both roles at the same time if bad things happen, but if bad things do happen,
as seems to be true, God necessarily violates his own rules. Moreover, "If he

[God] has the will but not the power, he is less strong than the cause which renders him unable to forethink." Those who persist in affirming God's positive influence despite this simple logic become themselves guilty of impiety one way or another. Sextus Empiricus does not bother to identify the author of this obvious paradox; its obvious antithetical emphasis suggests the likelihood of Carneades' authorship, especially in light of his several longer definitions of God elsewhere in Sextus Empiricus' text.

In his long segment, "Do Gods Exist," in the third volume, *Against the Physicists,* Sextus Empiricus offers several more elaborate syllogistic arguments to the same effect and once again the unidentified author could only have been Carneades, who seems to have frequently exercised his skill in formulating elongated syllogistic deductions called *sorites*: the demonstration of X, therefore Y, therefore Z, etc. Relevant to the identification of God(s), his argument began with the absurdity of X followed by the worse absurdity of Y, the bizarre absurdity of Z, etc. The first of these elongated atheistic deductions recorded in its entirety by Sextus Empiricus is quoted as follows:

> Again, if the Divine exists, it is either a body or incorporeal. But it will not be incorporeal for the reasons we have already stated [since the incorporeal is inanimate and insensitive and incapable of any action]. And if it is a body, it is either a compound of the simple elements or a simple and elemental body. And if it is a compound, it is perishable; for everything which is constructed by the union of things must necessarily dissolve and perish. And if it is a simple body, it is either fire or air or water or earth. But whichever of these it is, it is without soul or reason, which is absurd. If, then, God is neither a compound nor a simple body, and besides these there is no other alternative, one must declare that God is nothing. [20]

As an enlargement of *sorites* that can be quoted in this context (roughly half his longest example), Carneades is again quoted by Sextus Empiricus with a seemingly endless variety of extravagant comparisons to the effect that the usual traits attributed to God possess sufficient human resemblance not to be immortal, but that the elimination of such traits reduces God's identity to virtual non-existence. The second half of another of Carneades' elongated logical definitions of God can also be quoted here to confirm his unusual logical capabilities:

> But if God has not art, he will not have the art of living; and if so, neither will he have virtue. But if God has not virtue, he is non-existent—And again: God being rational, if he does not possess virtue, he certainly possesses its opposite, vice: but he does not possess its opposite, vice: therefore God possesses art, and there is something non-evident to God. From which it follows that he is perishable, as we argued before. But he is not perishable; therefore he does not exist. [21]

In summary, a perfect God can neither be speechless nor gifted with speech, artistic nor lacking in art, virtuous but not virtuous, etc. and therefore such a being is impossible. As explained by Carneades at the simplest level, "If, then, God is neither a compound nor a simple body, and besides these there is no other alternative, one must declare that God is nothing." Moreover, Carneades argues almost as an afterthought, there are too many gods to choose from. If Zeus is a god, so is Poseidon, but also countless minor deities can be added such as a sun God, a god for each month, for dawn, for the evening, and even worthless Phobos, "the god who shares in beauty least of all." Perhaps the better and more credible choice is no god at all.

In retrospect Carneades' theoretical dependence on the concept of probability seems to have had more influence on modern scientific methodology than the issue of atheism. Even in its earliest stage, well before its modern statistical application, its application seems to have been implicit Strato's empirical investigation as well as Arcesilaus' generalized principle of inductive thoroughness. Moreover, their shared perspective very likely afforded in combination what might be described as an overlooked but essential missing link between Aristotelian science and the inception of modern science as explained by Francis Bacon in his famous Preface to *Novum Organum*. Today they remain the most notorious atheists in ancient history—too aggressive in their commitment to disbelief to be identified by name or simply mentioned to be otherwise ignored. As perhaps to be expected, the memory of all three—Strato and Carneades as well as Arcesilaus—has continued to remain "untouched" well beyond the lifetime of Bacon. Yet they played a major role in the invention of inductive research.

Chapter Eight

Cicero (106-43 B.C.)

Cicero played a major role in the history of Rome. His speeches were re-markable, and as many as 800 of his letters have survived to document Roman civilization at the time. His so-called "Ciceronian" prose style be-came a unique standard of excellence, and he knew as much as any of his contemporaries about ancient philosophy. Moreover, he played a dominant role in the Roman Senate and he opposed Caesar's effort to become the emperor of Rome. The two knew each other well—Caesar as a successful general with ambitions of imperial authority and Cicero as an outstanding orator, statesman, and scholar, arguably the most eminent Roman citizen at the time. The two differed, however, on whether Rome would become an empire led by Caesar or remain a republic under rule of the Senate led by Cicero. Whether justified or not, Cicero was suspected of having supported Caesar's assassination to thwart the conversion of the republic into an em-pire. Aware of probable retaliation by Caesar's former lieutenant, Mark An-tony and his allies, Cicero withdrew from politics to write on a wide variety of fields, including Greek philosophy. As anticipated, he was murdered with-in two years, decapitated, and his skull and hands were sent as trophies to Mark Antony to be mutilated before a supportive crowd.

Fortunately, most of Cicero's writings escaped censorship because of his pivotal role in Roman history but also because of their excellence. As a result, his unique knowledge of ancient philosophy was preserved and helped to document its important but declining role at the time. Resulting from the effort to recover his writings by Petrarch, many centuries later his texts also helped to usher in the Renaissance. Others identified as philosophes, joined in the task, and soon their effort widened to include the recovery of texts by other classical authors, many of whom were all but forgotten. Whereas Cice-ro can be said to have failed in his attempt to preserve the Roman Republic, his writings seem to have become the single most important catalyst for the inception of the Renaissance fifteen centuries later.

Cicero was well qualified to explain Greek philosophy to his contemporaries in Rome. He had been taught Carneades' Academic skepticism as interpreted by Clitomachus. As disciples of Clitomachus, his tutors Philo and Antiochus were the leaders of the Fourth and Fifth Academies that pursued a synthesis with Platonism and Stoicism probably to soften Carneades' radical assumptions. In his mid-teens Cicero had also been a disciple of both the Stoic philosopher Diodorus and the Epicurean philosopher Phaedrus. Moreover, he was a close friend and former student of Posidonius, the eminent scientist who was then leader of the Stoic movement. And of course his editorial assistance to Lucretius in the composition of *De Rerum Natura* must have reinforced his familiarity with Epicurean philosophy. His remark in one of his letters regarding Lucretius' text, "many brilliant passages of genius," suggests his likely approval of the text's atheistic assumptions.[1]

Two of Cicero's final books, *Academica* and *De Natura Deorum,* were especially important in treating the issues of skepticism and natural philosophy as opposed to the existence of gods. *Academica* provided a sophisticated historical analysis of Academic skepticism. In turn, *De Natura Deorum* provided a hypothetical debate about religion and the existence of gods from the perspectives of the principal philosophical schools of the time as represented by a Stoic, an Epicurean, and an Academic skeptic. Cicero's treatment of philosophical issues was less persuasive than Plato's earlier debates, but he gave all the participants better opportunity to defend their assumptions.

I. *ACADEMICA*

Academica provides the single ancient text that explains in depth the principal issues of late Hellenistic skepticism. In the format of a debate, its text surveys a broad variety of theories and assumptions except for those of Carneades, whose theoretical views were later deleted from Cicero's manuscripts. Of the two elongated segments that survived, the second half of the first segment remains intact, as does the initial quarter of the second segment. The large gap between them is easily overlooked by modern readers, but this is at the cost of Cicero's full explanation of Carneades' version of atheism. The modern reader's knowledge of Carneade's arguments is thus limited almost exclusively to the much later summary by Sextus Empiricus.

Part I of *Academica* begins with a comparison between Plato and Aristotle by Varro, a friend and prestigious scholar whom Cicero conceded might be at least as informed as himself. In the context of the dialogue, Varro summarizes the ideas of Antiochus, Cicero's second tutor in Academic skepticism, but soon shifts to consider issues beyond the received assumptions of

Academic skepticism. He explains, for example, that Socrates' insistence that he knew he didn't know had inspired both Plato's sustained quest for transcendent truths and Aristotle's alternative quest for scientific truths through the systematic investigation of the physical universe based on empirical evidence. According to Varro, all philosophers at the time who came afterwards took Socrates' simple paradox into account one way or another, including both Arcesilaus and Carneades in their emphasis on common sense and probability. On the other hand, Varro concedes Aristotle's "copiousness of intellect" as well as his supposed invention of what amounted to a fifth element beyond earth, air, water, and fire-- a material "entirely formless and devoid of all quality."[2] He undoubtedly refers to the general concept of matter as already suggested by Anaximander and others preceding Aristotle. Varro further explains that the response of both Arcesilaus and Carneades to Socrates' paradox was simply to consider all supposed "truths" on a tentative basis by emphasizing the principle of *epoche* as suspended judgment. If no truth could be fully known, Varro asserts, let that be the final truth concerning all issues, by implication including the possible existence of gods, not that he specifically mentions such a possibility.

Upon the completion of Varro's elongated explanation, Cicero suggests the role of Carneades, and here, as earlier mentioned, the text suddenly terminates with the tantalizing words "incredible facility," very likely intended to describe Carneades' oratorical skills. Discussion resumes with Lucullus (a skeptic in Philo's school of Academic skepticism), explaining the issue of probability and the benefits of arguing on both sides of any question on all matters, including religious belief.[3] Lucullus goes on to summarize the historic importance of Carneades without referring to his ideas, and he rejects unnamed critics of Carneades' radical negativism as "thinkers who sanctioned nothing as proved."[4] Still later, however, he concedes that Carneades himself now and again softened his relentless stance hostile to religious belief as an invalid hypothesis.

Lucullus also criticizes Philo for his continuing arch-skeptical stance in having shared the conviction of Carneades that in the final analysis nothing can be known."[5] Lucullus himself asserts the effectiveness of reason itself as an appropriate alternative to arch-skepticism since it depends on the pursuit of research as a "process of reasoning that leads from things perceived to something not previously perceived.'[6] It is difficult to disagree with this argument. However, unexamined assent has been almost universally enforced in all societies and among all religions. As a result skepticism's negative methodology in addition to Carneades' atheistic certitude is discouraged and even prohibited in too many societies, and perhaps at too great a cost. What ancient skeptics provided for the first time was sufficient negation to make possible the valid pursuit of religious doubt despite continuing enforcement of shared beliefs among the population at large.

Lucullus draws his argument to a close with a brief discussion of Arcesilaus' concept of *epoche* on the assumption that whatever cannot be fully perceived cannot be granted full assent. On this basis Lucullus concludes that wisdom consists of withholding assent from anything either false or unknown. What is crucial, he argues, is to be guided by reason rather than received opinion. Then again, as insisted by Antiochus, also a former tutor of Cicero, Lucullus concedes that excessive skepticism can too easily become oppressive by preventing not only thought but all physical activity.[7] Even Carneades was said to have broken this stricture by now and again conceding, "that the wise man will occasionally hold an opinion, that is, commit an error."[8] In effect, he had sometimes compromised his systematic effort to reject all presumed truths that turned out not to be true.

Cicero devotes most of the second half of *Academica* to an extended explanation of his own theory of skepticism and his response to alternative sources. He qualifies his acceptance of Carneades' theory of probability, for example by declaring that his own interest in skepticism has not been combative. On the other hand, he asserts that he continues to be "fired up with zeal for the discovery of the truth," as Augustine much later conceded in his critique of Cicero in both *Against the Academics* and his *Confessions*. Cicero insists that it is entirely honorable to hold valid assumptions," and he holds the complementary opinion that it is even disgraceful to accept falsehoods as the truth. The chief virtue of the truly wise man, he suggests, is his ability to avoid being misguided and susceptible to deception." Cicero accordingly suggests the advantage of agnosticism by declaring that the "mere habit of assenting" is necessarily at risk, and to such an extent that it is preferable that "all assent be withheld." Cicero continues that nothing can be entirely perceived, and that it is precisely this limitation on which "all the controversy turns."[9] He rejects Pyrrho's concept that all truth is ultimately indeterminate, and instead proposes that truth does exist but can only be known indirectly and therefore on a tentative basis. He also cites Carneades distinction that many falsehoods might seem probable, but nothing truly false can be perceived and known. As a result, he suggests, the philosopher's task is to withhold assent as obliged by the principle of *epoche*, but also to be guided by the aspect of probability in finally granting qualified assent.[10] By implication he suggests that the god concept is more dependent on this necessity than any other concept.

As emphasized by both Arcesilaus and Carneades, Cicero concedes that doubt plays an important role in serious analysis rather than outright denial, and that sufficient doubt ultimately justifies what might be described as tentative denial. Cicero also explores in depth the necessity of withholding assent simply in order to weigh the merits of alternative theories as Strato recommended. Like others before him, he emphasizes the importance of arguing on both sides to arrive at the nearest approximation to the truth.[11]

Moreover, since the absolute truth is all but impossible to discern, he accepts the necessity that philosophers should refine the comparison of alternative "truths" based on what seems their likelihood. "The wise man," he argues in full accord with Carneades, will take into account whatever he encounters that seems probable if nothing presents itself contrary to that probability.[12] On this basis Cicero acknowledges the universal relevance of probability pertaining to every aspect of human experience as opposed to the act of assent dependent on "mere opinion and hasty thinking."[13]

Cicero summarizes almost all of the cosmic assumptions by early Greek philosophers through Plato and Aristotle to determine their relative validity as explanations of the universe. Of particular interest are those he lists as having proposed an eternal history of the universe devoid of initial creation. He specifically includes Anaximander and Xenophanes as well as Melissus and Aristotle. In particular he tells of Melissus' description of an infinite and unchangeable universe and of Aristotle's similar concept of a world that never had a beginning and would never "perish in dissolution."[14] Cicero also praises Strato's atheism in having dispensed with the notion of divine origin, instead confining his investigation to all existence that can be traced to natural causes. However, he is reluctant to accept Strato's radical hypothesis that existence in its entirety has been exclusively a product of the natural forces of gravitation and motion--an assumption anticipated by Aristotle's binarism of matter and motion that was obviously acceptable to Strato. There can be no doubt, however, that Cicero remains interested in Strato's theory, and to the extent that he concedes his inability to make a choice among credible alternatives.[15] Today Strato seems to have been far closer to the truth than Cicero had been willing to accept.

Academica ends on an ambivalent note. Cicero pays his obligatory respects to Rome's pagan gods and goddesses, but he also makes it plain that he remains an agnostic, if unwilling to make the final inductive leap by abandoning the concept of an afterlife and the benevolent authority of god(s). In retrospect, his choice seems to have been of unusual historic importance. He inspired St. Augustine's choice to cultivate unexamined faith as explained in the last paragraph of his first book, *Against the Academics*, and much later, he inspired Petrarch's efforts to recover Cicero's writings, which proved essential to the beginning of the Renaissance. Copernicus' heliocentric theory can also be traced to *Academica.* According to his Introduction to *On the Revolutions of the Heavenly Spheres,* Copernicus first encountered the concept of heliocentric motion in a copy of *Academica* that told of the ancient astronomer Hicetas's astronomical proposal to this effect.[16] Copernicus' later mathematical calculations were by general consensus the first major scientific breakthrough linked with the Renaissance. In effect, amazingly, the two principal figures responsible for this grand collective achievement— Petrarch and Copernicus—were inspired by Cicero, but so too was St. Au-

gustine's conversion to Christianity as a defiant response to Cicero's defense
of skepticism—effectively his own choice based on the comparison of prob-
abilities.

II. *ON THE NATURE OF THE GODS*

As the second of Cicero's two volumes relevant to the issue of disbelief, *The
Nature of the Gods* [*De Natura Deorum*] is supposedly limited in particular
to the validity of the god concept. At the very beginning, Cicero indicates
that he has already published *Academica* to examine the broad consideration
of "withholding assent," and that his specific purpose in this text is to explore
the possible existence of one or more gods as explained by contemporary
philosophers.[17] To suggest the potential difficulty in undertaking this task, he
asserts that there is such a wide range of beliefs about their existence that it is
difficult to arrive at a coherent final judgment. In order to cope with this task,
he explains that his organization of *De Natura Deorum* involves a tripartite
comparison of attitudes toward religious belief among the three most popular
philosophies in currency at the time—Epicureanism as explained by Velleius, Stoicism as explained by Balbus, and Academic skepticism as explained by Cotta, based on the teachings of Carneades interpreted by both
Philo and Antiochus. For Epicureanism, Cicero combines the perspective of
Zeno of Sidon with his friend Phaedrus, the author of *On Gods* (*Peri theon*).
For Stoicism he combines the perspectives of his personal friends Diodotus
and Posidonius. And finally, for skepticism he resorts to Cotta to elucidate
Philo and Antiochus' explanations of Carneades.[18]

Cicero divides theories that support the god concept into two categories--
those with deities totally indifferent to human experience and those with
intrusive gods who have created mankind as a species to be "controlled and
kept in motion."[19] As explained by Cicero, this difference has important
implications for the practice of religious belief, since the abandonment of this
practice may be at too great a cost, for individual integrity ultimately depends
on one's ability and confidence in making what seems a valid choice. This
principle, he suggests, applies to both the individual and society as a whole.
For this reason he praises the useful contribution of philosophers such as
Plato and Zeno, who believed "the whole world is ruled and governed by
divine intelligence and reason," as opposed to Carneades, who "contro-
verted" this orthodox perspective at great length.[20] He and his followers
might promote their seemingly valid theories with vigor and conviction, but
others less hostile to the god concept to make valid arguments that also
deserved consideration.

Two of the three participants, Velleius and Balbus, respond by suggesting
their support of religious belief to a certain extent, but also their willingness

to argue their opinions in the spirit of skepticism. The third, Cotta, concedes his recent temptation to consider the possible existence of gods, but insists that this is something that has never been proven. Cicero then mentions the outright disbelief of Diagoras of Melos and Theodorus of Cyrene as well as such figures as Strato and Carneades, if without identifying them by name. However, he also mentions "other philosophers . . . of eminence and note have proposed that a more sophisticated religion can be adopted based on the supposition that the world is ruled by "divine intelligence and reason." Thus, he proposes that it seems entirely possible that gods do "watch over the life of men," as perhaps suggested by the religious assumptions of Anaxagoras, Plato, Zeno, Chrysippus, and later Stoics. Cicero concludes by proposing that active dialogue—effectively a sequence of elongated statements--seems an appropriate means to explore and compare these possibilities. Cicero suggests that there is finally just one answer—either affirmative or negative— pertaining to God's existence, and that Carneades' willingness to declare his atheism had been based on evidence available at the time but that a new and more advanced perspective might have changed his mind. Cicero seems to be sympathetic with Antiochus's effort to soften skepticism but unable to ignore the earlier and more stringent skepticism of Carneades. The new and more advanced perspective he mentions probably referred to a recent effort of Stoic philosophers to obtain a synthesis between some of Aristotle's assumptions and an updated version of Platonism. Once debate resumes, however, Carneades is all but ignored, and it seems he has been quoted primarily to initiate the exchange.

The sequence of books in *De Natura Deorum* that follows is key to understanding it. Book I consists of two halves with a ten-page introduction plus Velleius' initial summary of Epicurean theory (sections 18 to 56), answered by Cotta's prolonged critique in light of skeptical assumptions (sections 57 to 124). In Book II, Balbus once again suggests the possibility of a viable synthesis of Stoicism and Aristotelian scientific findings, and Book III brings the exchange to a close with Cotta's skeptical arguments that reject the concept of religion based on ethical issues, if nothing else. It should be mentioned that Cicero grants Cotta as much space in Book I to attack Velleius as he has given Velleius' argument plus the introduction. Altogether Cotta and Balbus are allotted equal participation overall, each of them roughly four times as much as Velleius receives. Moreover, Veilleius' presentation is mostly limited to the relatively uncomplicated task of summarizing the religious implications of ancient Greek philosophers up to and including Plato. As a result, the Epicurean perspective receives far less attention than the others, suggesting that Cicero's principal effort is to contrast Carneades' version of Academic skepticism as explained by Cotta with Balbus' synthesis of Aristotelian science with Stoicism and Platonism. In fact such a combination suggests the earlier effort by Antiochus, a director of the so-called fifth academy as well as one of Cicero's instructors in skepticism.

The exchange begins in Book I with Velleius' historic summary of Greek philosophy in which he attributes religious views to pre-Socratic philosophers that are slightly different from earlier descriptions by Aristotle and others. For example, Velleius indicates that Thales had proposed that god consists of mind that has molded everything from water, and that Anaximenes had described the air as god in incessant motion. He also indicates that Anaxagoras first proposed that an infinite mind had designed and perfected the order of the universe, that Pythagoras first suggested that the entire universe consists of a soul of which our souls are but fragments, and that Parmenides identified God as a circle of glowing lights across the sky. Veillius also criticizes Empedocles for his religious naiveté, Protagoras for his lack of clarity, Plato for his concept of God's divine incorporeal existence, and Aristotle for various Platonic inconsistencies in his early but now lost essay, "Philosophy," whose arguments were entirely abandoned in his later writings. On the other hand, Velleius praises Democritus in having disentangled his theory from a "maze of errors" by proposing a "repudiation of deity so absolute as to leave no conception of a divine being remaining!"[21] He also mentions the contributions of such secondary figures as Antisthenes, Speusippus, Xenocrates, Heraclides of Pontus, Zeno, Aristo, Cleanthes, Persaeus, and Chrysippus.

With less justification, he dismisses Strato, Epicurus' contemporary, as a philosopher unworthy of serious consideration. He expresses his willingness to accept Strato's atheism but not his indifference to human experience: "In his [Strato's] view the sole repository of divine power is nature, which contains in itself the causes of birth, growth, and decay, but is entirely devoid of sensation and of form."[22] He also warns against "the insane mythology of Egypt" as well as the countless popular beliefs at the time that were typified by inconsistencies resulting from ignorance.[23] On the other hand, he reiterates his full support for Epicurus' assumption that the gods exist because nature itself has imprinted their concept on the minds of all mankind. In other words, if mankind's religious belief is necessarily almost universal, it must be conceded that the gods do in fact probably exist.

Next to speak is Cotta, and in the second half of Book I he rejects Velleius' assumptions, many of which seem to deviate from Epicurean doctrine as explained by both Epicurus and Lucretius. As an Academic skeptic Cotta confesses that he still believes in the gods despite his skepticism, but he rejects the argument that the world's entire population throughout history has believed in gods, since many ancient societies did not hold such beliefs, nor did the assortment of ancient Greek atheists and skeptics whose identities were common knowledge. Democritus himself, Cotta insists, had "no fixed attitude toward the existence of the gods."[24] He also challenges the theory of atomism as an eternal multiplicity of tiny particles suspended in a void that repeatedly swerve and collide with each other.[25] How, he asks, can such a realm be linked with the authority of godhead? In his opinion these and comparable suppositions suggest a lack of education on the part of Epicurus, whose philosophy did not display any trace whatsoever of influence by Plato's Academy, Aristotle's Lyceum, or even ordinary schools[26] Aside from having heard a few lectures by Nausiphanes, a follower of Democritus, Cotta argues, Epicurus' knowledge of philosophy was sparse, and his chronic disrespect of other philosophers was inexcusable.[27]

Moreover, Cotta explains, the gods suggested by Epicurus were "shadow deities," nothing more than the "counterfeit of substance."[28] He also expresses his astonishment that the theory of atomism is considered an adequate explanation of human existence in the form of gods.[29] Then again, he asks why do gods possess hands and feet if they don't really need them? He declares that it is absurd to believe in an optimistic God entirely occupied for all eternity in reflecting "What a good time I am having! How happy I am!"[30]

In the final analysis, Cotta declares, the whole purpose of religion is to guarantee loyal citizens: " . . . the entire notion of the immortal gods is a fiction invented by wise men in the interest of the state." He explains that this pragmatic intention, however beneficial it might seem at times, is finally destructive of religion as a supposedly transcendent experience. Cotta thereupon reminds Velleius, that as Posidonius has suggested in his earlier book with the same title, *De Natura Deorum,* that Epicurus did not really believe in the gods, and that he praised the immortal gods only to avoid public hostility. In his opinion, Epicurus was fully aware that the God concept is an impossibility, so he abolished them, though professedly retaining them.[31]

Third in sequence, Balbus is granted all of Book II for expounding a unique synthesis between Skepticism and Stoicism, and by implication, between Platonic metaphysics and scientific inquiry as promoted by Aristotle. Balbus indicates that he will only have time to discuss two basic issues, the proof of gods' existence or lack thereof, and the explanation of their nature. He begins by quoting Chrysippus, the most prolific of the early Stoic philosophers, to the effect that the dominant and final authority in the universe beyond human capability necessarily depends on the existence of one or more gods. He summarizes this more or less Platonic assumption in an eloquent passage that features the need for transcendent reason, whatever it consists of, that can be identified as superior ability usually identified with one or more gods. [32] If human intelligence, the most advanced achievement of the universe, is incapable of having created the universe and then having ruled it, a bigger and more dominant authority must fulfill this need. Whatever god consists of, he is to be identified with this enlarged authority. On the other hand, Balbus suggests, the difficulty with stoicism is that it can be used to justify the worship of any number of natural forces presumably superior to

human reason. With this reasoning the sun, fire, liquidity, can all be worshipped. Moreover, as earlier suggested by the Stoic philosopher Chrysippus,
polytheism and pantheism also become possible.

Balbus next proposes a pantheistic argument that anticipates Spinoza's
thesis that the entire universe may be considered a god. He also praises
design as the source of regular and rhythmical motion in the universe, and
then praises chance as well, though it seems antithetical to design. Finally he
declares the importance of Aristotle's emphasis on the "motion of all living
bodies" as the result of nature, force, or will, and declares that the physical
world is "necessarily the most excellent of all things . . . itself a living being
and a god.[33] Finally Balbus advocates the possibility of obtaining a synthesis
between Plato and Aristotle by treating science as justification for Platonic
beauty, ultimately suggesting Pythagoras' early concept of spherical perfection. [34] After an extended discussion of cosmic phenomena such as the sun,
moon, and sky as astronomical bodies of absolute regularity, Balbus shifts to
the perspective of Zeno, the founder of Stoicism who was willing to accept
Heraclitus' insistence on the special role of fire. This too, Balbus insists, is
indicative of God's foresight in planning the universe in every detail. Godhood can therefore be explained to manifest three principles . . . first, struc-
tures toward better survival as recommended by Zeno; second genuine com-
pleteness as demonstrated by Aristotelian science, and third, and most of all,
consummate beauty as suggested by Plato.[35] Balbus goes on to describe more
than a dozen classical gods and goddesses as credible deities, and then differ-
entiates religion from superstition based on appropriate levels of worship. He
also offers a proof of God's existence that anticipates St. Anselm's ontological argument by conceding nature's status as a separate realm somewhat
independent of the gods. If we fully accept divine intelligence, he concludes,
we must also concede the necessity of divine providence. Moreover, if god
knows all, he is presumably generous as well. Balbus also asserts that the
gods are comparable to humanity in their possession of reason, that both have
the same concept of truth, and that both have the same standard in enjoining
what is right and wrong. The logic seems plain that if mankind possesses
intelligence, faith, virtue and concord, these virtues could only have de-
scended from the powers above. [36]

Balbus attributes to supernatural power the grand design of the universe
as an enormous cosmic cycle that somehow combines Aristotelian cosmology with the pre-Socratic paradigm advocated by Empedocles with earth turning into water, water into air, air into aether, and finally with the process
somehow reversed. To this extent Balbus is willing to concede that nature
governs the world.[37] However, he also concedes the contradictory possibility
that if nature exceeds art, and if art is entirely governed by reason, nature
itself cannot be considered to lack reason."[38] Balbus goes on to praise the
principle of gravity—the distribution of weight as defined by Aristotle--as

the ultimate source of beauty. As already suggested by Strato and Archimedes, he goes on to maintain that weight is more credible as a unifying principle than the haphazard collision of atomic particles, though he seems to have been unable to recognize that the two might somehow coexist. He also concurs with Aristotle in describing the earth as a sphere produced by weight and bedecked with water and a plenitude of vegetation.[39] For a full page he enthusiastically praises the spherical explanation of the earth. In conclusion, he anticipates the common religious defense against post-Copernican secularism: "No one thinking of the earth in its entirety can doubt the divine reason."[40] Such a glorious world could not happen all by itself. Obviously, it needs a transcendent helping hand.

Without mentioning Lucretius' *De Rerum Natura*, which had been published just a few years earlier, Balbus concedes the possibility that the earth might eventually come to an end in an enormous fiery cataclysm that destroys all life, setting the stage for new worlds also under the cyclical guidance of gods. [41] Without suggesting the involvement of one or more gods, Balbus proposes the ultimate cataclysmic destiny of the universe when it completes its cycle of existence comparable to the cycle of life. Lucretius' cataclysmic vision is suggested, if without any reference to Lucretius himself.

Balbus concludes his argument with the thesis "that the world was created specifically for the benefit of gods and men," in other words " . . . that everything beneficial to humanity was created specifically for this purpose."[42] On the other hand, he avoids mentioning the alternative possibility that the god concept itself just might have been promoted by mankind on the same basis, "specifically for its own purpose," since "no great man ever existed who did not enjoy some portion of divine inspiration." Here he assigns all acts of intelligence to this inclusive perspective as opposed to becoming entangled in incessant religious debate encouraged by the Academy of Arcesilaus and Carneades. Sustained pursuit of such speculation, he suggests, can only bear harmful consequences: "For the habit of arguing in support of atheism, whether it be done from conviction or in pretense, is a wicked and an impious practice."[43] With this abrupt and seemingly decisive rejection of atheism, Balbus brings his exposition to a close, fully aware that Cotta, who is waiting to respond, typifies exactly what he rejects.

The fourth and last portion of *On the Nature of the Gods*, Cotta's defense of Academic skepticism, is relatively brief and seems to have been based on skeptical assumptions almost identical to those of Carneades. Cotta begins with the assurance that he too wants to believe in the gods and has done so since his childhood, but that he cannot accept Balbus' arguments as adequate proof of their existence. He confesses that he opposes all four of Balbus' assumptions--first regarding the existence of the gods, second their nature, third the governance of the world, and finally, their supposed concern about mankind's welfare.[44]

Apropos of the first point, Cotta raises again the issue of universal belief in immortal gods suggested by both Balbus and Velleius to demonstrate the validity of religion. Quite the opposite, his response is that religious belief by almost the entire population including both "foolish" and "mad" believers justifies the discomfort of serious philosophers. [45] Cotta goes on to insist that the question is not who or how many believe in the existence of gods. Quite the contrary, he asserts, the more basic question in and of itself is whether the gods do in fact exist. [46] Moreover, he suggests that cosmic regularity at every level does not confirm god's existence. Quite the opposite, it confirms that the universe runs on its own, further suggesting that genuine miracles—if such occur--might be a far better indicator of God's existence than physical uniformity.

Nor, Cotta argues, is it possible to accept the ontological thesis attributed to Chrysippus, the most influential of early Stoic philosophers, that if what can be observed in the universe could not have been created by man, some being must exist of a higher order than man, and this being can therefore be identified as god. [47] In response Cotta inverts Chrysippus' argument to prove the contrary, that the world cannot be identified with one or more gods, yet nothing is superior to the world," more beautiful, or more conducive to our health. [48] By implication, the world itself becomes a manifestation of God as suggested by the most basic assumption of pantheism. Cotta also expresses his agreement with Chrysippus' explanation of supposedly transcendent human faculties as gifts of nature. According to Cotta, nature's ability to impart these gifts is entirely the outcome of material force rather than divine reason. [49] Relevant to the question of an afterlife, he explains that aging necessarily occurs for all living species and unavoidably culminates in death. Cotta also links the capacity for sensation with the inevitability of death once there is no longer any need for sensation."[50] And finally, Cotta explains the comparison between life and fire based on the fact that both culminate in ashes, and each expires when its process exhausts itself. Cotta emphasizes this similitude and concludes that the two are similar at least in this respect. [51]

Cotta switches his argument by suggesting that all the gods necessarily lack the most important anthropomorphic traits that worshippers attribute to them, such as prudence, ethical choice, and the capacity for reason, if in fact they themselves lack experience with evil and have no need to choose between things good and evil. His logic is disarmingly simple and based on the assumption that gods probably do not possess human traits if they have no need for them. [52] Cotta then lists a wide assortment of such traits absent in the standard concept of God, including all the vices as well as the virtues of temperance, courage, and rational judgment. Moreover, he asserts that without these traits, "God then is neither rational nor possessed of any of the virtues." Based on this deficiency he accordingly maintains, "But such a God is inconceivable." [53] Cotta concludes by arguing that Stoic philosophers who argue otherwise share the "stupidity of the vulgar and the ignorant" in their effort to identify god(s) as "deified human beings." Thereupon he provides an elongated catalog of as many as sixty-eight ancient gods and goddesses who have been worshipped at one time or another. He ends by arguing that the further invention of such deities can only be a waste of time and should be abandoned. The unspoken deduction is that the acceptance of atheism is the only credible alternative.

Next Cotta questions the ethical aspect of religion that links divine providence with virtue and reason. Whereas these capabilities might seem to merge in the depiction of god(s), he argues, such a convergence tends to be violated in human society. Far too often, he suggests, there is a misuse of reason despite ethical considerations, especially through the misuse of intelligence to perform hostile and even criminal acts. Too often, moreover, greed typified by an excessive accumulation of wealth often depends on superior mental facility, as do other such transgressions for comparable reasons. He accordingly asks, "Is there a single act of lust, of avarice, or of crime, which is not entered on deliberately or which is not carried out with active exercise of thought, that is, by aid of the reason?"[54] Cotta's answer to his own question is devastating:

> For if the gods gave man reason, they gave him malice, for malice is the crafty and covert planning of harm; and likewise also the gods gave him trickery and crime and all the other wickednesses, none of which can be either planned or executed without reasoning. [55]

In contrast, Cotta provides an extended list of virtuous men in ancient times who have instead been "visited by misfortune" as compared to "the wicked who have prospered exceedingly." In his opinion, such ethical disparities suggest that the benevolent intervention of the gods in human affairs has been modest at best, further suggesting the obvious paradox that there is no such thing as the divine governance of the world if that governance makes no distinction between the good and the wicked. For emphasis Cotta quotes the philosopher Diogenes, a contemporary of Aristotle and the inventor of the relatively modest Cynical school of philosophy, that "the prosperity and good fortune of the wicked . . . disprove the might and power of the gods entirely." Cotta fully concurs: "If human rulers knowingly overlook a fault they are greatly to blame; but as for god, he cannot even offer the excuse of ignorance."[56]

Cotta finally reminds everybody of Carneades' cynical deduction, "Accordingly either providence does not know its own powers, or it does not regard human affairs, or it lacks power of judgment to discern what is the best. It does not care for individuals." Cotta ends his argument on a less strident note: "This more or less is what I have to say about the nature of the gods; it is not my design to disprove it, but to bring you to understand how obscure it is and how difficult to explain."[57]

Upon the conclusion of debate, Cicero and Velleius compare notes on their respective attitudes in response to the various arguments. Velleius declares his preference for Cotta's atheistic assumptions, and Cicero answers perhaps surprisingly that he feels Balbus' Stoic arguments were more credible in the final analysis.[58] Today, in contrast, it seems to convey the weakest perspective, and Aristotle's often hardly recognizable assumptions somehow prevailed over those of Carneades. The retrospective assessments assigned to both participants also seems misguided. As an Epicurean, Veilleius is predictably attracted by an atheistic stance, aside from his aversion to Strato's example that was to be expected in light of the sustained animosity between Epicureans and the Lyceum. On the other hand, Cicero's agreement with Balbus is perhaps a result of the impact of Aristotle's fresh influence at the time, having come into currency in Rome not more than a few decades earlier. Cicero certainly appreciates Aristotle's views explained by Balbus, but there is little evidence that he himself has explored Aristotle's analysis in any depth beyond the assumptions expressed by Balbus. Then again, perhaps Cicero's choice results from his earlier experience as a student of the late Academic skeptics, Philo and Antiochus, both of whom sought a synthesis beyond Carneades' reductive commitment to atheism. In any case, Cicero seems more tempted by Balbus' effort as a Stoic philosopher to revisit the possible validity of religion than might otherwise be expected.

At the beginning of his remarkable text, Cicero seems to have presented its arguments as a final history of skepticism and natural philosophy in a tradition that extended from Plato's transcendent truths to their wholesale rejection by Carneades and others. His tone is initially apologetic. "They wonder at my coming forward so unexpectedly as the champion of a derelict system and one that has long been given up."[59] It suggests both the crisis in Rome and the declining relevance of Greek philosophy at the time, just a few centuries before Christianity offered an entirely new version of orthodoxy, one that eliminated from consideration the possible validity of both skepticism and natural philosophy. Today, of course, Cicero's summary assessment of the collective interplay among Greek philosophers after perhaps six centuries of documented secular assumptions seems more valid than ever. Cicero himself was remarkably insightful in having described this history as a "negative dialectic" that would continue to be valid whatever its future prospects in Rome:

> Take for example the philosophical method referred to, that of a purely negative dialectic which refrains from pronouncing any positive judgment. This,

after being originated by Socrates, revived by Arcesilas, and reinforced by Carneades, has flourished right down to our own period; though I understand that in Greece itself it is now almost bereft of adherents. But this I ascribe not to the fault of the Academy but to the dullness of mankind. [60]

This remarkable achievement of Greek civilization had already fallen into decline, and whether Cicero realized it or not deterioration would soon spread to all aspects of existence in Rome itself, and to such an extent that his generation can be described as having provided the culmination of ancient civilization beyond anything that would follow over the next fifteen centuries. There is insufficient evidence based on textual scholarship as to which of Cicero's final texts was brought to its completion immediately preceded his assassination, but his last words in *De Natura Deorum*, strictly translated as "more nearly a semblance of the truth" [*veritatis similitudinem*], suggest his final definitive pronouncement.

Epilogue

The decline of secular philosophy can be linked with the ascent of the Roman Empire, but it was also partly a result of its own evolution. Natural philosophy had already fallen into decline well before the reign of Augustus, and in fact Cicero's two dialogues seem to have been a culmination of secular inquiry, as compared to the continuing growth of stoicism advocated by Seneca, Plotinus, and Marcus Aurelius, which gave new life to Platonism as well as anticipating the later acceptance of Christianity. There was also renewed interest in Pyrrhonian skepticism as revised by the Alexandrian skeptic, Aenisidemus, who effectively expanded Pyrrho's defense of benign ignorance to include the value of unexamined political allegiance. This, too, was a by-product of the overall transition of Rome from a republic to Augustus' imperial reign, exactly when political quietism tolerant of authority was welcome. Not surprisingly, for example, Augustus exiled Ovid from Rome because of his obvious disrespect for the gods, then commissioned Virgil's epic, *The Aeneid,* to mythologize the role of Roman gods on an anachronistic Homeric basis. While ancient Greek civilization had advanced from Homer to Aristotle, Rome's later transition seems to have regressed from Lucretius' epic secular pessimism to Virgil's renewed depictions of Homeric bravery.

Augustus ruled effectively for two decades, and Tiberius, his successor was largely successful. However, less competent emperors followed whose impact was harmful, most notably Caligula and Nero. In the second century AD, there was substantial improvement in governance during the so-called Antonine Age led by Trajan, Hadrian, Antoninus, and Marcus Aurelius--all of whom ruled effectively for two decades apiece. In particular, Marcus Aurelius played an effective double role as a stoic philosopher and benevolent ruler of Rome. However, his son Commodus succeeded him and was as ruinous as Caligula and Nero. More deterioration followed under the next twenty-nine emperors before Diocletian failed in his futile attempt to restore Rome's earlier authority by suppressing Christianity. Gibbon described this process of deterioration in his history, *The Decline and Fall of the Roman Empire,* and in his recent book *The Swerve,* Stephen Greenblatt captures the inevitable downward transformation of Roman "civilization" as a whole—

> As the empire crumbled, as cities decayed, trade declined, and the increasingly anxious populace scanned the horizon for barbarous armies, the whole Roman system of elementary and higher education fell apart. What began as downsizing went on to wholesale abandonment. Schools closed, libraries and academies shut their doors, professional grammarians and teachers of rhetoric found themselves out of work. There were more important things to worry about than the fate of books. [1]

Along with Rome's cultural decline and perhaps contributing to it, there was an influx of workers from across the empire who brought an assortment of sacrificial religions with them. The goddess Cybele had been granted respectability as early as 206 BC because of her supposed role in Rome's victory over Carthage. Later arrivals included Attis, Dionysus, Astarte, Demeter, Serapis, and Zoroaster. Several of the religions featured trinities already suggested by the Egyptian sacred family of Osiris, Isis and Horus— and the worship of many of these gods seems to have imitated rituals performed in the worship of Osiris, whose death and resurrection had been celebrated in Egypt as early as the twenty-fourth century BC.

Many Roman aristocrats were offended and repelled by what seemed the vulgarity of populist religion. In his essay, "Superstition," Plutarch criticized his less fortunate neighbors for their prostrations, their inability to reason on their own, their mixture of dread and worship in the idea of God, and their acceptance of the concept of human sacrifice. [2] These attitudes extended to early Christianity and were often linked with social class. Celsus was rigorous in his dismissal of Christianity as nothing more than "a fable that primarily appealed to the lower classes." [3] On the other hand, some Roman aristocrats considered religion to be useful in keeping an otherwise unruly multitude respectful of authority. They thought impoverished troublemakers were more likely to obey the law if they believed in a god who punished disobedience. The Roman historian Livy agreed, suggesting that there was historic precedence for this necessity based on the legend of the king of Rome, Numa Pompilius, who "put the fear of the gods upon the people as the most effective thing for an ignorant and rough multitude." Earlier, the Sicilian historian Diodorus wrote that this goal was best achieved by promising rewards and punishment in an afterlife: "Myths which are told of the affairs in Hades, though pure invention at bottom, contribute to make men pious and upright." [4] The fear of God provided an incentive for people who were unable to obey the law as an ethical necessity.

Although Christianity arrived in Rome later than most of the Near Eastern religions, it was better packaged as a belief system than any of them. It possessed a text of its own, as opposed to an almost complete lack of written verification among competitive religions. It also enlisted an effective priesthood, included women as well as men (especially as compared to Mithraism), and, perhaps most important, taught a doctrine that featured the worship of one God instead of an assortment of countless demigods and goddesses. Finally, Christians were prohibited from attending ceremonies for competitive deities, for example the lively pagan festivals held in Rome. This combination of factors ultimately prevailed. When the Emperor Constantine converted to Christianity in 312 AD, he was successful in imposing Christian conversion across Europe, and with an impact that lasted for the next twelve centuries.

There was a substantial difference between the more exclusive conceptual demands of Greek philosophy and the greater accessibility of Biblical scriptures, which were intended for a broad audience. Christ had addressed his message to the population of the Levant, an impoverished region located between the two most remarkable economic and cultural epicenters of ancient history preceding Rome--Athens as a wealthy port city where philosophy was brought to fruition at an unprecedented level, and Alexandria as an even wealthier port city where science and philology also flourished. In the lands between these two cities, Christianity addressed the needs of an essentially illiterate rural community oppressed by Roman occupation. Here, the complexity of Greek cosmology and Alexandrian science must have been irrelevant and difficult to grasp. Although he was successful as a missionary, is not surprising that Paul converted few, if any of Athens' populace to Christianity when he traveled there for that purpose.[5]

In his first book, *Contra-Academica,* St. Augustine addressed theoretical assumptions of Greek philosophy in order to refute them. With skill he turned Academic skepticism against itself to justify the rejection of all Greek philosophy for its erroneous assumptions. He argued, most notably, that whether he realized it not, Cicero proved that all ancient philosophy was indeterminate and therefore wrong. Moreover, he added, Cicero's skepticism itself could likewise be rejected with the argument, "If nothing can be proven, even this [the argument that nothing can be proved] cannot be proven."[6] But of course Augustine himself neglected to go a step further by extending this line of argument to reject his own "proof" that supported religious doctrine. For if what can't be proven can't be proven wrong, it can't even be proven that what can't be proven can't be proven wrong, ergo the question remains open.

Over time, Christian emperors came to strongly support Christian doctrine, often by suppressing alternatives. Most notably, Theodosius seems to have been responsible for the accidental destruction of the Library of Alexandria around 380. As mentioned in this book's Introduction, the destruction of numerous other libraries occurred over the next few hundred years. The Christian emperor Justinian closed down the schools of Athens and outlawed Greek philosophy there to prevent Aristotle's assumptions from being linked with Christian doctrine. On the other hand, Christian philosophers advanced what amounted to a mandatory version of orthodox metaphysics that conferred special status to scriptures, presumed miracles, and the spiritual needs of the populace. This striking theoretical reversal was entirely at odds with the original intent of ancient Greek philosophy, while the basic assumptions of Plato's dialogues later provided Christian eschatology with its metaphysical justification throughout the Dark and Middle Ages. In contrast, Aristotle's works remained far less accessible and only became available to scholars after St. Thomas Aquinas had successfully gained their acceptance. Meanwhile, most of the philosophy of ancient secular philosophers such as Democritus, Theophrastus, Strato, Epicurus, and Carneades had all but disappeared.

The enforcement of Christianity became bloodthirsty. The Crusades supposedly fulfilled the expansionist Christian mission to capture Jerusalem, Constantinople, and the region, and the Inquisition tortured and killed millions of suspected heretics and witches. In 1209, for example, the entire population of Beziers, a fortified town, was slaughtered on the assumption declared by Pope Innocent III that God would sort out those victims worthy of heaven from those who deserved otherwise.[7] There is little to no evidence today of secular philosophy in any guise during the Middle Ages. It had been effectively erased.

Fortunately, Arab civilization culminating in the twelfth century AD tolerated and even encouraged the investigation of Aristotle's version of materialism, taught by Avicenna and Averroes. These two philosophers in particular provided a theoretical stepping stone that provided a link between ancient secularism to its later recovery during the European Renaissance, when Italian humanists could reexamine the few Greek and Latin texts that had survived the Dark and Middle Ages.

True to its name, the Renaissance that began with Petrarch's effort to restore Cicero was a "rebirth" in which the newly acquired knowledge from ancient Greece led to a spread of inquiry and of secularism across Europe. The principal astronomers of the Renaissance--Copernicus, Kepler, and Galileo--were heavily beholden to ancient astronomy. In his Introduction to *On the Revolutions of Heavenly Spheres,* for example, Copernicus stated that his concept of a heliocentric universe had been inspired by a passage in Cicero's *Academica* about similar findings by the ancient astronomer Hicetas. Similarly, both Bacon and Gilbert employed experimentation comparable to the efforts of Strato, Montaigne sought to recapture the intellectual freedom of Academic skepticism by pasting Arcesileus' favorite word, *epoche,* on the ceiling above his desk, and Bruno obviously enlarged upon the materialist assumptions of Aristotle, Democritus, and their contemporaries. Moreover, Gassendi elaborated his own version of Democritus' atomism, and Descartes renewed the pursuit of mathematical philosophy as first suggested by Pythagoras.

The year 1600 was noteworthy in particular. Bruno was burned at the stake for impiety at about the same time as Gilbert's breakthrough announcement of his discovery of electricity and Shakespeare's production of *Hamlet*, in which cosmic doubt is suggested by his most famous line, " To be or not to be," a phrase first articulated word-for-word by Aristotle in both *Prior Analytics* [70a4] and *Metaphysics* [1006b19]. This seemingly empty abstraction—the question of existence in and of itself--had been under consideration among the natural philosophers of ancient Greece, and Shakespeare re-presented this choice in its dramatic version for an English audience. Although Bacon avoided mentioning anyone by name, he paid tribute in his introduction to *Novum Organum* to ancient scientists for having inspired his scientific methodology—"modern" science as opposed to medieval alchemy.

The English philosopher Hobbes was repeatedly accused of heresy and had the audacity to describe atheism as "the sin of imprudence." Four decades later Spinoza confessed, "I do not know how to teach philosophy without becoming a disturber of established religion."[8] Newton suggested an explanation of gravity, a modern equivalent of Aristotle's theory of weight in the final pages of *De Caelo*. In turn, Hume featured a modern version of Academic skepticism based on Locke's psychology, which itself had been anticipated by Aristotle, and major figures in France including Voltaire, Rousseau, Diderot, Helvetius, and Condorcet identified themselves as deists (i.e. believers in an entirely impersonal God) as opposed to the outright atheism promoted by Meslier and d'Holbach. Later philosophers such as Mill, Spencer, James, Dewey, Santayana, Heidegger, Sartre, Ayer and Carnap were discrete in avoiding the discussion of religion, as opposed to Schopenhauer, Nietzsche, Marx, Russell, Freud, and Sartre, all of whom were willing to admit their atheism. Meanwhile science flourished beyond the most extravagant expectations of ancient philosophers, with inductive findings relevant to astronomy, evolution, genetics, particle physics, molecular biology, and numerous other fields of inquiry, all on a strictly secular basis.

Outspoken atheists who authored books and articles specifically to declare their disbelief include Meslier, Bradlaugh, Ingersoll, Mencken, Richard Dawkins, and Christopher Hitchens. Also worth mentioning, are the two nineteenth century historians of science, Büchner and Haeckel, as well as the American historian of science, Andrew White, and two remarkably productive secular historians of the early twentieth century, J.M. Robertson, and Joseph McCabe. And of course hundreds of other individuals have been quoted as freethinkers, for example, in James Haught's excellent anthology, *2000 Years of Disbelief.*

Not that freethinkers comprise a large percentage of the population as a whole. According to the latest Pew poll in 2015, only 7 percent of the population of the United States were willing to identify themselves as atheists as opposed to the 23 percent who identify themselves as being unaffiliated in their religious choice, and the 73 percent willing to identify themselves as Christians.[9] Atheists seem a small minority though their number is perhaps comparable to the prevalent ratio in Athens during the Age of Pericles. The percentage of atheists seems to be more substantial in Europe, for example in France 23 percent, in Holland 20 percent, in Sweden 19 percent, and in England 18 percent.[10] In contrast, these statistics are reversed among scientists. Over the past century as published in *Nature*, religious belief among modern scientists has declined from 27.7 percent in 1914 to 15 percent in 1933, and to 7 percent in 1998.[11] Einstein has often been identified as an outstanding exception because of his oft-repeated public support of religion throughout his life. However, he finally confessed in a personal letter a year before he died, "The word 'god' is for me nothing more than the expression and product of human weaknesses, the *Bible* a collection of honorable, but still primitive legends which are nevertheless pretty childish."[12] Who could have said it better?

Notes

PREFACE

1. John Burnet, *Greek Philosophy: Thales to Plato* (London: Macmillan, 1914), 12.
2. W.K.C. Guthrie, *A History of Greek Philosophy: The Pre-Socratic Tradition from Parmenides to Democritus* (London: Cambridge University Press, 1965) vol. 2, 114.
3. Diogenes Laertius *Lives of the Eminent Philosophers* trans. R.D. Hicks (Cambridge, MA: Harvard University Press, 1979), vol. 2, 435.
4. Theodor Gomperz *Greek Thinkers: A History of Ancient Philosophy* (London: John Murray, Albemarle Street, 1964) vol. 1, p. 191.
5. The anachronistic effort to "clarify" Aristotle's concepts in effectively Christian terms is usually blatant. Ironically, perhaps these changes prevented the text from being entirely destroyed.

INTRODUCTION

1. The combination of the words *western* and *civilization* may be either capitalized or not, or, if an author chooses, the first of them may be capitalized and the second kept in the lower case. My choice is to capitalize both in order to emphasize the unique cultural and geographical identity of Western Civilization in its advance from ancient Greece and Rome to medieval Arab cities, the Renaissance, and everything since. That this transition did in fact play a crucial role preliminary to the modern world is exactly what I try to demonstrate in this paper.
2. H. Michell, *The Economics of Ancient Greece* (London: Cambridge University Press, 1940), 313; Gustave Glotz, *Ancient Greece at Work: An Economic History of Greece*, trans. M.R. Dobie (New York: Knopf, 1926), Part III, chap. 7; Chester Starr, *The Economic and Social Growth of Early Greece: 800-500 B.C.* (New York: Oxford University Press, 1977), 97-112; Johannes Hasebroek, *Trade and Politics in Ancient Greece* trans. L.M. Fraser and D.C. MacGregor (London: G. Bell & Sons, 1933), 140-45, *in passim.*
3. Carroll Quigley, *The Evolution of Civilizations* (Indianapolis, IN: Liberty Fund, 1961), 291.
4. Aristotle *Metaphysics, The Complete Works of Aristotle: The Revised Oxford Translation.* Edited by J. Barnes. 2 vols. Bollingen Series. Princeton, NJ: Princeton University Press, 1984), 982b23-25.

5. Georg Hegel, *Lectures on the History of Philosophy* trans. E.S. Haldane and Frances Simson vols. 1 and 2. (Atlantic Highlands, NJ: Humanities Press, 1974), sects. 340 and 350.
6. Karl Kautsky, *Foundations of Christianity* trans. Henry Mins (New York: S.A. Russell, 1953), 167; M.I. Finley, *Economy and Society in Ancient Greece* (London: Chatto and Windus, 1981), 18; H. Michell, *Economics of Ancient Greece*, 313; Marx discusses this economic benefit in his 1857 "Notebook," cited by M.I. Finley in *Economy and Society*, 81.
7. Luther's translation seems to have initiated the tenfold mistake to be found in the later English translations. In any case, the lower estimate is no less hard to believe, especially if five thousand pieces of silver in ancient times was worth perhaps $20,000 in modern currency. The $200,000 value of the Ephesus bonfire as suggested in the King James version seems an obvious exaggeration.
8. Lionel Casson, *Libraries in the Ancient World* (New Haven, CT: Yale University Press, 2001), 92. See also Lucien Polastron, *Books on Fire: The Destruction of Libraries Throughout History* (Rochester, NY: Inner Traditions, 2007).
9. Kathleen Freeman, *Ancilla to the Pre-Socratic Philosophers. A Complete Translatlion of the Fragments in Diels' Fragmente der Vorsokratiker* (Cambridge, MA: Harvard University Press, 1957).

1. THE PRE-SOCRATIC PHILOSOPHERS

1. Kathleen Freeman, *Ancilla to the Pre-Socratic Philosophers*, a translation of Hermann Diels, *Fragmente der* Vorsokratiker, 5th edition. Unless otherwise noted, all fragments cited are from Freeman's translation. Only four fragments of Thales are listed in the *Ancilla*. A more thorough account is provided by Diogenes Laertius in *Lives of the Eminent Philosophers*, trans. R.D. Hicks, Loeb Classical Library (Cambridge, MA: Harvard University Press, 1979), vol. 1, 23-47.
2. Aristotle, *De Anima* in *Complete Works of Aristotle: The Revised Oxford Translation*. ed. J. Barnes. Bollingen Series. (Princeton, NJ: Princeton University Press, 1984), 405a19; 411a8.
3. Plutarch, "Dinner of the Seven Wise Men," trans. Frank C. Babbitt, *Moralia* Loeb Classical Library 222 (Cambridge, MA: Harvard University Press, 1998), vol. 2, 163E21.
4. Aristotle, *Sense and Sensibilia*, trans. J.I. Beare, *Complete Works* (Princeton), 441a.22.
5. Aristotle, *Metaphysics*, trans. W.D. Ross, *Complete Works* (Princeton), 983b20-27. Recent astronomical research indicates that "water ices" probably existed in the interstellar medium preceding the formation of the sun and that at least half the water on the earth's surface can be traced to that particular source.
6. Cicero, *Acudemicu, De Nuturu Deorum. Acudemicu.* trans. H. Rackham, Loeb Classical Library 268 (Cambridge, MA: Harvard University Press, 1933), 118.
7. Aristotle, *Physics*, trans. R.P. Hardie and R.K. Gaye, *Complete Works* (Princeton), 187a21.
8. Anaximander, frag. 1 Freeman.
9. Philip Wheelwright, *Heraclitus* (Princeton, NJ: Princeton, 1959), 5.
10. Aristotle, *Physics*, trans. R.P. Hardie and R.K. Gaye, *Complete Works* (Princeton), 203b13-15.
11. Kathleen Freeman, *The Pre-Socratic Philosophers: A Companion to Diels, Fragmente der Vorsokratiker* (Cambridge, MA: Harvard, 1966), 58-62.
12. John Burnet, *Early Greek Philosophy* (London: Adam & Charles Black, 1930), 73-76; Richard D. McKirahan, Jr. *Philosophy Before Socrates* (Indianapolis, IN: Hackett Publishing, 1994), 48-54.
13. Hippolytus, *Refutations of all Heresies* i.7 cited by John Burnet in *Early Greek Philosophy*, 73.
14. Heraclitus, frags. 31 and 36 F. Heraclitus excludes air from his proposed cycle of the universe, but he includes it in frag. 76.
15. Xenophanes, frags. 23-26 F.

16. Ibid. frags. 27-29 F.

17. Diogenes Laertius, "Xenophenes," *Lives of Eminent Philosophers*, trans. R.D. Hicks, Loeb Classical Library 185 (Cambridge, MA: Harvard University Press, 1979), vol. 2, 19-20. See also Aristotle, *Metaphysics*, trans. W.D. Ross, *Complete Works* (Princeton), 986b17-30.

18. Xenophanes, frags. 7.4, 7.5, and 7.6, Richard D. McKirahan, Jr., *Philosophy Before Socrates* (Indianapolis, IN: Hackett Publishing, 1994).

19. Xenophanes, frags. 29, and 33 F.

20. Xenophanes, frag 7.16 McKirahan. The Freeman translation is obviously more cumbersome: "Let these things be stated as conjectural only, similar to the reality." (frag. 35).

21. Sextus Empiricus, *Against the Logicians*, trans. R.G. Bury, Loeb Classical Library 291 (Cambridge, MA: Harvard University Press, 1983), vol. 2, 326.

22. Diogenes Laertius, "*Pythagoras*," *Lives*, trans. R.D. Hicks (Loeb), 8.6.

23. Ibid., 8.8.

24. Diogenes Laertius, "*Pythagoras*" in *Lives*, trans. R.D. Hicks (Loeb), 25-27. Also useful are the summaries in Aristotle's *Metaphysics*, trans. W.D. Ross (Princeton), vol. 2, 985b23-987a19 and McKirahan's *Philosophy before Socrates*, 91-113.

25. Aristotle, *Physics*, trans. R.P. Hardie and R.K. Gaye, *Complete Works,* (Princeton), 213b22-26.

26. Diogenes Laertius, "*Pythagoras*," trans. R.D. Hicks, *Lives*, (Loeb), 35.

27. Aristotle, *On the Soul*, trans. W.S. Hett, (Loeb), 404a17-23.

28. Aristotle, *On the Heavens*, trans. J.L. Stocks, *Complete Works*, (Princeton), 293a19-294b3.

29. Philolaus, frag. 17 F. See also Plato, *Timaeus*, *The Collected Dialogues of Plato.* eds. Edith Hamilton and Huntington Cairns. Bollingen Series (Princeton, NJ: Princeton, 1961), 34a-b.

30. Philolaus, frag. 21 F; see also Aristotle, *On the Heavens,* trans. J.L. Stocks, *Complete Works* (Princeton), 293a17-293b22.

31. Diogenes Laertius, "*Philolaus*" in *Lives*, trans. R.D. Hicks (Loeb), 85-86.

32. Heraclitus, frag. 125a F.

33. Plato, "*Cratylus*," trans. Benjamin Jowett, *The Collected Dialogues,* (Princeton), 402a, 439; *Physics*, trans. R.P. Hardie and R.K. Gaye, *Complete Works*, (Princeton), 253a22-254a.

34. Heraclitus, frag. 103 F.

35. Aristotle, *Metaphysics*, trans. W.D. Ross, *Complete Works*, (Princeton), 1012a25-1012b1; 1078b14.

36. Heraclitus, frags. 6 and 60, F.

37. Ibid. frag. 76, F.

38. Ibid. respectively frags. 90, 66, and 65 F.

39. Ibid. frag. 64 F.

40. Ibid. frag. 36 F.

41. Ibid. frags. 54, 123 F.

42. Ibid. respectively frags. 53, 80 F.

43. Ibid. frags. 1, 8, 10, 45, 50, and 114 F.

44. Ibid. frag. 41 F.

45. Aristotle, *Nicomachean Ethics*, trans. W.D. Ross, *Complete Works*, (Princeton), 1146b31; *Metaphysics* trans. W.D. Ross, *Complete Works*, (Princeton), 983a2-11.

46. Heraclitus, frag. 114 F.

47. Ibid. frags. 67, 102 F.

48. Ibid. frag.14 F.

49. Ibid. frags. 32 and 41 F.

50. Parmenides, frag. 1 F.

51. Ibid. frag. 2 F.

52. Ibid. frags. 7, 8 F.

53. Ibid. frag. 12 F.

54. Ibid. frag. 13 F.

55. Ibid. frag. 11 F.

56. Diogenes Laertius, "*Parmenides*," trans. R.D. Hicks, *Lives*, 22.

57. Aristotle, *Metaphysics,* trans. W.D. Ross, *Complete Works,* (Princeton), 986b25. See also Cicero's explanation in *Academica*, trans. H. Rackham, (Loeb), 118.

58. Parmenides, frag. 9 F.

59. Diogenes Laertius, "*Zeno of Elea*," trans. R.D. Hicks, *Lives* (Loeb), 26-28.

60. Melissus, frag. 8(2) F.

61. Ibid. frags. 1 and 3 F.

62. Ibid. frag. 6 F.

63. Diogenes Laertius, "*Melissus*," trans. R.D. Hicks, *Lives* (Loeb), vol. 2, 24.

64. Melissus, frags. 1, 8, 8(2), 9 and 10 F.

65. Ibid. frag. 7 (7) F.

66. Ibid. frag 8 (2) F.

67. Aristotle, *Physics*, trans. R.P. Hardie and R.K. Gaye, *Complete Works* (Princeton), 213b12-14.

68. Aristotle, *Physics*, trans. R.P. Hardie and R.K. Gaye, *Complete Works* (Princeton), 186a8-10; *On the Heavens*, 298b18.

69. Empedocles, frag. 129 F.

70. Ibid. frag. 133 F.

71. Ibid. frag. 28 F.

72. Ibid. frag 135 F.

73. Ibid. frag 12 F.

74. Ibid. frag. 8 F.

75. Ibid. frag.15 F.

76. Ibid. frag. 110 F.

77. Ibid. frags. 26 and 28 F; see also Heraclitus frag. 103 F.

78. Ibid. frag. 26 F.

79. Sextus Empiricus, *Outlines of Pyrrhonism*, trans. R.G. Bury, Loeb Classical Library 273 (Cambridge, MA: Harvard University Press, 1983), Cpt. 3,.30.

80. As an incidental personal note that unavoidably colors my acceptance of this account, my wife and I were horrified when our nine-year old daughter Kristin almost fell into Mt. Aetna. Fortunately our guide saved her life, tearing her raincoat in pulling her back to safety from the edge of the volcano.

81. Anaxagoras, frag. 1 F.

82. Ibid. frag. 4 F.

83. Ibid. frag. 9 F.

84. Ibid. frags. 2, 4-6 F.

85. Aristotle, *Metaphysics*, trans. W.D. Ross, *Complete Works*, (Princeton), 984a12-16.

86. Anaxagoras, frag. 12 F.

87. Ibid. frag. 12 F.

88. Cicero, *De Natura Deorum*, trans. H. Rackham, (Loeb), 1.26.

89. Aristotle, *Metaphysics*, trans. W.D. Ross, *Complete Works*, (Princeton), 1075b8-12.

90. Plato, *Phaedo, The Collected Dialogues of Plato*, trans. Hugh Tredennick, (Loeb), 97c.

91. Aristotle, *On the Soul*, trans. J.A. Smith *Complete Works,* (Princeton), vol. 1, 413a12-26; 414a22-24; 415a17-30, 415b13-22, etc.

92. Anaxagoras, frag. 12 F.

93. Ibid.

94. Anaxagoras, frags. 12-16 F.

95. Aristotle, *On Generation and Corruption*, trans. J.L. Stocks, *Complete Works,* (Princeton, 322b14-22.

96. W. K. C. Guthrie "Diogenes of Apollonia," Stromateis record (A 6), cited in *A History of Greek Philosophy*, (Cambridge: Cambridge University Press, 1965), vol. 2, 370.

97. Kathleen Freeman, "Diogenes of Apollonia," *Ancilla to the Pre-Socratic Philosophers*, 88.

98. Diogenes of Apollonia, frag. 5 F.

99. Ibid. frags. 2,3, and 5 F.

100. Leucippus, frag. 2 F.

101. Diogenes Laertius, "*Leucippus*," trans. R.D. Hicks, *Lives* (Loeb), vol. 2, 30.

102. Simplicius, frag. (Commentaria in *De Caelo*, 294.33-295.22). Quoted in *Complete Works*, (Princeton), vol. 2, 2446. It can be mentioned here that the entire text, necessarily of essential importance in linking Democritus and Aristotle's respective philosophies, was lost as late as the sixth century AD, apparently while in the possession of Christian monks.

103. H. Ritter and L. Preller, *Historia Philosophiae Graecae*, quoted by John Burnet in *Early Greek Philosophy* (Adam & Charles Black), 194.

104. Diogenes Laertius, "*Leucippus*," trans. R.D. Hicks, *Lives* (Loeb), vol. 2, 31.

105. Ibid.

106. Christopher Conselice, "A Universe of Two Trillion Galaxies," Royal Astronomical Society, Oct. 24, 2016.

107. Diogenes Laertius, "*Leucippus,*" trans. R.D. Hicks, *Lives* (Loeb), vol. 2, 33.

108. Commentaria in *De Caelo* 294.33-295.22—Aristotle, *Complete Works*, (Princeton), vol. 2, 2446.

109. Aristotle, *De Anima* trans. J.A. Smith *Complete Works,* (Princeton) 405a8-15; see also Diogenes Laertius, trans. R.D. Hicks, *Lives* (Loeb), vol. 2, 45.

110. Diogenes Laertius, "*Democritus*," trans. R.D. Hicks, *Lives*, (Loeb), vol. 2, 45; Cicero, *Academica* (Loeb) 2.55. Supportive of Democritus' thesis, recent astronomical findings confirm the existence of at least two trillion galactic systems beyond our own galaxy. One can only guess how many of these galaxies contain stars with planets—apparently one apiece on the average--that sustain life on an evolutionary basis.

111. Aristotle, *On the Soul*, trans. J.A. Smith, *Complete Works* (Princeton), vol. 1, 1.405a7-13.

112. Ibid., 404a8-9, 404b3-6, 405b8-16.

113. Aristotle, *On the Soul*, trans. J.A. Smith, *Complete Works,* (Princeton), vol. 1, 1.405a7-13.

114. Aristotle, *Metaphysics,* trans. W.D. Ross, *Complete Works,* (Princeton), 1009b12-16.

115. Aristotle, "Sense and Sensibilia," trans. J.I. Beare, *Complete Works,* (Princeton), 442a29-442b2.

116. Cicero, *De Natura Deorum*, Loeb Classical Library 268 (Cambridge, MA: 1979), 1.29—see also 1.120.

117. Aristotle, *Metaphysics*, trans. W.D. Ross, *Complete Works,* (Princeton), 4.1009b11; Cicero, *Academica*, trans. H. Rackham, (Loeb) 1.44-45; 2.73.

118. NB Sextus Empiricus, *Against the Physicists* trans. R.G. Bury, Loeb Classical Library 311 (Cambridge, MA: Harvard University Press, 1936), vol. 3, 1.24.

119. Sextus Empiricus, *Against the Physicists* trans. R.G. Bury (Loeb), vol. 3, 17.

120. Diogenes Laertius,"*Democritus*," trans. R.D. Hicks, *Lives* (Loeb*)*, vol. 2, 40.

121. In the three texts combined, *De Caelo, On Generation and Corruption*, and *De Anima*, Aristotle referred by name to Democritus 14 times and Leucippus 4 times as compared to Anaxagoras 13 times and Plato 4 times. Interestingly, most of his references by name were to Empedocles (33 times), followed by the Pythagoreans (6 times), Thales (3 times), and with no reference whatsoever to Socrates.

122. A modern counterpart to this dilemma could well be illustrated by the unresolved distinction between quantum mechanics and Einstein's theory of relativity.

2. PLATO AND THE AGE OF PERICLES

1. Sextus Empiricus. *Against the Logicians*, trans. R.G. Bury, Loeb Classical Library 291 (Cambridge, MA: Harvard University Press, 1983) 1.65.

2. Ibid. 1.53.

3. Metrodorus, frags. 1 and 2. Kathleen Freeman, *Ancilla to the Pre-Socratic Philosophers*, a translation of Hermann Diels, *Fragmente der* Vorsokratiker, 5th ed. (Cambridge, MA: Harvard University Press, 1957), 120-121.

4. *Greek Lyric*, trans. David A. Campbell, Loeb Classical Library 476, (Cambridge, MA: Harvard University Press 1991), vol. 3, 363-4.

5. Critias, frag. 25 Freeman.

6. NB In his biography of Pericles, Plutarch incidentally mentions this reciprocal dislike since their service together in combat many years earlier.

7. Protagoras, frag. 1 F.

8. Ibid. frag. 4 F.

9. Diogenes Laertius, "Socrates," trans. R.D. Hicks, *Lives of Eminent Philosophers* (Cambridge, MA: Harvard University Press, 1979), vol. 1, 2.21-22. See also Plato, *Phaedo*, 96a and Plato *Apology,* 19a both in *The Dialogues of Plato*. trans. Benjamin Jowett. *Great Books of the Western World.* ed. Mortimer Adler (Chicago: Encyclopedia Britannica, 1952);

10. Plato, *Apology* trans. Benjamin Jowett, *Dialogues of Plato (Great Books)*, 27b.

11. Ibid., *Cratylus*, (Great Books), 400a-c.

12. Ibid., *Phaedo*, (Great Books), 97b-d.

13. Ibid., 96a-c.

14. Anaxagoras, frag. 12, F.

15. Plato, *Timaeus*, (Great Books), 30a.

16. Ibid., *The Republic, II*, (Great Books), 382e.

17. Ibid., *Laws, IV.*, (Great Books), 716c. This sentence bears obviously monotheistic implications, suggesting the likelihood of its later interpolation similar to those used to modify Aristotle's arguments as discussed in the next chapter. In fact several if not all the examples used here might also be Christian interpolations.

18. Ibid., *Laws, VII.*, (Great Books), 803c.

19. Ibid., *Timaeus*, (Great Books), 68d.

20. Ibid., *Crito*, (Great Books), 44e.

21. Ibid., *The Republic VII*, (Great Books), 514a-520a.

22. Ibid., *Theaetetus,* (Great Books), 166d and 171c.

23. Ibid., *Timaeus,* (Great Books), 28c.

24. Ibid., (Great Books), 58b.

25. Ibid., (Great Books), 92c.

26. Ibid. 48d-e.

27. Plato, *Theaetetus*, (Great Books), 172b.

28. Ibid., *Timaeus,* (Great Books), 40e.

29. Ibid, (Great Books), 30b.

30. Ibid, *Timaeus*, 40d-e.

31. Ibid., *Laws X, Plato: The Collected Dialogues,* trans. A.E. Taylor, ed. by Edith Hamilton and Huntington Cairns (Princeton, NJ: Princeton University Press, 1987), 891e-899d.

32. Ibid, 892c.

33. Ibid, 896e.

34. Ibid, 899b.

35. Ibid, 886a.

36. Ibid., 888c, p. 1444.

37. Ibid, 890a, p. 1445.

38. Ibid, 908 b-e, p. 1464,

39. Ibid, 910d, p. 1465.

40. At the ripe age of eighty-three I suggest this possibility with all due respect.

3. EARLY ARISTOTLE (384-322 BC)

1. Aristotle *Physics*, trans. R.P. Hardie and R.K. Gaye, *The Complete Works of Aristotle: The Revised Oxford Translation*. Edited by J. Barnes (Princeton, NJ: Princeton University Press, 1984), 188a16-17. See also *De Caelo*, trans. J.L. Stocks (Oxford: At the Clarendon Press, 1922), 302b27-30.

2. *Plutarch's Lives,* trans. John Dryden and Arthur H. Clough, *Great Books of the Western World*, Mortimer Adler. (Chicago: Encyclopedia Britannica, 1952), vol. 14, 543-542.

3. W.K.C. Guthrie, *A History of Greek Philosophy: VI. Aristotle An Encounter* (London: Cambridge University Press, 1981), 41, 50-52.

4. Aristotle, *Generation of Animals,* trans. A. Platt, *Complete Works* Princeton), 760b29-33.

5. The full implications of Aristotle's change in attitude toward Melissus will be discussed at greater length in Chapter 4 in the segment pertaining to *de Caelo.*

6. Aristotle *On the Heavens*, trans. J.L. Stocks, *Complete Works* (Princeton), 296b8-20.

7. Plato *Phaedo*, trans. Hugh Tredennick, *The Collected Dialogues of Plato,* . Edited by Edith Hamilton and Huntington Cairns (Princeton, NJ: Princeton, 1961), 109 b-c.

8. Plutarch, *"Reply to Colotes,"* *Moralia*. trans. Benedict Einarson and Phillip de Lacy, Loeb Classical Library 428 (Cambridge, MA: Harvard University Press, 1967), vol. 14, , 1115.

9. Ibid., 1115A-B.

10. Aristotle, *Nicomachean Ethics,* trans. W.D. Ross, *Complete Works* (Princeton) Aristotle, 1178b9-24.

11. Aristotle, *Eudemian Ethics* trans. J. Solomon, *Complete Works* (Princeton), 1248a25-29.

12. Other passages that can be submitted to similar scrutiny include 270b5-10; 399b19-24; and 1326a31-32.

13. Aristotle, *Metaphysics,* trans. Hugh Tredennick, Loeb Classical Library Cambridge, MA: Harvard University Press, 1947), 1072b27-31.

14. Aristotle, *Eudemian Ethics*, *Complete Works* (Princeton), 1178b9-24.

15. Aristotle, *Physics*, trans. R.P. Hardie and R.K. Gaye, *The Works of Aristotle,* (Oxford: Clarendon Press, 1930), 185a13-15. This translation is strikingly different from the P.H. Wick-steed and F.M. Cornford translation in the Loeb classics, "Let us then start from the datum that things of Nature, or (to put it at the lowest) some of them, do move and change, as is patent to observation."

16. Aristotle, *Physics* trans. R.P. Hardie and R.K. Gaye, *The Works of Aristotle,* (Oxford) Ibid., 185b26-27.

17. Ibid., 207a8.

18. Ibid., 185a14-15.

19. Ibid., 188b25.

20. Ibid., 188b24-190a13-14.

21. Ibid., 198a18-26

22. Ibid., 205b13-16, 26-27.

23. Ibid., 213b32.

24. Ibid., 214a29-30.

25. 236b33-237b22.

26. 250b10-14.

27. 251b17.

28. 251a28.

29. 252b7-20.

30. 259a7-14. The archaic translation "movent," by Hardie and Gaye refers to both a mover and whatever moves or is moved. The more recent translations by Stocks (in the Princeton edition) and Wicksteed (in Loeb) simply refer to a "mover," apparently suggestive of supernatural authority such as a god.

31. 265a6-27.

32. 266b5-6.

33. 267b18-26.

34. Aristotle, *Metaphysics*, trans. W.D. Ross, *The Works of Aristotle,* (Oxford: Clarendon Press, 1930). The three passages that reference *Physics* in *Metaphysics* include 993a11-12, 1042b8, 1059a35-37.

35. Aristotle, *Metaphysics*, trans. W.D. Ross, *The Works of Aristotle* (Oxford), 982b-983a10.

36. See *De Anima* 433a13-15. Much later David Hume dared to be less circumspect in his definition: Poets themselves, "tho liars by profession, always endeavour to give an air of truth to their fictions." *A Treatise of Human Nature*, (Oxford: Oxford University Press, 1960), 121.

37. Aristotle, *Metaphysics*, trans. W.D. Ross, *The Works of Aristotle* (Oxford), 997b10-11.

38. Ibid., 1015a13-19; 1026a25-32.
39. Simplicius, "Commentarius in de Anima," Frag. 46 in *Complete Works* (Princeton *The Complete Works of Aristotle*, vol 2, 2403.
40. Aristotle, *Metaphysics*, trans. W.D. Ross, *The Works of Aristotle* (Oxford), 1074b1-15.
41. Later disdainful references to the orthodox populace by secularists have included Juvenal's "thoughtless mob," Bruno's "rude populace," Tindal's "bulk of mankind," Rousseau's "common herd," Hume's "great mass of believers," Schopenhauer's "ordinary mind," and Haeckel's "credulous masses." Even Kant spoke of "common people."
42. Aristotle, *Metaphysics*, trans. W.D. Ross, *The Works of Aristotle* (Oxford: Clarendon Press, 1908-52), 1062b23.
43. Aristotle, *The Works of Aristotle,* ed. W.D. Ross (Oxford: Clarendon Press, 1908-52), 13. 149, 179
44. Aristotle, *Metaphysics*, trans. W.D. Ross, *The Works of Aristotle* (Oxford), 1069a16-1076a4.
45. Ibid., 1074a37-39.
46. Ibid., 1075a12-17.
47. Ibid., 1075a36-1075b1.
48. Ibid.,1075a9-10. Italics in the original.
49. Ibid.,1075b25.

4. LATE ARISTOTLE

1. Aristotle, *On the Heavens.* trans. W.K.C. Guthrie, Loeb Classical Library 338 (Cambridge, MA: Harvard University Press, 2006), 278b11-22. Plato's two references may be found in *Timaeus* 34ab and *Laws 10*, 893.
2. Ibid.
3. Ibid., 279b1-4.
4. Aristotle, *De Caelo*, trans. J.L. Stocks (Oxford: Clarendon Press, 1922), 269a31-35.
5. Ibid., 270b5-12. The Guthrie translation of the passage accentuates the logical discrepancies suggestive of interpolation relevant to the first of these passages: "From all these premises therefore it clearly follows that there exists some physical substance besides the four in our sublunary world, and moreover that it is more divine than, and prior to, all these."
6. Aristotle, *On Sophistical Refutations*, trans. E.S. Forster, Loeb Classical Library 400 (Cambridge: Harvard University Press, 2000),167b13-16.
7. Ibid, 181a27-30. See also 167b13-20.
8. Aristotle, *Physics,* trans. Philip H. Wicksteed and Francis M. Cornford, Loeb Classical Library 228 (Cambridge: Harvard University Press, 1957), 186a6-10.
9. Aristotle, *Metaphysics,* trans. Hugh Tredennick, Loeb Classical Library (Cambridge: Harvard University Press, 1957), 986b14-26.
10. Aristotle, *De Caelo*, trans. J.L. Stocks (Oxford at Clarendon), 298b15-20.
11. Heraclitus, frags., 12, 31, 41, Kathleen Freeman, *Ancilla to the Pre-Socratic Philosophers* (Cambridge, MA: Harvard University Press, 1957), translation of Hermann Diels, *Fragmente der Vorsokratiker..*
12. Aristotle, *Metaphysics*, trans. Hugh Tredennick, (London: William Heinemann, 1956), 986a19-20.
13. Aristotle, *De Caelo,* trans. J.L. Stocks (Oxford at Clarendon), 292a32-33.
14. Ibid, 279a6-11.
15. Ibid. 284a3-12.
16. Ibid. 279a6-11.
17. Ibid., 276a30-31.
18. Ibid., 278b15-17.
19. Aristotle, *Physics* trans., Philip H. Wicksteed and Francis M. Cornford, Loeb Classical Library 228 (Cambridge: Harvard University Press, 1957), 208b29-39.
20. Kathleen Freeman, *Ancilla*, (Harvard), frags. 41 and 103.

21. Aristotle, *De Caelo,* trans. J.L. Stocks (Oxford at Clarendon), 283b17-21.

22. Ibid., 283b26-284a.6.

23. Ibid., 284a23-27.

24. Ibid., 284a28-31.

25. Ibid., 301a18-20.

26. Ibid., 303a4-303b7.

27. Ibid., 309a.1-309b.25.

28. Ibid., 280a30, 293b32, 300a1, 300b18, 306b19, and 308b4.

29. Aristotle, *De Caelo*, trans. J.L. Stocks (Oxford at Clarendon), 313b24 and *On Generation and Corruption*, 314a1.

30. Ibid., *On Generation and Corruption*, 337a.17-22.

31. Ibid., 337a31-35.

32. Ibid., 314b27.

33. Ibid., 315a24-25.

34. Ibid., 316b.27-34.

35. Ibid., 318a23-25.

36. Ibid., 319a18-23.

37. Ibid., 331b2-4.

38. Ibid., 332b6-8.

39. Ibid., 333a7-9.

40. Ibid., 334a7-9.

41. Ibid., 334a10-11.

42. Ibid., 316a10-12.

43. Ibid., 336b31-35.

44. Ibid., 337a17-22.

45. Ibid., 337b29-31.

46. Ibid., 338b13-21.

47. Aristotle, *De Anima*, trans. R.D. Hicks (New York: Cosimo Classics, 2008), 408a35-38; 411b11.

48. Ibid., 415b17-25.

49. Ibid., see respectively 406b27; 407b10; .410b5.

50. Ibid., 407a33-35.

51. Aristotle. *De Caelo,* trans. J.L. Stocks (Oxford at Clarendon), 292a33-292b3.

52. Ibid., *On Generation of Animals*, trans. A. Platt, *The Complete Works of Aristotle: The Revised Oxford Translation.* Edited by J. Barnes. 2 vols. Bollingen Series. (Princeton, NJ: Princeton University Press, 1984), 731b31-39.

53. Aristotle, *De Anima*, trans. R.D. Hicks (Cosimo Classics), 403b24-27.

54. Ibid., 402a5-8.

55. Ibid., 414a16-29.

56. Ibid., in passim, 407b7-26.

57. Ibid., 412a17-28, 412b34-36.

58. Ibid., 432a3-6.

59. Ibid., 427b17-21. My earlier book *Negative Poetics* explores this Freudian aspect of the imagination relevant to literary experience.

60. Ibid., 433a8-13.

61. Ibid.,402b34 and 409b44—410a for oblique references to God.

62. Aristotle, *Metaphysics*, trans. W.D. Ross, *The Complete Works of Aristotle: The Revised Oxford Translation.* Edited by J. Barnes. 2 vols. (Princeton, NJ: Princeton University Press, 1984). 982b11-983a.11.

63. Aristotle, *De Anima*, trans. R.D. Hicks, (Cosimo), 427b9-427b22.

64. Ibid., 428b24-428b39.

65. Ibid., 427b18-22, 24-34.

66. Aristotle, *Nicomachean Ethics* in The Great Books, vol. 11, trans. by W.D. Ross, p. 352, 1106b7-28. The revision of this translation by J.O. Urmson in vol. 2 of the Princeton edition of Aristotle's writings substitutes the word "excellence" for "virtue."

67. Summarized by W.K.C. Guthrie, *A History of Greek Philosophy*. vols. 1-6 (London: Cambridge University Press, 1962-81), 59-61.
68. Bertrand Russell *A History of Western Philosophy*. (New York: Simon & Schuster, 1945), 159.

5. THE LYCEUM AFTER ARISTOTLE

1. Carroll Quigley *The Evolution of Civilizations* (Indianapolis, IN: Liberty Fund, 1961), 293-94. Quigley indicates that democracy declined at the time as the result of rationalism, not irrationalism.
2. Diogenes Laertius, *Lives of Eminent Philosophers* trans. R.D. Hicks, Loeb Classical Library 185 (Cambridge, MA: Harvard University Press, 1979), vol. 2, 431.
3. Theophrastus, *Metaphysics,* trans. W.D. Ross and F.H. Fobes (Chicago, IL: Ares Publishers, 1978), 1.4.
4. Ibid., 4.15.
5. Ibid., 4.16.
6. Ibid., 8.27-28.
7. Ibid., 9.30.
8. Ibid., 9, 32. Italics in the original.
9. Ibid., 9.33.
10. Theophrastus, *Metaphysics*, trans. W.D. Ross and F.H. Fobes (Ares) 9.34.
11. *Strato of Lampsacus: Text, Translation, and Discussion.* eds. Marie-Lauren Desclos and William Fortenbaugh. Series: Rutgers University Studies in Classical Humanities (New Brunswick, NJ: Transaction Pub., 2011), v.16. It should be mentioned here that this excellent volume provides a comprehensive summary of Strato's remaining fragments as well as comments by others, especially Simplicius.
12. Cicero, *De Natura Deorum: Academica.* trans. H. Rackham (Cambridge, MA: Harvard University Press, 1933). 1.35.
13. Antony Flew, *God & Philosophy* (New York: Harcourt, Brace, and World, 1966), 69.
14. Plutarch, *"Reply to Colotes,"* *Moralia.* trans. Benedict Einarson and Phillip de Lacy, Loeb Classical Library 428 (Cambridge, MA: Harvard University Press, 1967), vol. 14, 1115B.
15. Minucius Felix, *Octavius* 19.8, 19B and Lactantius, *On the Wrath of God* 10.1, 19C. Both in *Strato of Lampsacus*, trans. Desclos and Fortenbaughm, (Rutgers), 61.
16. Cicero, *Academica,* trans. H. Rackham (Harvard), 2.121.
17. Ibid.
18. Aristotle identified gravity in at least three contexts: *On The Heavens,* trans. J.L. Stocks, 311b5, 311b8-9, and *Metaphysics,* trans. W.D. Ross, 1052b28-29. All from *The Complete Works of Aristotle: The Revised Oxford Translation.* ed. J. Barnes. 2 vols. Bollingen Series. (Princeton, NJ: Princeton University Press, 1984).
19. Geoffrey E. Lloyd *Greek Science after Aristotle*. (London: Chatto & Windus, 1973), 15-17.
20. Ibid. Also *Strato of Lampsacus*, Desclos and Fortenbaugh, (Rutgers),103.
21. "On Motion" quoted by Simplicius in *Commentary on Aristotle's Physics* in Geoffrey E. Lloyd *Greek Science after Aristotle* (Chatto & Windus), 16.
22. *Strato of Lampsacus*, Desclos and Fortenbaugh, (Rutgers), 40, 50B.
23. Plato, *Timaeus*, trans. Benjamin Jowett, *The Dialogues of Plato, Great Books of the Western World.* ed. Mortimer Adler (Chicago: Encyclopedia Britannica, 1952), 68d,
24. Stobaeus, *Selections* 26B; Hero, *Pneumatica* 30B. Both in Desclos and Fortenbaugh, *Strato of Lampsacus* (Rutgers*).* Also see Kirk Sanders, "Strato on Microvoid," in *Strato of Lampsacus*, 263-276.
25. Hero, *Pneumatica Strato of Lampsacus*, 30B.
26. Geoffrey E. Lloyd, *Greek Science* (Chatto & Windus), 16-17.
27. Aristotle, *On the Heavens,* trans. J.L. Stocks, *The Complete Works of Aristotle* (Princeton), 312b13-20.

28. This debt to Strato as well as Arcesilaus and Carneades will be explored at greater length in Chapter Seven.

29. Geoffrey E. Lloyd, *Greek Science,* (Chatto & Windus) 49-50; 53-74.

6. THE EPICUREANS

1. Diogenes Laertius, "Epicurus," trans. R.D. Hicks, *Lives of Eminent Philosophers*, Loeb Classical Library 185 (Cambridge, MA: Harvard University Press, 1979), vol. 10, 26.

2. Plutarch, "A Pleasant Life Impossible," in *Moralia*, trans, Benedict Einarson and Phillip de Lacy, Loeb Classical Library 428 (Cambridge, MA: Harvard University Press, 1967), vol. 14, 1100.

3. Diogenes Laertius, "Epicurus," *Lives* (Loeb), vol. 10, 8; Cicero, *De Natura Deorum : Academica,* trans. H. Rackham, Loeb 268 (Cambridge, MA: Harvard University Press, 1979), vol. 19, 93 and 91.

4. Epicurus, "Letter to Menoeceus" in *The Stoic and Epicurean Philosophers*, trans. Cyril Bailey, ed. by Whitney Oates (New York: Modern Library, 1940), 30.

5. Ibid., 33.

6. Diogenes Laertius, "Epicurus," *Lives* (Harvard), bk.10,133.

7. Ibid., 125.

8. Sextus Empiricus, *Outlines of Pyrrhonism*, trans. R.G. Bury, Loeb Classical Library 273 (Cambridge, MA: Harvard University Press, 1976), vol.1, 229.

9. Pliny, *Natural History*, trans. H. Rackham, Loeb Classical Library 352 (Cambridge, MA: Harvard University Press, 1942), bk 7, 188.

10. Cicero. *Natura Deorum* , trans. H. Rackham, Loeb 268 (Cambridge, MA: Harvard University Press, 1979), bk.1, 123.

11. Ibid., bk. 3, 3.

12. Sextus Empiricus, *Against the Physicists* and *Against the Ethicists* trans. R.G. Bury Loeb Classical Library 311 (Cambridge, MA: Harvard University Press, 1968), bk. 1, 58-60.

13. Diogenes Laertius, "Epicurus," trans. R.D. Hicks, *Lives* (Harvard), bk. 10, 39-40.

14. Ibid., 40, 42.

15. Ibid., 41.

16. Cicero. *De Natura Deorum* (Harvard), bk. 1,69.

17. Diogenes Laertius, "Epicurus," *Lives* (Harvard), bk. 10, 40.

18. Ibid., 63-4.

19. Ibid., 66.

20. Ibid., 67.

21. Sextus Empiricus, *Against the Logicians*, trans. R.G. Bury (Cambridge, MA: Harvard University Press, 1983), bk 2, 355.

22. Diogenes Laertius, "Epicurus," *Lives* (Harvard), bk. 10, 69.

23. Ibid., 77-78.

24. G.B Townend, "The Poems," *Cicero,* ed. T.A. Dorey (New York: Basic Books, 1965), 123.

25. Lucretius. *On the Nature of Things.* trans. W. H. D. Rouse, rev. Martin F. Smith, Loeb Classical Library 18, (Cambridge, MA: Harvard University Press, 1992), bk. 4, 8-9. See also fn. a, 8.

26. Lucretius, "On the Nature of Things," *The Stoic and Epicurean Philosophers*, trans. by H.A.J. Munro (New York: Modern Library, 1940), bk. 1, 45-52.

27. Ibid., 55-61.

28. Lucretius. *On the Nature of Things.* trans. W. H. D. Rouse, rev. Martin F. Smith, Loeb Classical Library 18, (Cambridge, MA: Harvard University Press, 1992), bk. 1, 205-70.

29. Ibid., 328 and 270-71.

30. Ibid., 329.

31. Ibid., 383-85.

32. Ibid., 419-22.

33. Ibid., 445-49.
34. Ibid., 599-610.
35. Ibid., 630-639 and 705-715.
36. Ibid., 778-95.
37. Ibid., 830-40.
38. Ibid., 875-80.
39. Ibid., 894-6.
40. Ibid., 995-97.
41. Ibid., 1040-42.
42. Ibid., 1082.
43. Ibid., bk.2, 128, 105ff; and 184, 109ff.
44. Ibid., 216-24; 223-28; 403-8.
45. Ibid., 179-82.
46. Ibid., 646-48.
47. *The Stoic and Epicurean Philosophers*, (Modern Library), bk. 2, 1055-1066. Today of course this probability of life elsewhere in the universe seems highly likely if 300 billion stars have been counted in our galaxy, the Milky Way, and if stars are now estimated to have an average of one planet apiece, and if as many as 2 trillion other galaxies have recently been detected.
48. Lucretius, *On the Nature of Things*. trans. W. H. D. Rouse, rev. Martin F. Smith, Loeb Classical Library 18, (Cambridge, MA: Harvard University Press, 1992), bk. 2, 1110-20 and 1090-94.
49. Lucretius, *On the Nature of Things*, Translated by H.A.J. Munro, *The Stoic and Epicurean Philosophers* (New York: Modern Library, 1940), Book II, lines 1114-18; 1140-41.
50. Ibid., (Modern Library), bk. 3, 122-3.
51. Lucretius, *On the Nature of Things* (Harvard), bk. 3, 830.
52. Ibid., 1089-90.
53. Ibid., bk. 4, 478-90.
54. Lucretius, *On the Nature of Things* (Modern Library), bk. 4, 512.
55. Lucretius, *On the Nature of Things* (Harvard), bk. 5, 384.
56. Ibid., 330-31.
57. Ibid., 1183-88.
58. Ibid., bk. 6, 1000-2.
59. Ibid., 1024-41.
60. Ibid., 1119-24.
61. Ibid., bk. 5, 245-6.

7. SKEPTICISM

1. Richard Popkin. *The History of Skepticism from Erasmus to Spinoza*. (Berkeley: University of California Press, 1979). Popkin provides a useful history of Pyrrhonian skepticism. Also John Mackinnon Robertson, *A History of Freethought: Ancient and Modern to the Period of the French Revolution*. vol. 1, 4th ed. rev. (London: Watts & Co., 1936). Robertson provides the standard history of secularism.
2. Recent news stories tell of clouds of ice specks that floated through the universe billions of years ago, and that half the water on earth can be traced to these clouds. Nicholas St. Fleur. "The Water in Your Glass Might Be Older Than the Sun," *New York Times* (New York, NY), Apr. 15, 2016.
3. Diogenes Laertius, "Pyrrho," trans. R.D. Hicks, in *Lives of Eminent Philosophers,* Loeb Classical Library 185 (Cambridge: MA, Harvard University Press, 1979), vol. 2, bk. 9, 62-63. Pyrrho had also been a pupil of Bryson, of the Megaric School, and in turn Pyrrho's followers included Nausiphanes of Teos, a teacher of Epicurus, whose moderate version of hedonism seems to have inspired Pyrrho's concept of *ataraxia* as achieved tranquility.

Notes 185

4. *Epoche* is described by both Diogenes Laertius, *Lives of Eminent Philosophers* (Harvard), vol. 2, 9.108, 519; and by Sextus Empiricus, *Outlines of Pyrrhonism,* trans. R.G. Bury Loeb Classical Library 273 (Cambridge: MA, Harvard University Press, 1976), bk. 1, 29-30 and 234,.

5. The resemblance between *epoche* and other aspects of oriental philosophy is discussed by Jay Garfield in "Epoche and Suunyataa: Skepticism East and West," *Philosophy East and West,* vol. 40, no. 3 (July, 1990), 285-307. See also D.T. Suzuki's explanation of *satori* in *Zen Buddhism* (New York: Doubleday Anchor, 1956), 84-85, 95-96, and 103-108.

6. Diogenes Laertius, *Lives of Eminent Philosophers* (Harvard), bk. 9.61-62.

7. Ibid.

8. Sextus Empiricus, *Outlines of Empiricism* (Harvard), vol. 1.14.

9. Cicero, *Academica,* (Harvard), 1.45.

10. Sextus Empiricus, *Against the Logicians,* trans. R.G. Bury, Loeb Classical Library 291 (Cambridge, MA: Harvard University Press, 1983), bk. 1,155.

11. Plato, "Meno," trans. W.K.C Guthrie, in *The Collected Dialogues of Plato,* ed. by Edith Hamilton and Huntington Cairns (Princeton: NJ: Princeton University Press, 1961), 86e-87b.

12. Charles Saunders Peirce, "Pragmatism and Abduction," in *Collected Papers* (Cambridge, MA: Harvard University Press, 1934), vol. 5, 121-22 and John Dewey, *Logic: The Theory of Inquiry* (New York: Henry Holt, 1938), 7-9, 11, 13.

13. Edmund Husserl, *Ideas,* trans. W.R. Boyce Gibson (New York: Humanities Press, 1931), 107-11.

14. Sextus Empiricus *Against the Logicians* (Harvard), vol. 1.165-170. For the full summary see all of 1.159-189.

15. Plato, "Timaeus," trans. Benjamin Jowett, in *The Collected Dialogues of Plato,* ed. Edith Hamilton and Huntington Cairns (Princeton, NJ: Princeton University Press, 1987), 72d, 1195.

16. Aristotle, *Prior Analytics,* trans. A.J. Jenkinson in *The Basic Works of Aristotle* (New York: Random House, 1941), 70a3-5.

17. Sextus Empiricus, *Against the Logicians* (Harvard), bk. 1.166-182.

18. Sextus Empiricus, *Outlines of Pyrrhonism,* (Harvard), bk 3, 2-12.

19. Ibid., esp. bk. 3, 11.

20. Sextus Empiricus, *Against the Physicists,* trans. R.G. Bury in *Sextus Empericus* III , Loeb Classical Library (Cambridge, MA: Harvard University Press, 1936), bk. 1, 151-186.

21. Ibid., 1.172-173.

8. CICERO (106-43 B.C.)

1. G.B. Townend, "The Poems" in *Cicero,* ed. T.A. Dorey (Basic Books, 1965), 123.

2. Cicero, *De Natura Deorum: Academica,* trans. H. Rackham. Loeb Classical Library 268 (Cambridge, MA: Harvard University Press, 1979), 1.27.

3. Ibid., *Academica* bk 3,7-9.

4. Ibid., bk. 2, 16-17.

5. Ibid., bk. 2, 18.

6. Ibid., bk. 2, 26-27.

7. Ibid., bk. 2, 61-62.

8. Ibid., bk. 2, 59.

9. Ibid., bk. 2, 66-68.

10. Ibid., bk. 2, 103-105.

11. Ibid., bk.2, 7-8.

12. Ibid., bk. 2, 99.

13. Ibid., bk. 2, 108-109.

14. Ibid., bk. 2, 118-119.

15. Ibid., bk. 2, 121123.

16. Ibid., bk. 2, 123.

17. Ibid., *De Natura Deorum* bk. 1,.11.
18. It can be mentioned here that Diodotus lived in Cicero's house until his death in 59 BC. Posidonius, who died in 51 BC, seven years before the publication of Cicero's text, was one of Cicero's teachers and the dominant Stoic philosopher at the time. Just before his death, Posidonius authored his own book upon the gods with the identical title, *De Natura Deorum.* Cicero choice in adopting the same title for his text would seem a gesture of personal indebtedness.
19. Cicero, *De Natura Deorum,* trans. H. Rackham (Harvard), bk. 1, 2.
20. Ibid., 4.
21. Ibid., 25-29.
22. Ibid., 35-36.
23. Ibid., 43.
24. Ibid., 61. Cotta overlooks the probable atheism in two passages by Democritus quoted in this book's Chapter 1, fns. 118 and 119.
25. Ibid., 69-70.
26. Ibid., 72.
27. Ibid., 93-94.
28. Ibid., 75-76.
29. Ibid., 91.
30. Ibid., 113-114.
31. Ibid., 123.
32. Ibid., bk. 2, 16.
33. Ibid., 39-46, esp. 45.
34. Ibid., 47.
35. Ibid., 58.
36. Ibid., 78-79.
37. Ibid., 85.
38. Ibid., 87.
39. Ibid., 93-94.
40. Ibid., 99.
41. Ibid., 118.
42. Ibid., 154.
43. Ibid., 167-68.
44. Ibid., bk. 3, 6-7.
45. Ibid., 11.
46. Ibid., 17.
47. Ibid., 25.
48. Ibid., 23.
49. Ibid., 27-28.
50. Ibid., 33-34.
51. Ibid., 37.
52. Ibid., 38.
53. Ibid., 39.
54. Ibid., 70-71.
55. Ibid., 75.
56. Ibid., 90.
57. Ibid., 93.
58. Ibid., 95
59. Ibid., bk. 1, 6.
60. Ibid., 11.

EPILOGUE

1. Stephen Greenblatt, *The Swerve: How the World Became Modern,* (New York: W.W Norton, 2011), 25.

2. Plutarch, *Moralia*, trans. Frank Cole Babbitt. vol. 2. Loeb Classical Library (Cambridge: Harvard University Press, 1928, 455-95. Human sacrifice as a pagan practice is obscured in the ritual celebrations of Christ's crucifixion and the Eucharist.

3. Ibid., 75. Celsius' book is *On the True Doctrine: A Discourse Against the Christians*. trans. R. Joseph Hoffmann, Loeb Classical Library, (Oxford University Press, 1987).

4. All the relevant passages above are quoted in Homer Smith's. *Man and his Gods*, (Boston: Little, Brown and Company), 168-69.

5. Acts, 17:16-34; 19:18-20. Not long after his stay in Athens, Paul supposedly witnessed the destruction of pagan texts in a bonfire that may have been a test of allegiance to Christianity.

6. Saint Augustine, *Against the Academics* (Newman Press, 1951), chap. 5, 110.

7. Henry Leas' three-volume text, *A History of the Inquisition of the Middle Ages*, (1887) remains the standard reference on this topic. More recent assessments can be found on the Intenet, for example long pieces by David Plaisted and Kelsos.

8. James Haught, *2000 Years of Disbelief: Famous People with the Courage to Doubt* (Amherst, NY: Prometheus, 1996), 45.

9. Nate Cohn, "Big Drop in Share of Americans Calling Themselves Christian," *The New York Times* (May 12, 2015). This is based on a National Opinion Research Center poll conducted three years ago.

10. Jeanna Bryner, LiveScience Managing Editor, April 28, 2012.

11. "Leading Scientists Still Reject God," *Nature*, vol. 394, No. 6691 (1998), 313.

12. James Randerson's article, "Childish superstition: Einstein's letter makes view of religion relatively clear," in *The Guardian*, May 13, 2008.

Selective Bibliography

I. PRIMARY TEXTS

Aristotle. *The Complete Works of Aristotle: The Revised Oxford Translation*. Edited by J. Barnes. 2 vols. Bollingen Series. Princeton, NJ: Princeton University Press, 1984.
———. *De Anima*. Translated by R. D. Hicks. Cambridge: Cambridge University Press, 1907.
———. *De Anima*. Translated by R. D. Hicks. New York: Cosimo Classics, 2008.
———. *Metaphysics*. Translated by William Heinemann. 2 vols. Loeb Classical Library. Cambridge, MA: Harvard University Press, 1956.
———. *On the Heavens*. Translated by W.K.C. Guthrie. Loeb Classical Library. Cambridge, MA: Harvard University Press, 2006.
———. *On the Soul; Parva naturalia; On Breath*. Translated by W.S. Hett. Loeb Classical Library. Cambridge, MA: Harvard University Press, 1957.
———. *Physics*, vols. 1 and 2. Translated by Philip Wickstead and Francis Cornford Loeb Classical Library. Cambridge, MA: Harvard University Press,1957.
———. *Sophistical Refutations* and *The Coming to Be and Passing Away*. Translated by E.S. Forster Loeb Classical Library. Cambridge, MA: Harvard University Press, 1955.
———. *The Works of Aristotle Translated into English: De Caelo* and *De Generatione et Corruptione*. Translated by J.L. Stocks and Harold Joachim Oxford at Clarendon Press, 1922.
Celsus. *On the True Doctrine: A Discourse Against the Christians*. Translated by R. Joseph Hoffmann. Loeb Classical Library. New York: Oxford University Press, 1987.
Cicero. *De Natura Deoru* and *Academica*. Translated by H. Rackham. Loeb Classical Library. Cambridge, MA: Harvard University Press, 1933.
Diogenes Laertius. *Lives of Eminent Philosophers*. vols. 1 & 2. Translated by Robert Drew Hicks. Loeb Classical Library. Cambridge, MA: Harvard University Press, 1979.
Epicurus. "Letter to Herodotus," in Diogenes Laertius, *Lives of Eminent Philosophers*. Translated by Robert Drew Hicks. vol. 2. Loeb Classical Library. Cambridge, MA: Harvard University Press, 1979.
Freeman, Kathleen. *Ancilla to the Pre-Socratic Philosophers: A Complete Translation of the Fragments in Diels, Fragmente der Vorsokratiker*. Cambridge, MA: Harvard University Press, 1948.
Jaeger,Werner. *Aristotle: Fundamentals Of The History Of His Development*, 2nd ed. (Oxford at Clarendon Press, 1948).
Lucretius. *On the Nature of Things*. Translated by W. H. D. Rouse, rev. Martin F. Smith, Loeb Classical Library 18, Cambridge, MA: Harvard University Press, 1992.

————. *On the Nature of Things*, Translated by H.A.J. Munro. in *The Stoic and Epicurean Philosophers*. Modern Library, 1940.

Natali, Carlo. ARISTOTLE; HIS LIFE AND SCHOOL, ed. by D. S. Hutchinson (Princeton University Press, 2013).

Oates, Whitney, ed., *The Stoic and Epicurean Philosophers*. New York: Modern Library, 1940.

Plato. *The Dialogues of Plato*. Translated by Benjamin Jowett. *Great Books of the Western World*. Edited by Mortimer Adler. vol. 7. Chicago: Encyclopedia Britannica, 1952.

————. *The Collected Dialogues of Plato*. Edited by Edith Hamilton and Huntington Cairns. Bollingen Series. Princeton: Princeton University Press, 1961.

Plutarch. *Moralia*. Translated by Frank Cole Babbitt. vol. 2. Loeb Classical Library. Cambridge, MA: Harvard University Press, 1928.

————. *Moralia*. Translated by Benedict Einarson and Phillip de Lacy. vol. 14 Loeb Classical Library. Cambridge, MA: Harvard University Press, 1967.

Sextus Empiricus. vol. 1. *Outlines of Pyrrhonism*, Translated by R.G. Bury. Loeb Classical Library. Cambridge, MA: Harvard University Press, 1976.

————. vol. 2. *Against the Logicians*. Translated by R.G. Bury. Loeb Classical Library. Cambridge, MA: Harvard University Press, 1983.

————. vol. 3. *Against the Physicists* and *Against the Ethicists*. Translated by R.G. Bury. Loeb Classical Library. Cambridge, MA: Harvard University Press, 1968.

————. vol. 4. *Against the Professors*. Translated by R.G. Bury. Loeb Classical Library. Cambridge, MA: Harvard University Press, 1987.

Strato of Lampsacus: Text, Translation, and Discussion. Edited by Marie-Lauren Desclos and William Fortenbaugh. Series: Rutgers University Studies in Classical Humanities, v.16 New Brunswick, NJ: Transaction Pub, 2011.

Theophrastus. *Metaphysics*. Translated with commentary by W.D. Ross and F.H. Fobes. Chicago: Ares, 1978.

Wians, William, ed., *ARISTOTLE'S PHILOSOPHICAL DEVELOPMENT: PROBLEMS AND PROSPECTS* (Rowman & Littlefield Publishers, Inc., 1996).

II. SECONDARY TEXTS

Bailey, Cyril. *The Greek Atomists and Epicurus*. New York: Russell & Russell, 1964.

Benn, Alfred William. *The Greek Philosophers*. 2 vols. London: K. Paul, Trench,1882..

Burnet, John. *Early Greek Philosophy*. 4th ed. London: Adam & Charles Black,1930.

————. *Greek Philosophy: Thales to Plato*. London: Macmillan, 1914.

Burnyeat, Myles. Edited by *The Sceptical Tradition*. Berkeley: University of California Press, 1983.

Casson, Lionel. *Libraries in the Ancient World*. New Haven, CT: Yale University Press, 2001.

Copleston, Frederick. *A History of Philosophy*. vol.1 Westminster, MD: The Newman Press, 1953.

Cornford, Francis MacDonald. *From Religion to Philosophy: A Study in the Origins of Western Speculation*. New York: Harper & Row, 1912.

————. *Plato and Parmenides*. New York: The Humanities Press, 1951.

Curd, Patricia, and Daniel Graham, eds., *THE OXFORD HANDBOOK OF PRESOCRATIC PHILOSOPHY* (Oxford University Press, 1908).

Dorey, T.A., Edited by, *Cicero*. New York: Basic Books, 1965.

Drachman, A.B. *Atheism in Pagan Antiquity*. Ares Publishers, 1977.

Draper, John William. *History of the Intellectual Development of Europe*. vol. 1, New York: Harper & Brothers, 1905.

————. *History of the Conflict between Religion and Science*. New York: D.Appleton and Company, 1905.

Finley, M.I. *Economy and Society in Ancient Greece*. London: Chatto & Windus, 1981.

Flew, Anthony. *God and Philosophy*. New York: Harcourt Brace, 1966.

Freeman, Kathleen. *The Pre-Socratic Philosophers: A Companion to Diels, Fragmente der Vorsokratiker*. Cambridge, MA: Harvard, 1966.

Glotz, Gustave. *Ancient Greece at Work: An Economic History of Greece.* Translated by M.R. Dobie. New York: Knopf, 1926.

Gomperz, Theodor. *Greek Thinkers: A History of Ancient Philosophy.* 2 vols. London: John Murray, Albemarle Street, 1964.

Greenblatt, Stephen. *The Swerve: How the World Became.* Modern New York: W.W Norton, 2011.

Gregory, Andrew. *Ancient Greek Cosmogony. Bloomsbury Academic:* New York, 2007.

Groarke, Leo, ed. *Greek Scepticism: Anti-Realist Trends in Ancient Thought.* Montreal & Kingston: McGill-Queen's University Press, 1990.

Guthrie, W.K.C. *A History of Greek Philosophy.* vols. 1-6. London: Cambridge University Press, 1962-81.

Hankinson, R. J. *Cause and Explanation in Ancient Greek Thought.* New York: Oxford, 1998
———. *The Sceptics.* London: Routledge, 1995.

Hasebroek, Johannes. *Trade and Politics in Ancient Greece,* Translated by L.M. Fraser and D.C. MacGregor. London: G. Bell & Sons, 1933.

Haught, James. *2000 Years of Disbelief: Famous People with the Courage to Doubt.* Amherst, NY: Prometheus, 1996.

Hecht, Jennifer Michael. *Doubt: A History.* New York, HarperSanFrancisco: 2003.

Hegel, Georg. *Lectures on the History of Philosophy,* vols. 1 and 2, Translated by E.S. Haldane and Frances Simson. Atlantic Highlands, NJ: Humanities Press, 1974.

Hookway, Christopher. *Scepticism.* London: Routledge,1990.

Huberman, Jack. *The Quotable Atheist.* New York: Nation Books, 2007.

Kiernan, Thomas. Edited by *Aristotle Dictionary.* New York: Philosophical Library, 1962.

Kirk, G.S. & J. E. Raven. *The Pre-Socratic Philosophers.* London: Cambridge University Press, 1957.

Kristeller, Paul Oskar. *Greek Philosophers of the Hellenistic Age.* New York: Columbia University Press, 1991.

Lange, Fredrich Albert. *The History of Materialism and Criticism of its Present Importance.* 3rd ed. Translated by Ernest Chester Thomas. London: K. Paul, 1925.

Lloyd, Geoffrey Ernest. *Early Greek Science: Thales to Aristotle.* London: Chatto & Windus, 1970.

———. *Greek Science after Aristotle.* London: Chatto & Windus, 1973.

Long, A.A. and D.N. Sedley, 2 vols. *The Hellenistic Philosophers.* New York: Cambridge University Press, 1987.

McCabe, Joseph. *A Rationalist Encyclopaedia: A Book of Reference on Religion, Philosophy, Ethics, and Science.* London: Watts & Co., 1948.

McKeon, Richard. Edited by *The Basic Works of Aristotle.* New York: Random House, 1941.

McKirahan, Richard. *Philosophy Before Socrates: An Introduction with Texts and Commentary.* Indianapolis, IN: Hackett Publishing Company, 1994.

Michell, H. *The Economics of Ancient Greece.* London: Cambridge University Press, 1940.

Ober, Josiah. *The Rise and Fall of Classical Greece.* Princeton, NJ: Princeton University Press, 2015.

Polastron, Lucien X. *Books on Fire: The Destruction of Libraries throughout History.* Rochester, NY: Inner Traditions, 2007.

Popkin, Richard. *The History of Skepticism from Erasmus to Spinoza.* Berkeley: University of California Press, 1979.

Quigley, Carroll. *The Evolution of Civilizations.* Indianapolis, IN: Liberty Fund, 1961.

Popkin, Richard H., ed. *The Columbia History of Western Philosophy.* New York: Columbia University Press, 1999.

Randall, John Herman, Jr. *Aristotle.* New York: Columbia University Press, 1960.

Robertson, John Mackinnon. *A History of Freethought Ancient and Modern to the Period of the French Revolution.* vol. 1, 4th ed. rev. London: Watts & Co., 1936.

Robin, Léon. *Greek Thought and the Origins of the Scientific Spirit.* New York: A.A. Knopf 1928.

Robinson, John Mansley. *An Introduction to Early Greek Philosophy.* Cambridge, MA: Harvard University Press, 1968.

Ross, Sir David. *Aristotle*. London: Methuen & Co., 1949.

Russell, Bertrand. *A History of Western Philosophy*. New York: Simon & Schuster, 1945.

Schmitt, Charles. *Aristotle and the Renaissance*. Harvard University Press, 1983.

Schofield, Malcolm, Myles Burnyeat and Jonathan Barnes. eds. *Doubt and Dogmatism: Studies in Hellenistic Epistemology*. Oxford: Clarendon Press, 1980.

Sedley, David. *Creationism and its Critics in Antiquity*. Berkeley: University of California Press, 2007.

Smith, Homer W. *Man and his Gods*. Boston: Little, Brown and Company, 1952.

Stace, W.T. *A Critical History of Greek Philosophy*. London: Macmillan, 1924.

Starr, Chester. *The Economic and Social Growth of Early Greece: 800-500 B.C.* New York: Oxford University Press, 1977.

Stein, Gordon. *The Encyclopedia of Unbelief*. Edited by Gordon Stein. vols.1 and 2. Buffalo: Prometheus Books, 1985.

Stockhammer, Morris. *Plato Dictionary*. New York: Philosophical Library, 1963.

Thomson, George. *The First Philosophers*. London: Lawrence & Wishart, 1955.

———. *Studies in Ancient Greek Society*. vol. 2. London: Lawrence & Wishart, 1955.

Thrower, James. *Western Atheism: A Short History*. Amherst, NY: Pemberton Books, 1971.

Wheelwright, Philip. *Heraclitus*. Princeton, NJ: Princeton, 1959.

Whitmarsh, Tim. *Battling the Gods: Atheism in the Ancient World*. Knopf, 2015.

Also useful are *The Encyclopedia of Philosophy*. Edited by Paul Edwards. New York: MacMillan, 1967, vols. 1-8 and both the eleventh and fourteenth editions of the *Encyclopedia Britannica* have useful information. On the Internet the Stanford Encyclopedia of Philosophy (https://plato.stanford.edu/) can be indispensable.

Index

194 *Index*

universe, 18, 155
ataraxia, 139, 140, 142
atheism, 82, 123, 143, 149, 171
atheists, x, 106, 171–5
Athens, 1, 52, 54, 105, 169
Atlas, 88
atoms, 11, 37, 39, 73, 124, 129
attraction and repulsion, 28
Averroes, 170
Avicenna, 170

Bacon, Sir Francis, 111, 117, 149, 171
Baghdad Battery, 114
Balbus, 156, 157, 159, 160, 161
Big Bang, 74
binary opposition, 4
Bohr, Niels, 124
Bruno, 171
Burnet, John, vii

Caesar, 151
Carneades, 144–149; atheism, 106, 147,
    153; Cotta's explanation of, 157;
    credibility, 146; deleted from Cicero's
    writings, 152; irreversible, 146; opinion
    of providence, 163; oratorical skills,
    153; orthodoxy, 156; probability, 147;
    refutations of God, 147–149; truth,
    145–146
catharsis, 51
Catholic ecumenical councils, 69
chance, 73, 111, 113, 123, 160
Christian, 169
Christian scribes, 71
Christianity, xv, 168, 169
Chrysippus, 157, 159, 162
Cicero, 151–165; absolute truth, 155;
    agnosticism, 154, 155; Arcesilaus, 142;
    Carneades, 145; Democritus, 41; De
    Natura Deorum, 156; doubt, 154;
    Epicurus, 122; later influence of, 155;
    Lucretius, 126, 164; St. Augustine, 169;
    surviving dialogues, xviii; swerve, 124;
    tutors, 152
circular universe, 14
Clitomachus, xvii, 144, 145, 152
Confucius, xiii
consciousness, 93, 126
Constantine, 169

Copernicus, 155, 170
cosmos, 11, 88
Cotta, 156, 157, 158, 161
Cratylus, 50
creation: Aristotle, 74, 75, 86; Cicero, 155;
    Epicurus, 123; Lucretius, 132;
    Philolaus, 14; Plato, 60, 75
Critias, 51
cycles, 66, 76, 81–82, 85, 89–90, 91, 92,
    93, 94, 95, 96, 109–110; Anaxigoras,
    15, 16, 34; Anaximander, 4, 5, 15;
    Anaximenes, 4, 6; Aristotle, 15;
    Empedocles, 14; Heraclitus, 17, 31;
    Leucippus, 39; Plato, 15, 58; summary,
    46

Darwin, 32
De Natura Deorum, xix, 152
death, 17, 93, 132
deists, 171
Democritus, 40–46; Aristotle, 90, 99, 116;
    atoms, 42; Cicero, 44; ideas
    appropriated by Epicurus, 120; ideas
    summarized, 42; Lucretius, 129;
    perception, 43; Plato, 45; religion, 44;
    soul, 42–43; void among atoms, 25, 88
Descartes, 138, 171
Dewey, John, 144
Diagoras of Melos, 50, 157
Diels, Hermann, xviii
Diocletian, 168
Diodorus, 152, 168
Diogenes Laertius, xix, 141
Diogenes of Apollonia, 34–36
doubt, 49, 51, 58–59, 122, 137, 138, 140,
    142, 146

earth: sphere, 68, 161; destruction of, 161.
    See also elements
Einstein, 47, 117, 172
Eleatic school, 7, 20, 67, 123
elements, 5, 10, 11, 16, 18, 24, 28–29, 31,
    36, 58, 60, 115, 129, 148, 153; air, 4, 6,
    8, 9, 11, 12, 17, 27, 30, 31, 35, 35–36,
    36, 39, 68, 73, 116, 132, 158, 160;
    earth, 3, 4, 6, 8, 9, 13, 16, 17, 30, 33,
    46–47, 115, 160; fire, 6, 9, 13, 16, 17,
    18, 19, 21, 22, 28–29, 35, 42, 46, 60,
    87, 88, 109, 115, 125, 126, 129, 160,

Lactantius, 113
Lao'tze, xiii
Leucippus, 36–40; atoms in space, 42
libraries, destruction of, xvi; Herculaneum,
 xvi, xx, 120; Library at Alexandria,
 xvii, 105, 169; Library at
 Constantinople, xvii
Livy, 168
Locke, John, 99, 171
Logos, 18, 31
Lucretius, 126–135; *De Rerum Natura* ,
 xix, 127; destruction, 88, 131, 133;
 senses, 132
Lyceum, xix, 64, 107

magnetism, 2, 134
Marcus Aurelius, 167
Marx, Karl, xv, 124, 127
mass: Aristotle, 12, 19, 64, 67, 74, 83, 85,
 86, 87, 88, 89, 95, 99, 101; Diogenes,
 35–17; Einstein, 47, 64; Leucippus, 39,
 85; Lucretius, 129, 130; Melissus, 9,
 68; Pythagoras, 68; Strato, 116
mathematics, 10, 11, 20, 22, 47, 68, 170
matter, 6, 17, 20, 25, 36, 37, 66, 90;
 Aristotle, 72, 85, 90, 96; Lucretius, 127;
 Strato, 113; matter and motion, 155;
 matter in motion, 73
Melissus, 24–25; agnosticism, vii–viii;
 Aristotle, 66, 67, 84–85, 86; atoms, 25,
 38; Epicurus, 123; existence without
 boundaries, 25; infinitude of space and
 time, 24–25; universe, limitless, 20
Metaphysics. See Aristotle*, Metaphysics*
Metrodorus of Chios, 50
Michell, Humfrey, xv
Miletus, xiv, 1
mind: Anaxagoras, 31–33, 34, 158;
 Aristotle, 2, 70, 72, 93–94, 94, 96–97,
 99, 100; Diogenes, 36; Empedocles, 27;
 Lucretius, 132; Parmenides, 21;
 Pherecydes, 10; Philolaus, 14; Plato,
 56, 66; Protagoras, 52; Socrates, 54;
 Thales, 158; Xenophanes, 7, 8
monads, 11
monotheistic God, 10, 32, 77
Montaigne, 144, 171
motion, 7, 92, 95, 99, 113; incessant
 motion, 87

nature, 92, 160
Nausiphanes, 119, 120, 159
Newton, 171
Nicomachean Ethics, 70, 100, 101
nous, 31, 57

Ockham's razor, 64, 102
Oedipus Rex, 51
On the Heavens. See Aristotle*, De Caelo*
On the Soul. See Aristotle*, De Anima*
oral doctrine. *See acromata*
Osiris, 168
Ovid, 167

pantheism, 36, 86, 92, 160
paradox, 23
Parmenides, 20–22; Aristotle, 67, 84,
 84–85; cosmic cycle, 28; creation, 74,
 75, 87; Eleatic school, 20; love, 21;
 monist concept, 22, 25; soul and mind,
 21; universe, 24, 123
Peirce, Charles Sanders, 144
perception, 99
Pericles, 52
perpetual motion, 75
Petrarch, 151, 155, 170
Phaedrus, 152, 156
Pherecydes of Syros, 9
Phidias, 50
Philo of Larissa, 144, 145, 152
Philolaus, 14
philosopher, term or word, 11
Phoenician trade, xiv
Physics, 72–76
plague, 134
Plato, 55–61; Anaxagoras, 30, 34;
 Aristotle, 66–69, 99; atheists, execution
 of, 122; Democritus, 45; creationism,
 75; Heraclitus, influence of, 17, 18;
 God, 56, 57; Heraclitus, influence of,
 17, 18; *Laws X* , 59, 63, 81; motion, 15;
 Socrates, 55; soul, 60, 88, 132;
 Timaeus, 56, 58, 89; transcendence, 14,
 45; universal Mind, 56; virtue, 57
Pliny, 122
Plutarch, 69, 113, 168
Popper, Karl, 53, 114
Posidonius, 152, 156
probability, 146, 154, 155

www.ingramcontent.com/pod-product-compliance
Lightning Source LLC
Chambersburg PA
CBHW020357100426
42812CB00001B/97